T0246208

THE PICNIC

ALSO BY MATTHEW LONGO

The Politics of Borders:
Sovereignty, Security, and the Citizen after 9/11

THE PICNIC

A DREAM OF FREEDOM
AND THE COLLAPSE
OF THE IRON CURTAIN

Matthew Longo

W. W. NORTON & COMPANY
Celebrating a Century of Independent Publishing

The Picnic is a work of nonfiction. Certain names have been changed and some individuals are referred to by initials, according to their respective wishes.

For information about special discounts for bulk purchases, please contact W. W. Norton Special Sales at specialsales@wwnorton.com or 800-233-4830

Manufacturing by Lake Book Manufacturing
Book design by Daniel Lagin
Production manager: Lauren Abbate

ISBN 978-0-393-54077-2

W. W. Norton & Company, Inc.
500 Fifth Avenue, New York, N.Y. 10110
www.wwnorton.com

W. W. Norton & Company Ltd.
15 Carlisle Street, London W1D 3BS

1 2 3 4 5 6 7 8 9 0

For Genny & Gianni

SOVIET
SECTOR

French
Sector

SOVIET
SECTOR

British
Sector

Soviet
Sector

B E R L I N

American Sector

---- path of Berlin Wall, 1961–89

DENMARK

Copenhagen •

Gdansk

POLAND

Berlin •

Warsaw •

U.S.S.R.

EAST GERMANY

Leipzig •

Dresden •

• Bonn

• Prague

WEST GERMANY

CZECHOSLOVAKIA

Munich •

Vienna •

Sopron

Budapest •

Debrecen •

AUSTRIA

Zürich •

SWITZERLAND

HUNGARY

ROMANIA

YUGOSLAVIA

Bucharest •

ITALY

• Sophia

BULGARIA

• Rome

ALBANIA

GREECE

Athens •

KEY

+++ Iron Curtain
xxx

- - - Border of non-
aligned countries
outside Soviet
sphere

N

MILES
KILOMETERS

ST MARGARETHEN

to VIENNA

Lake
Fertö
(Neusiedler See)

SITE
OF
BREACH

MÖRBISCH
AM SEE

Sopronpuszta

PICNIC

FERTÖRÁKOS

CAMPSITE

SOPRON

HUNGARY

to BUDAPEST

AUSTRIA

N

KEY
✕✕✕✕ Iron Curtain
········· Border
～～～ Roads

5 MILES
8 KILOMETERS

Contents

Prologue

FREEDOM'S PROMISE

László gives me a tour of what is nowhere. How did the East Germans even find this place? he wonders aloud. It is *anus mundi*, he says. The asshole of the world.

No one knew about this part of the borderlands. On maps, only the line was represented, but not the vast stretch of no-go zones that comprised the Iron Curtain—the militarized frontier that emerged after World War II, dividing Europe between East (Soviet influence) and West (American influence). If the full boundary system wasn't shown, the logic went, people couldn't find it. Thus, the reality of the border was itself divided. For the military, the border regime was precise. For the average person, it was mysterious and threatening.

László takes me to the edge of the woods. We follow the tree line down a slope through tall grass. When we round a bend, a clearing opens up. This is where the picnickers parked, he says.

The field on which László and I are standing was the site of the Pan-European Picnic, held on August 19, 1989, on the Austrian-Hungarian border, a giant, open-air party celebrating European togetherness and freedom, which furnished the stage for the greatest breach of the border in Cold War history—hundreds of East

German refugees dashing toward freedom—the initial tug by which the entire Iron Curtain would unspool. Or, as Helmut Kohl, chancellor of a newly reunified Germany, would later put it, where the "first stone was removed from the Berlin Wall."

The picnic has largely been omitted from history books, pushed aside by the macroscopic politics of the end of the Cold War: Gorbachev and Reagan, the machinations of Moscow and Washington. This focus is understandable. But sometimes the most important moments in history are forged by ordinary people, under circumstances unexpected and strange. Sometimes in forgotten places too.

The field in Sopronpuszta today is utterly desolate: a sea of grass that obscures human pathways. It is a place filled with history but also emptied of it. A reminder that history cannot speak for itself; it must be given voice. Even *anus mundi*, if you listen to it, has a lot to say.

When I first heard the story of the picnic, I had just spent years researching the US-Mexico border and its security expansion after 9/11. After so much time studying how borders get built up, I was eager to learn how they might be torn down—and the Iron Curtain no less, among the most terrifying instruments of oppression ever devised.

I am a child of the 1980s. I remember seeing the fall of the Berlin Wall on TV—watching the celebrations, all those people dancing atop the carcass of Leviathan. It is an indelible image of freedom, even today. One government toppled after another—Czechoslovakia in November, Romania in December—ending with the collapse of the Soviet Union in 1991. Then, for many in the West, the 1990s were boom years. It was the age of globalization and life-changing technologies. The Cold War was over and we believed the world would become a more interconnected place, that the reactionary forces of the past would give way to the progressive minds of the future. With the victory of liberalism, we had found the best, most just system of political organization.

The year 1989 was a triumphant one, but from the vantage of today there is something hard to reconcile about it too. Across the East people are watching their liberties slip, especially in Hungary, under the increasingly authoritarian grip of Viktor Orbán; and the West, riven by inequality, seems to be splitting at the seams. Even that first day, listening to László in Sopronpuszta, I had the feeling that the story of the picnic wasn't just about the rush to freedom—the end of one era and the beginning of another—but something bigger, prefiguring the world we live in now. It marked a moment of ideological fracture we are still experiencing.

In our political discourse, we frequently throw around the word *freedom* as though its meaning is self-evident. It is a vision of doing what we want and going where we please, of voting booths and demonstrations, of large supermarkets with a dizzying array of colorful products and plentiful food.

But freedom is a complicated ideal. Over the course of this writing, in the United States, #BlackLivesMatter activism has been widespread in response to racist police brutality. At the same time, state responses to the COVID-19 pandemic have pitted antiestablishment groups against the federal government. These clashes emerge from different sides of the ideological divide. But they are also, each in their own way, about freedom—freedom to live in safety from state violence on the one hand; freedom from state paternalism on the other.

That is, people on both sides of the political spectrum are saying the same thing. They are also using the same word to say different things.

How did we get from the revolutionary fervor of 1989 to *this*? From tearing down the Berlin Wall to our new age of erecting barriers?

It is fall 2018, one of my first trips to the Hungarian borderlands. The mix of wonderment and confusion is present, I suspect, on my face. László Nagy looks at me skeptically. He is the secretary of the Pan-European Picnic '89 Foundation, and its unofficial ambassador.

You have no idea how messy it's been, he says. The infighting, the scandals . . . You'll see at the thirtieth.

He is referring to the thirtieth anniversary of the picnic, a giant gala planned for the coming summer.

The picnic was decades ago, I say. Why would there be scandals now?

László regards me, his expression dark and cynical.

There's a saying popular in Hungary, he says. The future is certain. It's the past that keeps changing.

PART I

JUST KIDS

Chapter One

It was June 20, 1989, a warm summer night; by all accounts a perfect occasion for dreaming.

The dinner table at the Grand Hotel Aranybika (the Golden Bull), housed in a stately Art Nouveau building in Debrecen, Hungary, brought together an odd assembly of guests: Ferenc Mészáros—broad-shouldered, scraggly haired, eyes seemingly focused on something beyond the present—and a group of other young, would-be activists from the East, alongside a family of aristocrats from the West. For Ferenc and many of the other Hungarians present, this was the most elegant dinner they had ever been invited to.

Ferenc had been in and out of gangs in his teenage years. He and his friends had engaged in petty mischief and hosted boxing matches outside the city with the other gangs, defending their turf and roughing up anyone who got caught in the middle. The high walls and chandeliers of the hotel—the building was commissioned by Alfréd Hajós, Hungary's first Olympic gold medalist; Béla Bartók played concerts there— its starched linens and wine that flowed unbidden into their glasses, all this was new and exciting.

So too was political activism. The Hungarians came from a wide range of backgrounds. What united them was their membership in the

MDF (*Magyar Demokrata Fórum*, or Hungarian Democratic Forum), a newly formed opposition group. Political parties were illegal in Communist Hungary, but as of the previous fall, some organizing was tolerated. The MDF advocated democratic elections and returning power to the people. This platform spoke to Ferenc. According to the Communist ideal, everyday workers were supposed to be empowered. But Ferenc knew this was just propaganda. His people had never enjoyed any kind of leadership, and many intellectuals expressed outright prejudice against them. When the MDF had started its chapter in Debrecen, Ferenc joined.

The occasion of the meal at the Aranybika was the arrival of Austrian diplomat Otto von Habsburg, then vice president of the European Parliament and would-be heir to the Austro-Hungarian Empire had it not folded half a century earlier. He was in town to deliver a lecture entitled "Hungary's Chances of Catching Up," at the Kossuth Lajos University, founded before the First World War by his father.

Habsburg was a frequent visitor to Hungary, given the historical connections between the two states that once formed the empire over which his family had presided—long before the Soviet Union took over after World War II, before the Communist era began. Hungary, now on the other side of the Iron Curtain, had fallen into economic disrepair and Habsburg was eager to discuss how it might forge a path forward. His speech at the university was packed; more than two thousand students attended.

The dinner after the talk was small and select, mostly friends of Lukács Szabó, a member of the MDF who had family connections to Habsburg and had invited him to come speak. Among the activists, reaction to the event was mixed. Some were eager to meet the famous scion; others were dubious. How could a man like that understand our situation? Ferenc had wondered. He decided to go anyway.

He carried his doubts about Habsburg through the talk and into the dinner. Conversation over the table began timidly. Political matters weren't openly discussed at that time in Hungary—certainly not in public. But something about the night, the fact that Habsburg was there, lent the air around them a kind of magic. Habsburg spoke in fluent Hungarian, a gesture to their shared past, and talked in terms of "we" and "our"—enough to temper even the hardest cynic.

Shortly, one by one, the young Hungarians jumped into the conversation, building upon Habsburg's vision for a borderless Europe, a space of freedom and community that would bridge the Iron Curtain and reunite East and West. The night grew long, and cheerful, drunk as everyone was from the setting, this still-too-uncommon meeting of minds across the political divide. Eventually, the young activists began calling the elderly aristocrat Uncle Otto. When the conversation turned to Hungary, they waxed poetic about the reforms underway, how far they had come, how far they still had to go.

It was a good time for such imaginings. Since the rise of Mikhail Gorbachev in 1985 and the rhetoric of glasnost (political openness) and perestroika (economic restructuring) there was a feeling that the very foundation of the Soviet Union was trembling and something new was emerging. But it was a time steeped in uncertainty too. If the Soviet Union did fall, would it go quietly or in a paroxysm of violence? For all the talk of change, by the summer of 1989, Europe was still physically cut in half. On one side was the West, land of free movement and democracy; on the other, the Soviet Union's unique brand of Communist authoritarianism. And between them, an Iron Curtain of munitions, cameras, and barbed wire that extended from the Baltic to the Black Sea.

From the vantage of Debrecen, a leafy, wide-avenued city close to the Romanian border, the Cold War remained hauntingly present. Surrounding the city were three Soviet barracks, a training area, and the second biggest military airport in the country. As a border city, Debrecen operated as a transit hub for the more than one hundred thousand Soviet troops stationed on Hungarian soil. No one expected them to do anything, but the last time they had, in 1956, there had been a massacre.

This was only a generation ago. Many of the activists present had parents who'd taken part in the uprising, had grown up listening to stories of the brutal Soviet crackdown that followed.

As the evening at the Aranybika drew to its close, an uncomfortable silence set in. Everyone knew how challenging it was to affect political change. They were all too aware of the barriers that still circumscribed their lives—the Wall that divided Berlin; the Iron Curtain, which despite recent reforms felt as uncompromising as ever.

At this point, Ferenc spoke up. He shared the grand vision of a united Europe, where peoples were not separated by barbed wire and a spirit of togetherness could reign. But he felt that a fancy hotel was no place to talk about it. We should be out with the people, he said, out by the Iron Curtain itself.

We should throw a party, he said. A picnic.

Ferenc had big dreams. He envisioned a gathering at the border, with Austrians on one side and Hungarians on the other. Maybe they could have a bonfire, roasting pigs on either side. Or maybe they could pass pieces of sausage or cold beers back and forth across the barbed wire. After his proposal the conversation took off, the others parrying ideas in wine-soaked fervor, each coming up with something more ridiculous than the last.

Everyone had a good laugh and went home. Surely the state would never actually allow such a thing. And what could they even do to set it up? After all, they lived about four hundred kilometers east of the Austrian border—a long distance in any era, let alone one without basic telecommunications. Ferenc hadn't understood yet that the Iron Curtain was not really a line but a several kilometers-wide expanse of electric fencing and military installations. He had never been to the Austrian border. Before his dinner with Habsburg, he had never even met an Austrian.

Still, the thought lingered. What better way to thumb their nose at this most despised institution—the Iron Curtain—emblematic of the freedoms forbidden them. But how could they do it? It seemed impossible.

IN AUTHORITARIAN SOCIETIES, PEOPLE GROW USED TO LIVING off their dreams. In many parts of the Eastern Bloc, political repression was so ruthless that activism of any sort was almost unimaginable. In Hungary, conditions were a bit better—it was the most open of the eastern states. But overt political organizing was still a terra incognita. Certainly there was no protocol that would-be activists like Ferenc could point to. They had to be guarded—their meetings were infiltrated by the secret police and its informants, including friends and family members.

And yet, the more Ferenc thought about the picnic, the larger it grew in his mind. On June 30, a little over a week after the dinner with Habsburg, Ferenc raised the idea at a meeting of the Debrecen chapter of the MDF, held at their usual spot, a cozy, unassuming beerhouse called Kisdebrecen (Little Debrecen), with a scratched-up, wood paneled interior and a patio out back. Ferenc spoke excitedly about the idea, the dramatic spectacle it would be.

The picnic would represent community and freedom, he said—the dream of life without political constraints, of not being told where one could or couldn't go, what one could or couldn't do.

When Ferenc finished his oration, he looked expectantly around the room but his words were met coolly. There were much more important things to be working on than a picnic, the MDF leadership told him. They were trying to become a real political party, after all.

Ferenc might have given up on the idea then and there, if not for a young woman who stood up from her seat in the back of the crowded chamber. I'll help organize it, she said.

Mária Filep came from a long line of anti-Communist dissidents. Her father had fought in the uprising against Soviet rule in 1956 as a messenger delivering secret news among the insurgents. Though only a child then, Mária remembers it vividly, even watching the Soviet tanks as they rolled in. Her family remained political even after the revolution was suppressed. They listened together to the illegal radio broadcasts, usually on low volume with the windows closed, even in the summer. The broadcasts were on in the background when Mária went to sleep.

Radio Free Europe was my bedtime story, she likes to say.

By 1989, Mária had already been politically active for some time. That previous fall she'd begun organizing support for the persecuted Hungarian minority in Transylvania, a mountainous region in neighboring Romania, living under the brutal dictator Nicolae Ceaușescu. She had been looking for a new cause to rally behind. *A picnic at the Iron Curtain?* The idea was so outlandish—she was instantly hooked.

Mária and Ferenc became the nucleus of a team. Whereas Ferenc was a dreamer, Mária was a doer. She worked at a construction company with access to a telephone—a rarity in Communist Hungary, which had the fewest telephones per capita in the whole Eastern Bloc. (The Hungarian state decided the people didn't need them, a restrictive but shortsighted move. By contrast, Ceaușescu's Romania encouraged phone use; that way the state could listen in.)

Awhirl with energy, Mária soon took charge. She thought Ferenc's plan should be broader and suggested inviting the participants of a group she was involved in—the Sorsközösség, or Common Fate Camp—which gathered reform-minded peoples from across the East, from Estonia to Yugoslavia. The Iron Curtain was despised by everyone, she thought, so they should all protest it together.

Soon they had a name—the Pan-European Picnic—and a draft program. They even had a logo, a dove bursting through barbed wire. The target date was mid-August, less than two months away.

Ferenc and Mária knew the challenges of staging such an event would be immense. The borderland was a dangerous, prohibited place. And they had neither people nor funds. But they decided to go ahead anyway. Once they started planning others would join in, they reasoned.

But now came the hard part: What would it mean to actually organize a picnic across the Iron Curtain?

———

WE TEND TO THINK OF THE IRON CURTAIN IN BINARY TERMS: IT was the world's harshest border, until it wasn't. But thinking in this way obscures the shifting tectonics taking place beneath the surface, rife with friction. In Hungary, reform had been brewing for some time behind the scenes, with upstarts within the ruling Communist Party (officially the Magyar Szocialista Munkáspárt (MSZMP), or the Hungarian Socialist Workers' Party) embracing some of the same ideas—freedom and democracy, ending the Soviet occupation—as those toiling on the outside. Communication was thin between these groups and the path marked with obstacles. But the ground for activism was fertile.

Even so, at the picnic the line between redemption and bloodshed was razor thin. To understand how it came together, we have to rewind to November 1988 and the rise of Miklós Németh—the last Communist prime minister of Hungary—perhaps the most important figure of the last days of the Iron Curtain, but someone few have heard of. The story of Hungary's transition begins with him.

Chapter Two

The close of 1988 was bitter cold, even by the standards of Hungary, situated on a flat, windy plain that stretches from the foothills of the Alps on the west, all the way to the Carpathians to the east. In the halls of power in Budapest, it was colder still. Hungary was in the midst of a massive economic downturn, with spiking inflation rates and astronomical foreign debt—the highest per capita in Europe. There was a lot of handwringing in Parliament but at root, no one knew what to do.

This wasn't the Soviet Union: food remained on the shelves and queues didn't extend interminably from every shop. But prices were rising and wages were falling. Discontent was growing in every sector, with factory workers warming their hands over coffee, and soldiers rationing coal in the barracks.

The state was in a downward spiral. It had to borrow large sums of money from the West just to keep the heat on—gas was purchased from the Soviet Union in hard currency, which Hungary didn't have. The government was in a bind. If it went bankrupt, there would be riots. But so might there be if it cut off the gas.

And amid this frayed economy, the opposition was beginning to grow. As a placatory measure, earlier that year, the government had passed a law that authorized political opposition—officially, the Association and Assembly Act. The reform was limited—these groups were not technically "parties," as they didn't have the capacity to compete in elections—but now they could legally organize. This had been a watershed, and the opposition ranks swelled.

Political activism was quite contained at this point, as most people were afraid to speak out. But a number of recent gatherings had turned into sizable rallies. Earlier that year, on June 27, 1988, as many as thirty thousand people packed the Heroes' Square in central Budapest to protest the actions of Romanian dictator Nicolae Ceaușescu, who had been persecuting ethnic Hungarians in Transylvania—the very cause that Mária Filep was simultaneously protesting in Debrecen. This was the largest demonstration anywhere in the Eastern Bloc for more than a generation.

For Communist Party elites, this was a dangerous development. Because of the national affection many Hungarians felt for their brethren, these rallies could not be simply suppressed; but nor could their democratic character be denied.

On October 23, students gathered at the Budapest Technical University to commemorate the quashed uprising against Soviet occupation in 1956. Thousands took to the streets; thousands more stood by their windows applauding, some brazenly on their balconies, others more furtively peeking out behind the glass. In principle, this rally was to honor reformers of the past, but everyone could read between the lines.

Elites within the ruling Hungarian Communist Party were growing nervous. They needed a solution to their economic woes, someone who could come in and right the ship. The answer arrived in the form of a talented young economist named Miklós Németh. At an extraordinary and contentious Party conference in May, the Central Committee removed the aging autocrat, János Kádár, from his perch as general secretary—he had been appointed by Moscow in 1956 after the revolution was suppressed—substituting another Party functionary, then prime minister Károly Grósz. Like Kádár, Grósz was vehemently against political reform, but he was younger and better able to appreciate Hungary's economic straits. The Party then selected Németh to take over as head of the government.

This was not an easy decision. Németh had for years been a loyal comrade, climbing Party ranks and proving his mettle. But he was a reformer, in favor of free markets and democratic elections; he had spent time in the United States, having won an economics scholarship to Harvard. Still, Party brass felt they had no choice. If things went well, they reasoned, Németh could save the system. And if not, they could blame him—and the other reformers—for their failure.

Németh took over as prime minister on November 24, 1988. At just forty years old, he was the youngest prime minister in the Eastern Bloc (and the second youngest in the world).

The path to reform wouldn't be easy. As head of the government, Németh had some authority, but the real center of power was the Party, headed by Grósz. From the outset, rivalry between them was fierce. Németh wanted to be able to appoint his own cabinet, filling it with technocrats like himself, rather than politburo appointees. But Grósz wouldn't tolerate this. He and the other Party hardliners were distrustful of Németh and had no appetite for radical reform. They wanted him on a tight leash.

For Németh, this lack of autonomy was crippling. He quickly understood he had been set up to fail. Privately, he referred to his appointment as prime minister as the kiss of death. He also discovered he was being spied on. There were bugs in his office; during one meeting of the Central Committee, snippets from private conversations with his aides were read aloud. Thereafter, Németh took to staging fictitious conversations in his office. He would engage in sensitive subjects only during walks outside, along the shores of the Danube.

Németh hadn't been in power for a week when on November 29, Grósz gave an address to the Party faithful warning about reformers in government and the aggressive agenda they sought. He stoked fear of a "White Terror," or violence against Communists, that might commence if they—the Party, including the Worker's Guard (Munkásőrség), its armed wing—were not vigilant. He referred to Németh and his fellow reformers as enemies within.

Political transitions are usually not easy, or unilinear, and flash-points are manifold. And the broad geopolitical turmoil of the time only exacerbated conditions on the ground. To those in the West, Gorbachev rocketed to prominence as the reformer who would help bring an end to half a century of nuclear stalemate. But in the East, Gorbachev's rise was regarded with skepticism. He was not like the Soviet leaders of the past. He came as if out of nowhere. This made it hard to know what to expect.

Reformers wondered whether Gorbachev really held power in the Kremlin. Might he be replaced by someone who would undo his reforms and punish those who stepped out of line? Hardliners had doubts too. What would happen if opposition rallies got out of hand? Would Moscow help them keep power—by force, if necessary—as it had done in the past? Gorbachev had stepped back somewhat from the Warsaw Pact states, intimating without saying outright that their futures were to be their own. This seemed to offer a great deal of autonomy to the satellites, but because they were still under a military occupation they had to look to Moscow. This meant that at any given moment, ruling elites weren't sure what they were responsible for, or to whom.

In Budapest, this generated a climate of stasis and distrust. For Németh, it presented a challenge. If he was going to execute reforms, he had to find a way to wrestle free from the gridlock.

Just before Christmas, Németh went home to Monok, the village where he'd grown up. But if he had been hoping for respite, instead he arrived to find his mother a nervous wreck. I don't go to the market anymore, she told him; I can't bear hearing what people are saying about you.

One day Németh came back from a walk to find his mother in tears, clutching a letter in her hands. In the envelope was a photograph of her son with a noose drawn around his neck. The paper stank of shit.

Németh took his father aside and told him not to open unfamiliar envelopes anymore.

Just as Grósz and his cronies had intended, the villagers blamed Németh for the poor economy. Fearful of Moscow's reaction, they were also angry that he tolerated public demonstrations. Most were old enough to remember 1956, when the Soviet tanks rolled in across the eastern border, not far away.

Those first months, November–December 1988, were a trial by fire. Németh's trip home was especially illuminating, given the popular fear that he was inviting a Soviet response. He realized then that he couldn't just negotiate power internally. He would have to go to Moscow. He would have to talk to Gorbachev.

WITH THE COMING OF THE NEW YEAR, 1989, NÉMETH BEGAN TO work out a plan to bring before the Soviet premier, to see how far he could push his agenda before he met resistance. Gorbachev was a reformer too, but there were differences. While they saw eye to eye on economic reforms (perestroika), they disagreed about politics (glasnost). Gorbachev was cautious—his aims fell far short of Németh's vision of multiparty democracy. Still, would Gorbachev resort to violence to stop him?

Németh prepared an expansive list of policy priorities, centering on the status of the Iron Curtain. Németh saw the problem of Soviet occupation clearly: reform didn't just require economic restructuring; it required agency. The Soviet control of Hungary's border, he believed, was the crux of their economic troubles. This was illustrated most clearly by a policy initiative set up by Grósz the previous year, on January 1, 1988, the so-called World Passport, which allowed Hungarians to request a travel document from the Interior Ministry, as well as $350 US that could be spent abroad. This was not the kind of policy usually favored by Soviet authorities, but it was tolerated as an attempt by the Hungarian Communist Party to appease the stirring masses.

Soon whole families were applying for this special travel permit—mother, father, grandma, grandpa—gathering together a large sum of money, then squeezing everyone into the car and crossing the border into Austria for a shopping spree. They would buy a nice refrigerator or air conditioner from the West—the kind of item you couldn't find in the East—and strap it onto the top of the car and drive back. The system was ideal for such happy spenders, but not for state coffers. Pretty soon all their hard currency ended up in Austria with no system of reciprocal trade by which they could get it back.

For Németh, this was a catastrophe. He had to put a stop to the policy immediately or the country would go bankrupt. But simply cutting off travel was impossible as it would run afoul of the people. Németh couldn't present himself as a reformer if his rule was as draconian as everyone else's. Instead he had to cut to the heart of the problem: the closed system of which the World Passport policy and indeed all Hungarian institutions were a part. He had to start chipping away at the Iron Curtain, the tool by which the Soviet Union kept the country locked in its grip. But how? He couldn't just blow past it—he didn't have that kind of authority. And anyway, Gorbachev would never allow it. So he needed a different tack.

Németh settled on the problem of the physical barrier and its exorbitant cost. Once an impenetrable security zone, the Iron Curtain in recent years had fallen into disrepair. The wiring of the electric fence had become frayed, going off all the time, no longer distinguishing humans from rabbits or deer, littering the borderlands with the detritus of animals and destroying the morale of the guards. Too expensive to maintain given how poorly it functioned, it had to be either completely revamped or eliminated.

This was the case Németh would bring to Moscow—financial hardship was something Gorbachev would appreciate. Obviously, anything involving changes at the border would be a sensitive subject. But disabling its physical infrastructure was a good first step toward undermining the authority of its rule. Németh felt that if he went and

explained things to Gorbachev in person, if he looked him in the eye, he could persuade him and trust he would keep his word.

Trust is dangerous in politics. But Németh had met Gorbachev before, in 1984, right before Gorbachev took power, during an official visit to Hungary. They were working in the agricultural divisions of their respective agencies and spent several days together in a car, visiting cooperatives and state farms. Németh felt there was something kindred about Gorbachev, something he could believe in. A nice reminder that all politics is local. Even at the top.

Gorbachev had been impressed by Hungary's agronomy, which was far more productive than the Soviet Union's, despite inferior soil. In a moment of candor, he'd turned to Németh: Tell me, he said, what is the secret? Németh described the reforms he and his unit had put in place, severing aspects of the economic system from central planning, even offering some market incentives. Hungary had already enacted some economic liberalization—essentially a mini-perestroika—precisely what Gorbachev would soon propose for the Soviet Union.

What impressed Németh about Gorbachev was his character.

Gorbachev didn't accept gifts or drink vodka, as was typical of other Soviet dignitaries. His mind was open and his thinking clear. They spent those days talking, listening, arguing. By the end of the trip, they were on a first name basis.

Mikhail Sergeyevich. Németh still uses the patronymic when he speaks of Gorbachev today.

But of course in politics, friendship—like trust—only goes so far. What Németh needed were concessions. The date of their next meeting was set for March 3, 1989.

———

THE FLIGHT FROM BUDAPEST TO MOSCOW IS JUST A FEW HOURS, but politically Moscow was a different world.

Németh was nervous on multiple fronts. He insisted on bringing one of his trusted aides to bear witness to the events and to take notes in case Gorbachev later reneged on his word. But Németh was also concerned about prying eyes within his own politburo. So he asked that the translators be provided by the Soviet Union rather than Hungary, to prevent leaks.

The trip got off to an inauspicious start. Németh had big plans, but the meeting was allotted only twenty minutes. He would have to be quick. In fact, the whole thing was rushed to begin with. Németh had pushed for a meeting so soon in part because Grósz was due to travel to Moscow later that month. If Grósz got there first, Németh feared he might undercut him—warning Gorbachev of the scope of his plans, which might have put an end to the project before it started.

The meeting was formal. They sat together in a small room, flanked by advisors and translators. There were no hugs or kisses. But Gorbachev remembered Németh from their prior conversations. This was evident to Németh immediately—in his gaze, and the warmth of their handshake.

Wasting no time, Németh cut straight to their issue of broad ideological disagreement: I want to move toward free elections, he said.

The ramifications of this were obvious: in free elections, the Communist Party might lose, and if they did, they would have to relinquish power. The conversation immediately soured. Gorbachev did not want to push toward a post-Communist future. He wanted to return to the Communism of Lenin and the New Economic Policy (from 1922)—a system of market incentives that would work within the Communist system, not against it.

Soon the men were arguing. Németh put an end to this by posing a question, sharp and direct: If we hold an election and the Communists are voted out, what will be your reaction, Mikhail?

Gorbachev replied just as forcefully: Miklós, he said, as long as I am sitting in this chair, 1956 will never happen again.

Not exactly a blessing, but a promise. The Soviets would not send tanks.

With this out of the way, Németh could focus on specifics. He started with the withdrawal of nuclear warheads and Soviet troops from Hungarian soil. This was a delicate subject. Gorbachev commanded everyone in the room to stop taking notes.

Now off the record, Gorbachev described a bleak picture. The Defense Council in the Soviet politburo was filled overwhelmingly with hardliners opposed to anything that might weaken their military standing, and were eager to put an end to Gorbachev's talk of reform. There would be no negotiating about nuclear matters.

If news gets out that we even discussed this, Gorbachev said, I will be destroyed.

Officially, the USSR denied there were nuclear warheads in Hungary. Until he became prime minister, Németh himself hadn't known about them. They were hidden in silos outside Lake Balaton, right in the middle of the country.

Németh pledged never to mention them. But he did ask Gorbachev to withdraw a unit of Soviet forces from Hungarian soil—a trifle, perhaps, but something that could be reported to the Hungarian press.

(Both men kept their word. On April 26, ten thousand troops left Hungary, and Németh never spoke of the country's nuclear arsenal.)

Now that the conversation had settled into calmer waters, Németh made his move: Hungary has decided to begin tearing down the Iron Curtain, he told Gorbachev. Németh did not ask this, he declared it—he calls this his *force-item*. If the Warsaw Pact wants to keep the Curtain, he said, they should pay for it.

Németh had steeled himself for a fight. But Gorbachev merely responded: That's your responsibility.

Németh was stunned. He had achieved virtually all he had hoped for. And for all the friction at the outset, the meeting ended amicably. Rather than twenty minutes, they spoke for two and half hours. Whenever an aide called Gorbachev to another meeting, he said to cancel it.

Németh left relieved, but a bit unsteady on his feet. He saw Gorbachev, still, as a person he could trust. But he understood now just how vulnerable Gorbachev was to the hardliners within his own Party. Indeed, the issue was less that Gorbachev might betray him, and more that Gorbachev himself might be betrayed. This was a threat Németh intuitively understood, given the line he was also treading. Both men in different ways worried that their days were numbered.

Németh realized then that he had to start executing reforms immediately. Specifically, he had to cut the electric wiring of the Iron Curtain before Gorbachev changed his mind or was replaced by someone less benevolent.

This was now his main fear: that he didn't have enough time.

Chapter Three

L ike so many things, political ideas begin mysteriously and build slowly, almost imperceptibly—until they suddenly seem unstoppable.

So it was for many in the opposition when, in March 1989, around the time of Németh's trip to Moscow, the political change they'd so long envisioned suddenly seemed not just possible, but very real. That month, the often-fractious opposition groups formed a round table, briefly putting their differences aside in their common struggle, lest the state divide them up and devour them one by one.

It was at this time that László Magas, leader of the MDF in Sopron, began traveling to Budapest for meetings at MDF headquarters. Far from the hinterlands of Sopron, out by the western border with Austria, Budapest was the political and cultural capital of the country and the center of opposition activity. By early spring 1989, demonstrations in the capital were not uncommon; still, for Magas, the experience was thrilling.

Even just a year before, such gatherings would have been broken up violently, usually with beatings and imprisonments. But now the police simply stood back and observed, as though waiting for a call that never came. If such events were possible, it was natural to wonder what else might be.

On March 15, the power of the people was no longer left in doubt. It was the anniversary of the 1848 revolution against the Habsburgs, and in addition to the official state ceremony, the opposition held one of its own—as much as three times larger than the state affair, an explosion of color and energy. The opposition crowd was loud; it was also fearless. At one point, a student read out Gyula Illyés's censored poem, "A Sentence about Tyranny."

"Where there is tyranny, there is tyranny . . ." the student recited, "in the 'sh' of the finger sealing the mouth."

Illyés was a critical voice from the period of Hungary's darkest days, following the Soviet takeover, under the authority of Stalinist puppet Mátyás Rákosi. During those years, especially 1948–1956, hundreds of thousands of dissidents and critics were jailed or killed, land was forcibly stripped from farmers, democratic institutions were shuttered or corrupted, and all power was removed thousands of kilometers away, to Moscow, an alien capital in an alien land.

Illyés penned his famous poem in 1950, but it was immediately banned, surfacing a few years later, in 1956 during the revolution, after which it was censored anew. For a whole generation, Illyés's words were unutterable. But here was a student, reading them aloud.

Standing there in that sea of bodies, listening to these words, Magas was awed. It was his own life read back to him, touched by the horrors of state oppression in the very ways that Illyés described.

For Magas, like so many of the opposition, that day in March was definitive. It was a time of words theretofore unspoken, thoughts previously kept inside, now pushing forcefully into the bright of day.

On that afternoon in Budapest, Magas got a glimpse of the future, free of coercive state power. But returning home to Sopron was affecting too, leaving the center and going back to the periphery. In Sopron, the view was different, pressed up as it was against the Iron Curtain. Here, coercive state power was everywhere.

THE BORDER IS JUST OUTSIDE THE CITY OF SOPRON, MAKING
something of a hook around it. As with most borders, this is not oblique
to politics. In 1920, Hungarian territory was divided up according to
the Treaty of Trianon, after the Austro-Hungarian Empire was broken
up by the victors of the First World War. Overnight, two-thirds of Hungary's land and half its people were distributed among its neighbors—
with millions of Hungarians consigned to live outside the state rather
than within it—a tragedy that still looms large in the national psyche.

Sopron is a nice footnote to this painful history. The western Hungarian borderlands, Sopron included, were initially to be awarded to
Austria. But this met with unrest in the city, leading finally to a plebi-
scite, held on December 14, 1921, where the inhabitants opted to stay
in Hungary. It has been called the City of Fidelity, Civitas Fidelis-
sima, ever since. Like every border, this one is thus a human artifact;
but unlike most borders it was, at least in part, drawn by the people
themselves.

After the Second World War and the division of Europe between
East and West—between the Soviet area of influence (covering what
became known as the Eastern Bloc, or the Warsaw Pact states, principally East Germany, Poland, Czechoslovakia, Hungary, Romania, and
Bulgaria) and the American sphere of influence (Western Europe), first
adumbrated at the Yalta Conference in February 1945—Sopron soon
found itself as a western outpost of Soviet territory.

"From Stettin in the Baltic to Trieste in the Adriatic, an iron curtain has descended across the continent." The words are Churchill's,
delivered in a now-famous speech on March 5, 1946, at Westminster
College in Missouri. The term *Iron Curtain* was originally a metaphor
for the limit of Soviet dominion. It didn't stay metaphorical for long;
soon it came to represent a sequence of actual barriers—a restricted
security zone, enforced by layers of barbed wire fencing, watchtowers,
and patrols—that became among the most militarized boundaries in
the world.

In Hungary, its first iteration was a minefield; later, in 1953, after a brutal sequence of border guard deaths, the mines were replaced with an electric fence. In May 1965, it was fully refurbished, thanks to a new fencing system, the sz-100 provided by the Soviet Union. For citizens of the East, the Iron Curtain soon became an uncrossable divide, powerful not just in its scale, but also in the mythology that justified its rule. In the official ideology of the Soviet satellite states, the Curtain was envisaged as a shield defending them from the forces of capitalism and unrepentant fascism inherent to the West.

Across the Hungarian opposition, this boundary system was a repository for their feelings of unfreedom and constraint. But for the people of Sopron who toiled in its shadow, this was especially so. Growing up, Magas spent a lot of time thinking about the border, the tangible limit of his world. He was especially taken by Lake Fertő, a sliver of water that cuts across the Hungarian-Austrian divide, just north of Sopron. The lake provided an imaginative landscape for his longings—for freedom, the West, everything that lay on the other shore, just beyond reach. He lived just a few minutes' drive from the lake, but because it was part of the Iron Curtain, he could never go see it.

In some ways, the story of the lake, and the slow, stepwise access to it provided by the state, offers a mirror to the liberalization of the country at large. Until the 1970s, all access to Lake Fertő was forbidden. Then in 1977 the government began to ease restrictions, and residents of Sopron and the nearby village of Fertőrákos could go visit for the weekend, lie on the beach, even swim. You had to give your ID when you showed up; you got it back on the way out. There were strict curfews, and those who lost track of time or overstayed were brought back by force.

Predictably, there were some attempts to flee. The lake was tantalizing—there in front of you was the border, Austrian flags visible only a few, swimmable kilometers away. Out on the water were watchtowers and border guards on boats. Some people tried their chances, hiding in the reeds, waiting until nightfall. There were some epic chases. But most people were caught and brought back.

After a time, not only citizens of Sopron but all Hungarians could go to the lake. Later still, you didn't even have to relinquish your ID.

On one of my first trips to the Hungarian borderlands, I decided to drive out to Lake Fertő. I wanted to experience the landscape, to try and understand something of what the border meant to those who grew up beside it.

The lake lies right beyond Fertőrákos. It is long, and so slender that no matter where you drive or walk alongside it, you can always see the other side. It is also very shallow. These days there is a yearly competition where people over a certain height gather to walk from one side to the other, because at no point will their heads go under.

I pull up into a flat, open parking lot of the sort common to picnic grounds worldwide. There is plenty of space for cars, even on a sunny day, along with refreshment stands and public toilets. As you dip down toward the water you find a beach, with a playground set up right against the shore and a flat stretch of grass where families spread out their blankets and dogs chase about.

It is late in the afternoon when I arrive and the sun is already past the midpoint in the sky, its light beginning to shift toward the pale amber of summer evenings, illuminating the opposite shore: Austria, basking in possibility. It looks so close; the water, so inviting. How could anyone resist?

I walk now through extensive docklands, where countless small sailboats are moored. The sheer serenity of the scene is striking, given the context of the recent past. At one point, I pass a ferry landing. A small wooden plaque in Hungarian, German, and English, proclaims "To Austria."

The big shift in travel came in 1988, with the World Passport policy that Németh so despised. Many of the Hungarian activists I interviewed spoke giddily about those times. From Sopron, you could go to Austria three times a day if you wanted. No one had much money, so there wasn't a whole lot they could do; still, just the fact of such travel was exhilarating.

László Nagy another activist from Sopron—who first introduced me to the story of the picnic out in the field at Sopronpuszta—recalls a moment that spring, when he and some friends made a plan to hop in the car and go to Austria, to Eisenstadt, thirty kilometers away, but then decided against it. The wine at home was good and they were feeling lazy. They were happy to sit around and talk about the fact that they could have gone if they wanted to.

This was a stage altogether new. Not the euphoria of freedoms gained; but the banality of freedoms gotten used to. The next stage was still far away. Even in László's dreamy reflections about those days, there is always a shadow. The fear that at any moment, without cause, it could all be taken away.

All they had to do was look around to realize the precariousness of their situation. In the neighboring states, East Germany, Czechoslovakia, and Romania, conditions weren't just as bad as ever. They were getting worse.

GYULA ILLYÉS'S POEM WAS A DARING UTTERANCE. THE FACT THAT such a thing was even possible was a testament to how far Hungary had come. Still, a lot was left unspoken, at least formally, most of all, the story of 1956 itself. But this too was about to change. While Németh spent the spring concerned about a reprise of 1956, his fellow reformer, Minister of State Imre Pozsgay, was looking for ways to revisit it.

In the decades since the uprising, all critical discussion of the subject was prohibited. Certainly there was no commemoration of the freedom fighters or condemnation of Soviet aggression. But just as 1989 brought wind of a progressive political future, it also perhaps allowed for a reconsideration of the past. At least that's how Pozsgay saw it. You can't have political transition without a historical reckoning, he argued. If the government suppressed the people—as it no doubt did—it was a crisis not just of history, but of the present, of the very legitimacy of the Communist regime.

It was in January 1989 that Pozsgay started to kick about the silt of history and ask questions of 1956, culminating in a provocative public radio address. The uprising, he declared, was not a treasonous counter-revolution, as the Party had for decades maintained. It was a popular movement, a "legitimate uprising of a people whose national sensibility and self-esteem had been crushed by dictatorship."

Across the country, people listened to their radios in stunned silence, disbelieving what they had just heard; they dashed outside, hoping to catch a friend or neighbor, someone who might have heard it too.

After his address, Pozsgay was summoned before a committee of decorated Communists, people who had won awards for their service in putting down the rebellion, who had drawn their weapons on their own people and profited from it. In short: the very people whose heroism Pozsgay was out to deny.

Pozsgay was told by his security detail that there would be weapons in the room, that the police wouldn't be able to control the situation if it got out of hand. They feared he wouldn't survive. Pozsgay said he would go anyway. His deputy, László Vass, escorted him to the meeting and recorded the exchange with the secret service on a tape recorder, in case something were to happen. On his way home, Vass stopped by his office in Parliament and put the cassette in a safe.

Pozsgay made it out alive; but the next morning when they opened the safe, the cassette was gone. Pozsgay instructed Vass not to leave anything in the office again.

This was February, just before Németh's trip to Moscow. As Pozsgay unveiled the secrets of 1956, he was rapidly making enemies. Party chief Károly Grósz was livid when he heard what Pozsgay was up to. Grósz confronted him, told him he was acting irresponsibly, that he was moving too fast.

From that point on, Pozsgay walked about with a target on his back. But he was content with his intervention and the reform it encouraged. Indeed, things *were* moving very fast. That was the point.

BY EARLY SPRING, HUNGARY'S POLITICAL CLASS WAS RIVEN BY infighting. Such a chasm had opened up between the reform and hardline wings of the Party that it was hard for the two sides to control their vitriol. Given the rise of opposition activity, the fact that the state would undergo reform was no longer possible to suppress or deny. But no turf would be conceded without a fight. Németh several times received word from his security detail that Grósz was planning a coup. This made for many sleepless nights.

One may make myriad mistakes in retelling history; it is a minefield of misinference and omission. In Hungary, the difficulty lies in untangling the chaos of actors, angry stars vying for a place in a petulant, paranoid sky. Too frequently we forge a Manichean divide between the forces of good—"the people"—and evil—"the state." And maybe this was how it was in Poland—the other country in the East Bloc treading a similar path of reform—but in Hungary there were three sets of actors: the opposition groups, the reformers in government, and the Party hardliners. Power in such a context has many faces; many anxieties too.

For those on the outside, the fissures within the state—and the uncertainty of its positioning—added to the arbitrariness of its power, and the feeling that everything they had achieved could be taken from them. But this is also how things felt on the inside. In a way, arbitrariness and uncertainty are two sides of the same coin. This condition of indefinite stalemate defined the Hungarian transition. The three sides were in a standoff, with each side waiting to see if someone would blink.

And it was in the midst of this morass that Németh enacted his plan to start cutting the electrical wiring of the Iron Curtain. The date was set for May 2 and the event would be public, staged outside Hegyeshalom, by the tripartite border of Hungary, Czechoslovakia, and Austria. The weeks beforehand were a scramble to get everything ready.

At this point all their actions took place under a shroud of secrecy—deliberately kept from the prying eyes of Party hardliners. These were nervous days around the capital, with a lot of averted eyes and brisk handshakes. Plans were not discussed, except in private.

The driving force was the conviction shared by Németh and other reformers—principally Imre Pozsgay, Interior Minister István Horváth, and Balázs Nováky, commander of the border patrol—that this was the right plan of action.

With everything in place, Németh was ready to make his move.

Chapter Four

The press conference was held under the cloak of a cloud-thick sky, with journalists transported in for the occasion. As spectacles go, the May 2 event was a muted one—there was only so much the Németh government could do without the Party catching wind.

It was dramatic nevertheless: a circuit breaker was pulled, a bit of electrical wiring rolled up. Rows of border guards, young men in dark green uniforms with white, heavy-duty gloves and large wire clippers, made their way across the stretch of fencing, snipping the wires from their concrete posts and rolling them up into bundles, like metal bales of hay.

Balázs Nováky of the border patrol took questions from the press. He was in a good mood, outlining the economic reasoning behind the cutting of the wires, even flashing some wit. When a journalist asked whether they had informed Austria of their decision, he said no, then added: Why should we? We didn't tell them when we put it up.

The audience was sparse, but the message was clear: from that day forward, the current that made the Iron Curtain so deadly would be switched off.

This sent a shockwave around the world—including within the Hungarian Communist Party. Németh's event blindsided Grósz. All

the planning and coordination had happened under his nose, but he
knew nothing. It was all over before Grósz had time to react. On the
outside, it was a triumph of political theatre; on the inside, it was a heist.

Németh's timing was intentional: the event took place the day
after May Day, one of the most important dates on the Communist
calendar—celebrating laborers, and by extension the Party for whom
they putatively toiled. In the preceding weeks, Party leadership was
kept busy with the May Day planning, Grósz included. This provided
Németh all the cover he needed.

The May Day festivities were viewed as a chance for the Party to
rekindle confidence in its vision. Tens of thousands of people were
anticipated to attend. But the weather didn't cooperate—sheets of rain
poured over the venue, turning the fairgrounds into a mudded lagoon.
Few but Party functionaries showed up. When it came time for speeches,
Németh stood on the damp, cheerless stage beside Grósz, who sermon-
ized about the glories of Communism and hectored Németh for his
reckless reforms. If Németh took any solace, it was in knowing what
was to come the following day.

The wire-cutting event went off without a hitch. Eager journalists
sped home to write up the shocking news. Border guards soaked up
the attention of the world, so rarely cast upon their far-flung stretch of
it. That evening, news of the event was aired on Hungarian television.

Németh spent the evening alone with his thoughts. He imagined
a phone call, the hotline ringing: Gorbachev angry, shouting, telling
him to stop the whole process. Németh was all but alone in the Eastern
Bloc, with only a handful of allies. One word of displeasure from Moscow might have been enough to tip the scales—for Grósz, or any of the
other hardliners—to put a stop to Németh and his reforms. They were
already looking for reasons.

He thought of the nearly one hundred thousand remaining
Soviet troops on Hungarian soil. Who knew how they might react?
All it would take was for one to feel threatened, to get defensive or
go rogue.

Such were the scenarios that played out in Németh's mind as he lay awake in bed, the night of May 2. He also thought about his father, a staunch anti-Communist, who had resisted Németh's ascent to power. In 1988, before he decided to take the office of prime minister, he went back to his village to ask his advice. If you feel the strength inside, you should accept the position, his father told him. But I don't want to see my son hung up like Imre Nagy, he said, invoking the prime minister during the 1956 uprising. We've had some bad experiences with reformers in the past.

The morning of May 3, news of the wire cutting was splashed across the pages of the world press. And still there was no reaction from Moscow. Later that week, Németh bumped into the Soviet ambassador in the Parliament building. The issue was not raised.

Emboldened by this calm, on May 10, Németh cut his remaining ties with the Party, kicking out the last handful of cabinet members he had inherited from Grósz and putting in his own men. He didn't ask permission from the Central Committee or await their response. Finally, his government was fully free of the Party—the first autonomous regime in the entire Communist world.

A week later, on May 18, Németh signed an official decree that the Iron Curtain would be dismantled in Hungary. The declaration had been written out and planned since February, but the time hadn't been right. Now Németh was ready. He knew where he stood.

—————

MY CONVERSATIONS WITH NÉMETH TAKE PLACE AT HIS COTTAGE perched among vineyards in the hills outside Lake Balaton. Szonja, a student of mine, is with us to help with translation and to look through documents. Németh's wife, Erzsébet, offers us coffee and almonds from the trees near their house.

Németh is a fairly reserved man, a private citizen now and getting on in years. He spends a lot of time fussing over his grandchildren, far from the cauldron of politics. But when revisiting his days in office, he becomes animated. When the political drama escalates he paces; occasionally he smacks the table and pushes his fingers into his chest.

How do we get a leader like Németh, I wonder, a politician of such integrity and equanimity? This is one of the oldest questions of politics, usually posed as something of a riddle: Do good leaders produce good laws, or do good laws produce good leaders?

Of course, the question is a tricky one. Citizens and laws are not discrete from one another, but co-constitutive. When bad rulers arise, they do not just emerge, as if, from nowhere—however much they sometimes seem to. Rather, they are endogenous to the societies that produce them. This is why social change is so hard to bring about. When leaders do enact reform, they tend to do so in a manner that fulfils their own interests too.

In Plato's *Republic*, the problem of leadership is posed by Socrates: "Where will we find a disposition at the same time gentle and great-spirited?" His answer is well known: the leader cannot just be a king, he must also be a philosopher; he must be a philosopher king.

Tempted by power, only the worst people will seek to rule—the vain, the ignorant, the greedy. The only way you will get good people, Plato tells us, is by selecting them at birth and raising them on a lie—a Noble Lie—that within their veins flows golden blood, by dint of which it is their duty to serve. Those anointed are to be educated at the highest levels and are to live without property or wealth. He likens their training to a kind of dyeing process—as though the soul were imprinted with virtue, like an article of clothing, such that even faced with temptation, the "dye could not be washed out."

In other words, justice only obtains when philosophy and politics align—a rare occurrence. Plato is doubtful it can be sustained.

Plato is not alone in being skeptical of the possibilities of good leadership. Rousseau comes to a similar point, that only a man without interest in the outcome of laws will write good ones. He is so pessimistic that such a person could emerge internal to the state, he suggests the leader should come from the outside, as good societies must "entrust the establishment of their laws to foreigners."

So how do we explain a man like Németh? The risks he took for others gain. And the oddness of his legacy. He still feels warmly about Communism, despite having done perhaps more than anyone else in Hungary to bring it down. I ask him about this, his trajectory to power. Why he chose to enter the Communist Party, rather than pursue a course of reform from the outside—by joining one of the budding opposition groups, like Fidesz (the Alliance of Young Democrats, or Fiatal Demokraták Szövetsége), alongside Viktor Orbán, for example.

My question is a real one: How does one decide to fight the system from within, rather than from without? But it is untactful of me to mention Orbán, a sore point in contemporary Hungary. Németh gets exercised by this. Don't compare me with the Fidesz generation, he snaps. I didn't come of age in an era of change.

He continues calmly: You know how many times I've asked myself that question? It was impossible.

Németh was born in a village with only a few thousand residents, tucked into the northeast of the country. There was only one school in town and the children would rotate between morning and afternoon classes so everyone would have a spot. Németh's family was Catholic and anti-Communist. Sometimes he would wake up with his grandmother at 5 a.m. for mass and then go to school afterward. But Németh always understood that education—official, Communist education— was the way forward.

This is one of the enduring legacies of Communism, that state-funded schooling was available to everyone. There was a lot of accommodation in the process—saying the right things, toeing the line, looking the other way. But if you wanted to go places in Hungary, this was your best bet.

Németh did eventually make it out of the village, going first to a grammar school in Miskolc, the nearest city, then to Karl Marx

University, where he studied economics. He excelled and soon found himself drawn into the political machine. One day, the rector invited the top students of the program into his office and offered them membership in the Party. You are the best and brightest, he said. We want you on the inside.

Németh accepted. The Party had helped him get this far, and he wasn't going to stop now. But he was torn up—he knew his father would not approve. When he first returned to the village with his Party membership, his father wouldn't speak to him. Not a word for six months.

For years, Németh's loyalty to the Party was unwavering. An intelligent, hard-working young man, he steadily ascended the ranks. But in 1981, he was promoted to an elevated position in the economics division of the Central Committee, and there everything changed. In this new office, he gained access to state economic records through which he learned the Party had been lying—specifically about debt. There before him, Németh had the internal figures in one hand and the reported figures in the other. The difference was *billions* of dollars. The economic trajectory of the state was unsustainable. Indeed, the country was headed for collapse.

Németh understood then that the only path forward was reform. He also knew that if the millions of Hungarians outside knew what he now did, they would want change too. He was in on a secret and had to find a way to tell it. But he had neither the authority nor the platform. To change the economic direction of the country he needed first to rise to a position of power. This would take time.

IN OUR DAYS TOGETHER, NÉMETH SHOWS ME REAMS OF FILES from those tumultuous first months in office. Formal briefs typed up by his secretary as well as private notes, scribbled in shorthand along the margins. This is where he kept his most precious, intimate thoughts, the off-the-record stuff that no one could see—like his discussion with Gorbachev about the nuclear warheads. These personal papers were closely guarded. He carried them around with him wherever he went, wouldn't show them even to his closest associates.

He pretends now to be aloof about his records, as though they are merely the detritus of a bygone era; but he curates them meticulously. These are probably useless to you, he says, looking at the stack of papers he is rummaging through.

I smile and photograph them anyway. To me these scribbles are everything. His thoughts and worries; the space between how he remembers things and how they unfurled. Not the chess game, per se, but the thinking and rethinking of every move, even those that never happened. The idle daydreams of a man in power, sitting on the precipice of a changing world.

I try to imagine what it would have felt like, living in the Communist system—the dreams people harbored, their banalities and stresses. It isn't easy, in part because of my own biases, borne of the ideological system of which I too am a part. I recall a joke I used to think was funny. "What is the contract of Communism? You pretend to work, and we pretend to pay you."

I realize now the ideological work the joke was doing. Of course people worked incredibly hard in Communist times. And the problem wasn't about payment. Even to think of Communism in terms of contracts was our invention, the ideological tool of the West. It was a joke made by us, for us. It cast a world we didn't know into terms we did.

I try to remember when I first heard it, but I can't. At home, we wouldn't have made fun of Communism in such a flippant way. More likely I learned it in high school; our curriculum did little to disabuse us of such prejudice. The first two years of our history education were dedicated to the United States, the third to Europe, and the fourth to what we then called "the third world." It wasn't a terrible course, but there was one country clearly omitted: the Soviet Union. It wasn't American or European. It was "second world," another bygone concept, and thus outside the mandate of our final year. In other words: the "world" was everywhere else.

This eluded me then. It is only now, so many years later, that I am beginning to understand what that omission meant, the kind of American it shaped me to become. We are all products of our national frame—me in my American high school, Németh ascending to state power, as Mária Filep and Ferenc Mészáros and all the others laboring on the outside. We learn what the state wants us to, and we become the citizens this curriculum creates. It's a black box, sealed shut, until something comes along to prize it open.

That something came along for Németh in 1981, when he saw inside the books the state was cooking, his *eureka* moment, positioning him briefly outside of the office in which he sat, seeing the world anew. It was this experience that conditioned the leader he was to become. A clarity of vision we all long for but infrequently find.

It is similar somehow, this moment, to what Ferenc felt over dinner in Debrecen in June 1989, and what Magas experienced at the demonstration just a few months prior in March. An instance that captures the chaos of the world we live in and distills it to a point of perfect clarity. Not all revolutions have this; those that do still often fail. But it's a beginning. A portal out of received time.

One evening, late into our talk, Erzsébet, Németh's wife, comes outside where we are sitting and brings us lamps, as it has grown dark. You know, she says before leaving, it would be a lot more relevant for you to write a book about the DMZ.

She is referring to the militarized border between the Koreas, perhaps the closest analog we have to the Iron Curtain today. I shrug the comment off lightly. I prefer to stay in the past, I tell her, although this is not entirely true. What I am most after is the trace the past has on the present. And Németh's story is part of this. So are his scribblings. So is this idle chatter, ours now, as much as his then.

————

IT WAS NOT RANDOM THAT NÉMETH SETTLED ON THE BORDER AS his nexus of change; the issue that most required compromise from

Gorbachev. It is an important institution, no doubt. But it is also a symbol, an idea, emblematic of sovereignty, of self-determination. Of freedom too.

What Németh did that day, May 2, 1989, when he cut the electric fencing of the Iron Curtain, was shift the logic of possibility for opposition activity, like a magician lifting the curtain on a trick. His words were unspoken, but he used a language every single Hungarian would understand.

After the news broadcast on Hungarian television on the evening of May 2, the whole nation waited to see if the Soviets would respond—precisely what Németh feared that sleepless night, and what Pozsgay felt when he revisited 1956 in front of the room of decorated Communists.

But the Soviet Union, the great giant, did not stir. This was the moment, for activists across the opposition, when they knew. The door was open. Not just for demonstrations, but for concrete collective action. The time to organize was now.

Chapter Five

History is always a story of ghosts, figures of the past haunting the present. For the '89ers in Hungary, visions of 1956 and the failed Hungarian uprising against Soviet rule weighed heavily. That moment of brutal repression, when freedom fighters were crushed beneath the tread of Soviet tanks; of blood in the streets, where shrapnel marks pocked plaster facades on the avenues. It is the point around which all narratives of this period coalesce, the lodestar that guides political imagination.

I am in László Nagy's office in Sopron, seated on the floor, surrounded by papers. László was one of the organizers of the picnic and very much the keeper of its records. We are going through documents—photographs, memorabilia, and other such items, as dusty and time-worn as the memories they capture. László speaks quickly, the flush of boyhood still on his cheeks despite being in his early sixties.

It was he who first introduced me, now many months back, to the story of the picnic. We corresponded about meeting. Come to my office, he said. I have everything you need.

It is a cluttered room, yet more crowded with my presence. Where the shelves end, the floor accommodates. Stacks of books teeter around us. László calls it the history room. It is his personal office, and also the address for the Pan-European Picnic '89 Foundation, of which he is the secretary and, seemingly, its only member. We are on the second floor of a stately house where László lives with his wife. Stand-alone and offset from the road, it is the same building he inhabited through the turmoil in 1989.

That woman, László explains pointing at a photograph of the picnic, she's Hungarian but lives in Austria. She fled in 1956. She went crazy at the picnic. She saw the refugees, the East Germans, and it all came back to her: everyone was afraid, the soldiers, what they might do. She relived it all, as though she went back in time.

László has photographs from 1956 too, black and white. That's Stalin, he says of a fallen statue. Freedom fighters, they threw down the red star, you see?

The stage for 1956 was set a few years earlier, in 1953, when Hungary's Soviet puppet Mátyás Rákosi was summoned to Moscow

to account for his paltry economic record. This was a grave issue in Moscow's eyes. As a satellite, you couldn't just be subservient to the metropole, you had to be productive for it. Thereafter, Rákosi was to share power with Imre Nagy, a moderate, who became prime minister, while Rákosi remained general secretary of the Hungarian Communist Party.

Nagy's attempts to tone down some of the harsher aspects of the Rákosi regime were quickly overruled by Party hardliners—which, by summer of 1956, sparked an outcry of public support for Nagy. Students at the Technical University of Budapest put out a letter demanding reform, and on October 23 there was a massive demonstration.

The students were unarmed, but the crowd quickly grew in size and when the police tried to contain the situation by firing shots into the crowd, a revolt broke out. The army was called in to control the protestors, but rather than contain them, they joined in. What began as a peaceful protest quickly snowballed into an armed insurrection. Nagy spoke in front of the Parliament building to try and calm the unrest, but the crowd only became more boisterous. On the afternoon of October 24, the Soviet army invaded Budapest.

In the days that followed, thousands were killed and scores more wounded as the Soviet forces overwhelmed the protestors. Nagy tried to restore order, begging the protestors to stand down so he could negotiate a cease-fire. He succeeded, and within a few days the Soviet army withdrew and Nagy took control of the government, promising to restore the multiparty system that had existed in Hungary prior to the Soviet takeover.

It seemed to be a new day for Hungary. But the Kremlin decided Nagy had gone too far, and ordered him to step aside, in favor of the new, Moscow-sanctioned prime minister, János Kádár. Nagy refused. The next morning, on November 4, the Soviet forces attacked without mercy.

After the revolution was suppressed, Kádár took over and cleaned house, embarking on a reign of terror similar in style to Rákosi's, ferreting out leaders of the revolution, who were executed or imprisoned—

including Imre Nagy, executed by hanging in 1958. Kádár consolidated power quickly and stayed atop the government for thirty-two years.

Most of the opposition members in 1989 were children of the late 1950s and early '60s, the generation that came of age right after the passage of Soviet tanks. The horrors of that violence were close to mind in their childhoods, but so was the hope of redemption, the idea that one day they would rise up and right the wrongs of that failed revolution.

László was born in 1957, at the beginning of the Kádár years, and grew up in Sopron listening to Radio Free Europe with his father. The broadcast would be interrupted every few minutes by a siren. When it came, his father wiggled the dial a bit to the left now to the right, hoping to recapture the signal. If that was achieved, he could hear something silenced everywhere else: the news, the story of the present.

As far as politics went, this was the extent of it. Certainly, you were never to act or be political in any way, or even talk about such things outside the house. Sometimes László did, but only to his closest friends. His parents scolded him for this. *Soha, sehol, senkinek*, they said, quoting a familiar phrase. Never, nowhere, to nobody. That was when you should speak about politics.

László's family had reason to be worried, as they were under constant state pressure due to his father's insufficient loyalty. He was an engineer and thus a resource for the state, but an anti-Communist, so someone they kept an eye on. In 1970, when László was thirteen, his father was relocated to Nigeria with his family. They spent several years there, as part of a community of about two hundred Hungarian expats, all but three of whom—his father, a math professor, and an eye doctor—were devoted Communists.

László's father was always at risk of being punished. Sometimes a delegation would be sent from Budapest to check on him. Such was the state's power, it followed you wherever you went. At any moment, you felt a black car might stop in front of your house—this was the governing idiom of the period—and take you away.

This is the thing we cannot explain to our children, László says about those days. Your generation cannot understand, he says also to me.

Fraught dreamscapes were common across the social spectrum. In his novel, *The Case Worker* (1969), György Konrád depicts the life of a bureaucrat in the Communist infrastructure. Even though his protagonist works for the state, he shares in the torment felt by regular citizens—replete with nightmares of trading places with the subjects he lorded power over.

> [I] dreamed about him: handcuffed, he led me along a barred-off corridor where, at regular intervals, jack-booted guards brooded outside gray, felt-padded doors. In another dream he was sitting bolt upright at my desk, his long fingers rested on the keys of my typewriter; he warned me that I must tell the truth, and started a file on my case.

Konrád revisits these tense, locked down years—the "consolidated '60s"—in his memoir, *A Guest in My Own Country* (2002). "After 1956 people no longer tacked their thoughts up on trees," he writes. "Once informing has become common currency—and the informer the model citizen—what is left to inform about? Where is the truth whereby we can recognize the liar?"

The government hold on power was ruthless, especially in the beginning. But Kádár proved to be a more able governor than his predecessor, slowly easing his terror tactics and settling into a moderate style of governance. Starting in the 1970s, Hungary began to liberalize, at least economically—the very scheme that Németh explained to Gorbachev during his trip in 1984, sometimes called Goulash Communism, named after the iconic local stew. Political freedoms remained minimal, but Hungary flourished, relative to its neighbors. This brought something of a renaissance, a mini-thaw, just enough to spark hope that one day real reform might be possible.

László returned to Hungary in 1977 to go to university. He studied chemistry at the Technical University of Budapest—the same institution where the 1956 uprising began—and quickly became obsessed with politics. He bought a special radio with a wide band just for Radio Free Europe. Every night, when he finished his schoolwork, he would go home, shut the door, and listen.

The late '70s were an exciting time to be a student. The university campus was electric with latent political fervor. Increasingly students were daring to talk about politics, dissembling just enough to get by. This was especially true at the István Bibó College, a dormitory, where this energy was at its peak.

László was entranced. The feeling of being part of something, of possibly *doing* something. It was there, at university, surrounded by so many eager minds like his own, that he began to figure out how.

NAMES CARRY A CERTAIN WEIGHT IN POLITICS, SOMETIMES EVEN a talismanic power; in Hungary, István Bibó is one such example. Bibó, the minister of state under Imre Nagy during the 1956 uprising, is a relatively unknown figure in European political thought. But when opposition members speak today about the heroes that inspired them, it is to him they most often refer.

An image is frequently drawn: Bibó is seated at his typewriter in his office in Parliament, while the Soviet forces plow into Budapest and take over the building. Rather than run and hide or lie prostrate before the invading powers, he stays at his desk typing, finishing his work. The Soviets allowed this—he was not the leader they were after, nor a revolutionary in the streets.

But what he was typing was no simple daily brief. It was an open letter to the Hungarian people, a Declaration of Independence of sorts, called "For Freedom and Truth." "Hungarians," it begins, and proceeds to describe the world unfurling around him, seated as he was that day, November 4, 1956, as the lone representative of the Hungarian government in a Parliament under siege.

In the letter, he echoes the insurgents' demand to live in a "free, just, and exploitationless society" and declares his support for the revolution, which has brought Hungarians together "irrespective of class or denomination." The document is not expressly hostile to the Soviet Union, but it calls for a sovereign Hungary. The activities of the revolutionaries, he explains, were a legitimate expression of popular will. It was not the people who had acted unjustly, but the Soviet troops that had crushed them.

Bibó was arrested on May 23, 1957, and sentenced to life in prison, but was released in 1963 as part of an amnesty (he died in 1979, in Budapest). After his death, a student movement named a university dormitory after him, the István Bibó College.

It was about this time, in 1980, that László and a friend, Berci Dichazi, started a political society—the 405 Circle, they called it, after the room in their own dorm. They weren't explicitly critical of Communism; they couldn't be or they would have been shut down. But they invited politicians, historians, and other intellectuals to speak. They also had poetry readings and folk concerts, which were formally banned by the Party but sometimes tolerated.

The events started small, just a few dozen students crammed into a common room on the floor in which they lived. But as their gatherings swelled in size, they switched to a large lecture hall, situated on the ground floor of the building. This could fit several hundred people. Soon this too was packed.

Often the events would last for hours. They would start out with a talk, and then a conversation with László or Berci or one of their friends. Afterward, they would continue with drinks up in their room, where they could talk more freely.

It was all pretty relaxed and low-key. They were just kids, living away from home and stirring up trouble. Kids: shaggy haired, drinking beer by the bottle—Pepsi-Cola, too—and wearing large square-rimmed glasses, and patterned, untucked button-ups, as was fashionable at the time. But from the beginning, their meetings were infiltrated by the secret police. Once they got a letter from a young journalist, sympathetic to their project. Be careful, he told them. Not everyone is happy with what you are doing.

They were lucky to have gotten by. At the same time, a similar conversation circle at the Karl Marx University was broken up, and its leader given the choice of prison or exile. He fled to Canada.

Their most uncomfortable moment came in the fall of 1981, when László's political society hosted a debate between the editor of the official Communist Party newspaper, *Népszabadság* (*People's Freedom*), and an opposition-minded magazine, *Mozgó Világ* (*Moving World*), which would soon be banned. As many as three hundred students showed up to watch the old Communist be humiliated, unable to answer even basic questions.

This was a big day, perhaps too big. For weeks afterward, the air felt frozen around them. Later László learned that the editor of the Party paper had written a letter demanding they be thrown out of university. In a great twist of irony, it turned out to be the Party secretary of the Faculty of Chemistry (where László studied) who refused the request—the man László was most concerned about, his Communist overlord, in the final hour covered his back.

When opposition groups finally began to mobilize—nearly a decade later, in 1988—the MDF (Magyar Demokrata Fórum, or Hungarian Democratic Forum), led by Zoltán Bíró, was the first to declare itself. Many of its members had been part of László's 405 Circle in the early 1980s. By this point, László had moved back to Sopron, far from the ferment of Budapest. He was in his mid-thirties and had a family now. But when the MDF formed a local chapter, László—along with László Magas—was a founding member.

The inaugural meeting of the MDF in Sopron was convened on November 4, 1988—the very date, in 1956, that the Soviet Union invaded Hungary, when Bibó penned his letter in a Parliament under siege. This wasn't intended as a provocation, but the secret service flooded the venue just in case. The historical resonance of the date wasn't lost on the crowd. At the end of the presentation, a man in the audience rose and suggested everyone stand in silence to honor the dead of '56. The room fell into a stunned hush, but one by one, nearly everybody stood.

And so, the MDF in Sopron was born, baptized with words that should not have been uttered, in a room with organizers standing beside undercover agents, everyone exercised and confused, each in their own way cognizant of the change they were experiencing but equally unsure of what it meant.

In that room, 1956 was everywhere present. Except now it was no longer just a story of past aggression, but of present agency too, embodied by local activists and informants. Pozsgay was right: if real change was to occur, history couldn't be avoided. It had to be confronted. And in fact, a reckoning was on the horizon.

Chapter Six

The weeks after Miklós Németh's power play at the Iron Curtain were relatively quiet. But there was little doubt about the contest to come. Fast approaching, on June 16, 1989, was the day commemorating the death of Imre Nagy, the leader of the counterinsurgency of 1956. Nagy was still considered an enemy of the Communist Party, and scarcely a word had been spoken of him for a generation. But for the opposition he was a hero. This was the day he would be reborn.

In the generation since his death, Nagy's legacy, like that of most martyrs, had grown to mythological proportions, magnified further by the scandal surrounding his death. After the revolution was squashed by Soviet tanks, Nagy fled to the Yugoslav Embassy where he was promised sanctuary and safe passage out of Hungary—with the written promise from new, Soviet-appointed Prime Minister János Kádár. But in an act of almost Shakespearean backstabbing, Nagy was arrested when he set foot outside the Embassy, and in 1958, he was tried in secret, found guilty of treason, and hung.

And as Nagy rotted, Kádár rose to the highest office in the land.

Nagy's body was deposited in an unmarked grave. Its location was officially a secret, although many knew where it was, a faraway corner of the Rákoskeresztúri Cemetery in Budapest, Plot 301. The secrecy

of it all, the ferment and shadow, lent Nagy's body a latent power, rep-
resenting the myriad deceptions and rewritten truths that the Party
had promulgated about the uprising. The body was physical evidence
of that wrongdoing. And for a generation it had lain in the earth gathering force.

For years, observances of this ignominious day were held in secret,
expressly forbidden by the state. Just a year earlier, in 1988, a group of
about four hundred people commemorating the thirtieth anniversary
of Nagy's death were beaten by police and forcibly dispersed. But a lot
had changed in a year's time. Not least because of the steady disappearance of Kádár himself, driven first out of office and then, on May 8,
1989, stricken by illness, out of politics altogether.

The political lives of the two men were inextricably intertwined.
In being resuscitated, Nagy would be given a justice denied by his show
trial; at the same time, Kádár was being, you might say, put on trial. This
fact was not lost on Kádár. When first pushed to resign at the extraordinary Party conference that previous May, he had shouted angrily at
his aids. *If I step down, they will rehabilitate Nagy!*

In fact, this year something big was planned. Nagy's body wasn't
just going to be honored. It was going to be exhumed.

By early morning, June 16, Heroes' Square in central Budapest
was thronged with people, many brandishing Hungarian flags with
the centers cut out—a nod to the flags used by the revolutionaries of
1956, who had knifed out the red star and hammer and sickle of their
Soviet masters. A stage was set up in front of the steps of the Budapest
Palace of Art, a contemporary art museum, its columns clad in black.
At the top of the steps were six coffins draped in cloth surrounded by
flames—one for Nagy, four for the others executed alongside him, and
one empty, standing in for the unknown martyrs who'd given their lives
to freedom.

The event was laden everywhere with symbolism—especially the
last coffin. It was a marker of something unidentified: a gesture to possibility itself, to uncertainty and change. In that sense it was the perfect

emblem for a moment that had not yet constituted itself, the transition to a post-Communist future that was felt, and believed in, but which had not yet come.

Nagy's reburial was organized by a small group of activists, mostly family members of Nagy and a smattering of survivors from the '56 uprising, who gave themselves the weighty title The Committee for Historical Justice. Pozsgay and Németh were both involved in authorizing the ceremony, but stayed behind the scenes. They supported the message: if Nagy was a patriot, so too were they. And of course, if Kádár was a villain, so was Grósz—and every other hardliner. The risks were considerable.

On the day of the reburial, Németh received death threats—explicit ones, by telephone, but also covert ones, retrieved by his secret service and confirmed by the Soviet Embassy. There might be an assassination attempt, they warned him, perhaps emanating from the Romanian Embassy. In the case of a megalomaniacal dictator like Ceaușescu, you never knew.

As they left Parliament, one of Németh's security team offered a piece of advice. You will be standing in broad view beside the casket, which is an easy target, he told Németh. Don't stand still, try to change position constantly, and move your head and body in different directions.

More than two hundred thousand people showed up. Németh and Pozsgay stood on the stage beside relatives of the martyrs as well as some leaders of the opposition. They were the only members of the politburo present. This was no surprise. A few days earlier, Grósz had ordered Party members not to attend. He was angry that the ceremony had been authorized. Németh wasn't at that meeting. Instead, Pozsgay spoke on Németh's behalf, stating their intention to go. Grósz stormed out of the room. At that point, what lingering unclarity there might have been about the division within the Hungarian ruling class was definitively erased. There were two sides and between them, an abyss.

However much drama preceded the ceremony in Parliament, nothing compared to the event itself. There were speeches about the deceased, about the importance of democracy and tolerance. Most powerfully, there were also recordings of Nagy from 1956 and readings of his texts.

Nagy's words were well known, at least among the opposition. This was true of his speeches, but also his writings, dossiers passed about even though they were contraband. Especially resonant were those from the Snagov prison in Romania where he was kept before being executed. "What I betrayed was not the ideal," he proclaimed, "but the system which betrayed the ideal." He railed against the government's portrayal of him as a traitor and spoke in favor of the protestors' revolutionary vision "of national independence, sovereignty, equality and non-interference."

Nagy didn't mince words about who he thought was to blame. The Soviet Union, sure, but also the Hungarian leadership who did its bidding. In a word: Kádár. In his prison diaries, Nagy wrote that Kádár committed "a crime against the nation he can never set right: he is a traitor."

After Nagy was transferred from Snagov to the Gyorskocsi prison in Budapest, on June 14, 1958, he wrote directly to the Hungarian people, stating that although his death sentence was unjust, he knew he would one day be redeemed—not by the court, but by the people. It is the Hungarian nation, he wrote, that "will clear me of these grave charges," by whose decree "justice can be made."

Up until this point in the reburial proceedings, with Nagy's words broadcast to the assembled crowd, the ceremony remained fairly sober, a celebration of the memory of the deceased. Everyone stuck to the script. But then came the last speaker, a young man, only twenty-six, with wild black hair and fire in his eyes. This was Viktor Orbán of Fidesz, the Alliance of Young Democrats. He had no interest in sermonizing the deceased. *"In the sixth casket,"* he screamed, *"we bury Communism!"*

The Communists had betrayed the nation, Orbán declared. Now it was time for a change. He demanded free elections and an end to the occupation. If we are to honor the ideals of 1956, he said, we must "demand the withdrawal of Soviet troops!"

And so it was that Orbán said the unthinkable—Soviets get out! The crowd erupted, a motley cheering mass, broadcast on national television.

This was a moment that changed the course of the transition. Hungary was now a pressure cooker. The question was how it could be managed without bursting. Németh was concerned. He felt Orbán had gone too far by mentioning the Soviets directly. Now all the reform he had worked for might be compromised.

Németh feared Moscow's response. But more than this, he now felt a threat from a new direction. Orbán didn't just go after the Soviets. He condemned all Communists as antidemocratic—not bothering to distinguish between the reformers in the government and the hardliners in the Party. They were all Communists to him. By Orbán's logic, Németh was as guilty as all the rest.

The fallout from the Nagy reburial was considerable. On June 24, a little over a week later, the Central Committee of the Hungarian Communist Party held a contentious session in which Grósz was removed from his perch atop the Party and forced to share power with the reformers in a joint presidium. Just a year before, he was the most powerful person in Hungary, and viewed by many leaders in the West as a welcome change from the elderly Kádár—British prime minister Margaret Thatcher described Grósz as a man in her own image. Now he was a minority voice at the top of the Party, sure to be outvoted and humiliated on every measure.

History has its satisfying symmetries. Just as the removal of Nagy paved the ground for the rise of Kádár, so did Nagy's reburial furnish Kádár's fall and that of his successor. Grósz now joined Kádár ignominiously on the sidelines.

The politics of death is for every society revealing: how we mourn, for whom; the language and iconography we use to justify our grief. Nagy's exhumed body was a visual expression of this grief, a material truth that no propaganda could cut through, making plain that the nation would not heal until this historical injustice was rectified.

IT WAS PRECISELY INTO THIS MOMENT OF INSIGHT, FEAR, AND upheaval, that Otto von Habsburg's entourage inserted itself, on the balmy evening of June 20, 1989, out in far-flung Debrecen, a comparatively quiet place where young activists were nonetheless stirring.

Ferenc Mészáros, the activist who first came up with the idea of the picnic, took a circuitous path to politics. After the police had cracked down on the gang he was in as a teenager, in the mid-1970s, Ferenc was directionless—filled with anger toward the authorities, but not knowing how or where to channel it. It was sometime later that he found himself in a circle surrounding György Túróczi, an older intellectual who ran a theater group in Debrecen. He became a mentor to Ferenc. Afternoons of stage work ended in evenings of conversation about politics and literature.

It took time and work for Ferenc to fit in. He burrowed into the library, where he could read poetry and philosophy (whatever books weren't restricted) and listen to classical music. He found himself grappling with the great thinkers—especially German philosopher Friedrich Nietzsche. Ferenc had already for years been writing poems. But now he started to think more about the world of politics, and the change he sought. This was when, in 1989, the MDF (Hungarian Democratic Forum) came into his life.

It was also at this point that Ferenc started looking to the West, a place he dreamed of but struggled to envision. The Soviet presence was more pronounced in Debrecen than most places, due to a preponderance of military bases. This was a restricting condition, a parameter beyond which thought could not cross. For Ferenc, the West was simply the place without The Army—as he calls the Soviet forces. Hungary could be a place of free thinking too, he began to believe. If only The Army would go away.

Such were the thoughts that filled Ferenc's mind when he met Habsburg at dinner.

Interesting the turns that history takes: in Debrecen, the city where a century and a half earlier his family was stripped of its throne, the crown prince now returned as a guest, swept in as though from a fantastical past that had nothing to do with Communism. Otto von Habsburg: the man whose family might have been thought of as The Army before the Soviets showed up.

At dinner, they spent much of their time talking about the Iron Curtain. The original picnic idea was just to re-create their conversation in a place where Hungarians and Austrians could sit and talk and by the simple fact of their doing so—a reasonable if seemingly impossible act—demonstrate how senseless the border barrier was.

It was to be an act of political theatre. Ferenc wanted to make the Iron Curtain look ridiculous.

IN COMMUNIST TIMES, THEY USED TO SAY THE WALLS HAD EARS; maybe the borders did too. The morning after Ferenc's dinner with Habsburg, on June 21, the Romanian government started to place barbed wire along its perimeter with Hungary. This was a provocation in response to Hungary's handling of the Transylvanian refugee crisis. There was an uptick in violence too, with several Hungarian refugees shot by Romanian border guards.

The perversity of Ceaușescu's move was not lost on anyone. Just as Németh was trying to dismantle the border in the west, a new one was rising in the east. The difference between the two borders could not have been more stark: in the month and a half since Németh's decision to cut the electric wiring of the Iron Curtain, steady progress had been made on its demolition, with many kilometers of fencing already rolled up and stowed away.

Németh now decided it was time for another event at the Iron Curtain—this time bigger and more public than the last. On June 27, the foreign ministers of Austria and Hungary, Alois Mock and Gyula Horn, staged a joint action of cutting a stretch of fencing. With big smiles and comically giant wire cutters, the two ministers posed for photographs as they made the ceremonial snip. Then they shook hands before distributing pieces of defunct wiring to journalists present for the show.

The event was once again largely symbolic. A section of the Curtain had to be rebuilt for the two ministers to cut through, since they couldn't find a suitably photogenic site in which the fencing was still intact. No restrictions on Warsaw Pact travel were lifted, and the border itself between Austria and Hungary would stay as it was. Still, in a year full of symbols, this one was unmistakable. It was a propitious time to consider other border provocations, even absurd ones. Or at least that's how it seemed.

Chapter Seven

Having an idea, as Ferenc Mészáros was soon to find out, was just the beginning. And his partnership with Mária Filep quickly developed cracks. A few days after they agreed to plan the picnic together, Ferenc turned up at Mária's office only to discover she had started work without him. Ferenc was offended. He didn't like her tone, found her rude and uncompromising, showing little regard for his ideas. Mária, on the other hand, felt Ferenc was too starry-eyed. If he wasn't going to take initiative, she would.

At a subsequent MDF gathering, on July 6. Mária showed up armed with papers, and she and Ferenc outlined the plan they had drawn up. Once again, MDF leadership was unmoved.

Mária refused to be deterred. Her office quickly became a hub of activity, with Mária doing fourteen-hour shifts, covertly planning the picnic when she should have been doing her job.

Mária's officemate, Márta Magos, kept a diary. "Mari is working day and night," she wrote. "She is going to end up in jail, she will be fired . . . [Our Boss] is suspecting something, but he hasn't yet said anything . . . The secret calls in the afternoon, secret faxes. This woman is getting braver by the day."

Mária was lucky to have gotten this far, sneaking around the system. But progress was halting. She reached out to the foreign affairs division of the MDF, to two historians who she hoped might help her navigate the government bureaucracy. Instead, they told her off, mocking her amateur meddling in politics.

Mária was livid. How lucky you historians only write history, rather than do it, she told them.

For funding they sought out the Soros Foundation—by that point, George Soros, himself a Hungarian, was already a prominent humanitarian and anti-Communist agitator—but when Mária went to request sponsorship, the response was, as she puts it, "unfriendly."

These failures were disappointing, but also perplexing. It had seemed the perfect time to stage such an event. But in fact, the national scene had grown increasingly tense. After the Nagy reburial, political actors across Hungary took some time to reassess their positioning. No one was taking risks. Indeed, for all the bombast of Orbán's speech, the next weeks were dominated by an uncomfortable quiet. There were no major opposition moves, nor state crackdowns. Just the slow churn of a machine grinding itself into paralysis.

On July 6, 1989, the precise day that the Supreme Court of Hungary formally rehabilitated the heroes of 1956, János Kádár died in his sleep. The following day, Németh went to Bucharest for what would end up being the last meeting of the Warsaw Pact. The summit would bring together leaders from around the East, including Gorbachev; it also set the stage for a dangerous confrontation with Romanian dictator Nicolae Ceaușescu.

Unbeknownst to all but a handful of state officials, word had been circulating around the intelligence wires that Romania was planning a military operation against Hungary as early as the coming fall. The Romanian decision to build up its border with Hungary was part of this escalation.

This news increased Németh's sense of isolation. Certainly, he had made enemies across the Eastern Bloc—Németh was considered by most Warsaw Pact leaders to be a pariah, chipping away at the foundations that supported their rule. But Hungary's most proximate ally in the West also made clear that it was not going to help. Earlier that year, Austrian chancellor Franz Vranitzky warned Németh against "reform euphoria," a pace of change that could spin out of control.

For Németh, en route to Romania, where his aggressive pace of reform would be on the top of the agenda, this contributed to the eerie feeling that he was being set up, lured into a deadly trap. That, despite his entourage of aides and security personnel, he was traveling alone.

———

THE HUNGARIAN DELEGATION TO THE WARSAW PACT SUMMIT was assigned a cluster of villas in Bucharest. Németh was told not to enter. His security team went ahead and screened for threats. They returned with unsettling news: the villas tested positive for radioactive material—nothing explosive, but toxic enough that sustained exposure would be fatal. Such tactics were familiar in those days.

Németh and his team slept outside in the garden. They didn't have tents, so they rolled out mats on the ground. This wasn't so bad, as it was a balmy summer night. And anyway, they had no choice.

At the meeting, Ceaușescu could barely constrain his rage. He banged on the table, shouted about Hungary's "dangerous experiment" that would "destroy socialism." Ceaușescu wanted the Warsaw Pact to stop Hungary's "counterrevolution," using force if necessary—just as they had in 1956, in Prague in 1968, Poland in 1981. As though entranced by these visions of power and forgetful of the devastation they wrought, pretty soon other leaders were chiming in.

Ceaușescu spoke dismissively of Németh, referring to him as "Mister," rather than "Comrade." Even the Polish delegates were better regarded. As far as Ceaușescu and the other hardliners were concerned, the Polish model, in which the opposition movement Solidarity and the Polish Communist Party worked together, was more acceptable than what the reformers in Hungary were trying to do—especially when it came to decisions about the Iron Curtain, which would affect them all.

For Németh, the meeting was terrifying. He was the youngest leader in the room. It was his first time encountering such abuse. The only solace he took was that Gorbachev was there with him. Gorbachev—*Mikhail Sergeyevich*—the man he trusted, a reformer like himself, was the most powerful person there. Németh knew there was nothing the other leaders could do without his support.

At one point during Ceaușescu's tirade, Németh looked over at the Soviet leader. He didn't know what he was searching for exactly, just some reassurance, a smile, anything to make him feel less vulnerable out there. Gorbachev did one better. He calmly regarded Németh across the room. Then he winked.

With that simple gesture, the weight of the world lifted from Németh's shoulders. Throughout the day, each time he looked over at Gorbachev, he found the same smiling eyes, untouched by the vitriol that swirled around them.

Németh returned to Budapest feeling relieved. But the geopolitical climate remained volatile. A few days later, on July 11, US president George H. W. Bush paid an extraordinary visit to Hungary—the first ever by an American president—a move received coldly in Moscow. This was Soviet turf, after all. The next day, in an event whose optics were as mixed as its message, President Bush spoke at the Karl Marx University, carrying the banner of democracy, but ultimately declaring his support for the status quo. In private sessions with elites, Bush made clear that his principal objective was to maintain security in the region, and thus to keep the Hungarian Communist Party from being destabilized.

This was demoralizing for the opposition. The United States, putative beacon of democracy, was punting. Despite the changes on the ground and in the air, the precariousness of the opposition position seemed to redouble. The same uncertain conditions that had given them hope now gave them pause.

It was in this climate of disillusionment that Mária and Ferenc toiled, out east in Debrecen, a place adrift, politically undefined, less than an hour's drive from Romania. Sure, Németh had made it out of

Bucharest unscathed. But what about them, out there where the border violence beckoned? Who would protect them if clashes spread? They felt alone too.

———

I MEET MÁRIA FILEP AT DEBRECEN CENTRAL STATION. WE ARE close enough to the Romanian border that the departure board lists foreign destinations and touts sell smuggled cigarettes—a frontier staple.

This is my first trip out east. I had been west, on the road to Vienna, and south to Lake Balaton, beautiful swaths of countryside preened by centuries of care. By 2018, the roads were up to any standard; the train cars, silvery and new. Heading east is a different story: the trip from Budapest could have taken an hour and a half but takes nearly five. I sit in an old train car. The stained yellow and orange drapery and faux-wood wallpapering of the cabin seem unchanged from my first forays into Eastern Europe, some twenty years earlier. Riding such a train today conveys a sense of atemporality, as though it is going forward and backward at once.

Mária too carries the mark of another era: the cadence of her speech, perhaps, the lock of her gaze. She remembers 1956, but the roots of her activism reach back further, to 1920, the Treaty of Trianon, when, after the Austro-Hungarian Empire was broken up, Hungary lost huge swaths of territory—especially to Romania. To this day, she bears a heritage of anger passed down by her grandfather, who had fought in World War I in Transylvania.

The tragedy of Trianon has captivated the minds of the Hungarian public ever since. Likewise, its intellectuals. István Bibó wrote extensively about the treaties after World War I, how they ran roughshod over the principle of self-determination. The treaty forced Hungary to relinquish not only vast territories it once controlled but also ones that were predominantly Hungarian—like Transylvania. Already in the first years after the treaty, this led to violence and the forced displacement of those who were newly seen as ethnic minorities.

Bibó described the devastating effect of this loss on the Hungarian population, who were thrust into a state of national defensiveness, shuttered into narrow, solipsistic views of community and what he called political hysteria, a condition that sows the ground for fascism and dictatorship.

The social and political consequences of these treaties also had a powerful effect on the political philosopher Hannah Arendt. In *The Origins of Totalitarianism*, she writes about how they created a world in which nations—ethnic groupings—triumphed over states (political units), forcing minorities to live without protection. It also set the stage for the conflict to come. "National interest had priority over law," she wrote, "long before Hitler could pronounce 'right is what is good for the German people.'"

Arendt's purpose in this instance is to proclaim the importance of rights—in the universal sense, as something all people are due by dint of their humanness, what she calls "the right to have rights"—over national whim. Hungarians in Transylvania were a good example of the problem: without the nation to protect them or an international regime to intervene on their behalf they were ripe for abuse.

Six decades later, the same historical injustice structured Mária Filep's world—manifest, in the autumn of 1988, with Hungarian refugees fleeing the brutality of Ceaușescu. Images splashed across the newspapers of Hungarian villages in Transylvania being torn down. Scores of people were cast onto the street into the bitter cold without much to eat. It all made Mária sick. At this point, the Hungarians weren't just being persecuted; they were being eradicated.

This was the spark that set her in motion. Once those villages were demolished, the whole system had to fall. The road to Berlin, the fall of the Wall and everything else, for Mária, thus began in Romania, in those outer villages, central to nowhere, nearly impossible to categorize, that lay unheralded on the map. The Hungary that was not Hungary. It is a story that makes no sense if you think of injustice only in the language of Soviet rule. But those Hungarians in Transylvania were the wounded heart of the nation.

When the MDF formed in Debrecen, Mária decided to get involved. At the time, she was one of only two people in her firm, which had several thousand employees, who joined the opposition.

I ask her if she was scared. She says no, so I ask the question in a different way. Why did your coworkers not join?

Here, a flicker of a smile. She says: because they were afraid.

AS AN ORGANIZER, MÁRIA WAS UNFLAPPABLE. THIS WAS FORTU-
nate because the obstacles didn't cease. What they needed was a patron—*védnök*, in Hungarian—someone high up to watch over them, ideally the highest ranked person they could find. Mária proposed Imre Pozsgay, the minister of state and respected reformer. It was an obvious choice, but the local Debrecen branch of the MDF had no connection to him, and the headquarters in Budapest wouldn't spend such a politically costly favor on something they deemed frivolous.

Mária decided to try and call him on her own, but this proved harder than anticipated. Aside from the obvious fact that no one could know that she was using the office telephone, she quickly discovered that the phone itself was only suitable for calls within Debrecen city limits. Pozsgay's office in Budapest was a world apart.

The system was designed to stymie communication, especially the unsanctioned kind. But if you poked around, you could often find a way through. Through a campaign of whispers and some trial and error, Mária learned that if she called a colleague who worked in the city government, she could stay on the line after they hung up and the line would stay "live," after which she could dial out-of-city numbers. Despite its storied omniscience, the state wasn't always looking; sometimes it even looked the other way.

Mária's first attempts bordered on farce. It was hard to get the

timing right, to intercept calls and hold the line. And when she succeeded, she often had to hang up anyway to avoid the prying eyes of
her boss. But with time she managed to get through to Pozsgay's office
and was told her message would be relayed to the minister. Then she
had to wait.

Meanwhile, the picnic planners needed to find a site at the Austrian
border. Since neither Ferenc nor Mária had been out there, this initially
meant guesswork, dragging fingers haphazardly along the map. They
settled on the city of Kőszeg and then contacted the local chapter of the
MDF—only to have their letters and phone calls go unanswered. This
was disheartening.

On July 11, Mária was seated in a meeting presided over by her
boss, when a knock sounded on the door. It was the office secretary.
There was an urgent phone call, she said. It was Minister of State Imre
Pozsgay, calling from Budapest. He was asking for Mária Filep.

The room fell silent. Mária flushed as she stood to take the call, and
walked slowly from the room. She recognized the voice immediately—
she'd heard him on the radio. There he was, bursting through the little
receiver, pressed against her ear. Speaking not to the millions of Hungarians who hung on his every word; nor to the politicians he enter-
tained or visited. Just to her.

The call was brief. When she hung up, she returned discreetly to her
seat. For some time a hush followed her around the office. She wasn't
in the Party, so everyone assumed she was in trouble. In those days,
such matters were not openly discussed so no one asked questions—
not even her boss. But now she had a real secret to keep. Pozsgay had
said yes.

She couldn't wait to tell Ferenc. They had a patron now, someone they could call for help—if they needed an official letter, perhaps,
bearing his seal. Or get formal permissions from the border command,
clearance that might take months had they tried to obtain it on their
own, if they heard back at all.

Armed with this news, Mária reached out to the Habsburg fam-

ily to secure the same commitment. Márta Magos captured the absur-
dity of the moment in her diary: "If Ottó Habsburg saw this! That he
received a phone call from a stolen line in a small office of a construction
company in Debrecen, from the 4th floor, room 411! Do these important people take our amateur ideas seriously?"

Emboldened, Mária and Ferenc settled on a name—the Pan-
European Picnic—which captured their aspirations of an event not
just for Hungary, but as Mária put it, for all of Europe "round and
complete"—and a precise date, August 19. But they still needed a place.
On July 15, they tried out the MDF office in a new city, Sopron.

As it turned out, this would also be a challenge. They were lucky
their letter even arrived—the secret police had intercepted it, a standard practice at the time. Had a different officer been in the bureau that
day, that might have been the end of their plans. Instead, the agent let
the letter through, but alerted the authorities. Indeed, the border guards
knew of the picnic before its would-be host.

Such is the tango of authoritarian politics. Inasmuch as the organizers planned the event, the state also allowed it to happen. It was an
elaborate dance of "step *here* but no farther" except no one knew exactly
where *here* was. Everything was about intuition: you had to feel it out
as you went along.

Mária and Ferenc were also lucky in another way. The MDF had
no listed office in Sopron, nor a public roll of officers. So they sent the
letter blindly to the home address of the person they were told might be
in charge—a man named László Magas.

Magas, who had stood out in the crowds that day in March when
the censored poem of Gyula Illyés was read aloud; who grew up in the
borderlands of western Hungary looking out upon the Iron Curtain,
which he dreamed he would one day live to tear down. Magas had been
looking for the right occasion to mobilize at the border. When he got
the letter, he knew this was it.

PART II

EUROPE'S PRISON

Chapter Eight

Regina Webert was sprawled on the couch with her husband, Lars, in their flat in Friedrichshain, a working class neighborhood in Communist East Berlin. It was spring, May 2, and it was light out. They were at home, illegally watching West German news, a common practice in those days as the West's transmission stations were so close that their feed could easily be picked up in the East. The volume was low and whatever they heard they did not talk openly about. But at six o'clock most nights, Regina and Lars, along with so many others across the eastern half of the city, adjourned to their separate halls and living rooms to tune in to the *Tagesschau* news broadcast.

The television flickered images of a field in Hungary, of soldiers rolling up giant sheets of metal fencing, which on the screen looked like brittle fishing nets. The anchorwoman delivered the news evenly, but her face registered excitement and alarm: the Hungarian government had just begun cutting the electric wiring of the Iron Curtain.

Regina shot upright, reached for Lars's hand. They looked at each other and although no words passed between them, the implications were clear. Maybe this was it, what they had been waiting for.

It wasn't until Regina had met Lars, that previous spring, that the idea of trying to run away from East Germany—the Deutsche

Demokratische Republik (German Democratic Republic or GDR)—
had even occurred to her. They had been together less than a year before
getting married. This was normal in those days—unmarried couples in
East Germany were unable to rent or buy apartments or be put on the
waiting list for a car. Regina was young, just twenty years old. She was
just beginning her adult life in the GDR, how could she even imagine
doing something as rash as try to escape?

Growing up, she'd taken the Wall for a given. It was just there. It
would always be there. It wasn't something to be overcome.

For Lars it was different. He was a few years older and worked as
a taxi driver. Every day he drove by the Wall, that broad flank of dull
concrete that sliced the city in half—that cut off neighborhoods and
commercial districts, transformed avenues into cul-de-sacs. The Wall
was something he couldn't get away from, and it bothered him.

They talked about this sometimes when they were alone, mostly
on walks through the park when they felt sure nobody was listening in.
Soon the dream of escape was Regina's as much as Lars's.

Nothing came of it, of course. Traveling to the West was strictly
forbidden in the GDR. People that tried their hand at the Wall—by
scaling over it or burrowing beneath it; by stowing away in authorized vehicles—were mostly caught and imprisoned, sometimes even
killed. But on May 2, the news from Hungary shook them out of their
dreamworld. Sure, they could never make it over the Wall. But crossing into the West from Hungary? For Regina, the idea stirred senti-
ments long repressed.

Regina had grown up in East Berlin with parents who were unpolit-
ical, at least outwardly. As a cellist, her father was allowed to travel with
his orchestra to nonsocialist destinations abroad—a great privilege—
provided he toed the Party line. This was the way forward in the GDR,
a path Regina quickly learned to tread. But he returned with stories of
the West—it was filled with ordinary people, he would tell her, not the
exploitative monsters depicted in GDR propaganda. *Sie kochen auch
nur mit Wasser*, he explained. They too cook with water.

Regina wasn't exactly unhappy with life in the GDR. What she felt was something abstract, the residual bitterness of a life stuck in standstill. When she was young she had wanted to study music, but because her father was an artist she was barred entry into the academy. The GDR did whatever it could to restrict the power of artists and intellectuals who might be critical of the regime. This often meant crippling their children, preventing them from building on the legacy of their parents. Regina had taken the message to heart: basic freedoms—to play music, to travel like her father—were not for her.

Making education a political weapon was one of the most myopic features of the GDR, inspiring resentment in ordinary people, even those without ideological contempt. But keeping citizens in line and in place was a GDR specialty.

The GDR was Europe's prison, a walled fortress led by Prime Minister Erich Honecker, with the help of the infamous Stasi—the Staatssicherheitsdienst, or State Security Service, under Erich Mielke. The Stasi penetrated all aspects of daily life. Agents were positioned in every housing block, hospital, and school, even in the clubs and social venues where citizens went to relax. Newspapers, radio, and television broadcasts were monitored; books were run through censors before being published.

The Stasi's role was to be all-seeing and all-knowing—this is what made it stand out from other secret services. Under a normal regime of policing, it is one's actions that are measured and constrained; under the Stasi, it was one's thoughts. This produced a never-ending spiral of information gathering: digging into peoples' lives generated the threats that justified further digging. The Stasi looked around for any evidence of disloyalty—watching Western TV for example, or talking politics with one's friends—and punished it as summarily as an ordinary police regime might punish theft or graft.

Almost all social relations filtered through the Stasi, as citizens were recruited to inform on one another—even within families, and among coworkers and friends. This is partly why the state was so effective. How could you mobilize against it if you couldn't band together? And how could you believe what anyone said to you if you couldn't even trust the ones you loved?

It was a regime of total surveillance, where the Stasi watched everyone and everyone watched each other—a system of control like the infamous *panopticon*, a prison in which a tower stands in the center of a circular courtyard. While the officials in the tower can see all subjects—positioned along the perimeter—the officers themselves cannot be seen, so at no point can the inmates be certain whether they are being observed. Thus, they come to police their own behavior and internalize control.

French philosopher Michel Foucault notably described this model of authority as "the oldest dream of the oldest sovereign." In the panopticon, the sovereign says: "none of my subjects can escape *and none of their actions is unknown to me.*"

By the end of the 1980s, the Stasi had grown to monstrous proportions, with over ninety thousand employees, as well as nearly two hundred thousand registered informers, not to mention scores of informal ones. Files were kept on more than six million people—roughly a third of the total population (seventeen million). This degree of social infiltration was unprecedented—higher than the Soviet Union at the height of Stalin, more expansive than the Gestapo under Hitler. Locally, the Stasi headquarters was dubbed the House of One Thousand Eyes.

And while by 1989 some states in the Eastern Bloc—notably Hungary and Poland—had begun to liberalize, the GDR was frozen in time under leaders Erich Honecker and Erich Mielke, both well into their twilight years. Their positions were fixed: socialism was the only just path; capitalism was a gateway to fascism. Reform was considered a threat to the very ground on which they stood. And just as Stalin grew more paranoid the more powerful he became, so it was with the two Erichs. With every perceived threat—real or otherwise—the secret police expanded.

For most citizens of the GDR, the end of the 1980s was a period of great cynicism. And yet, on May 2, many like Regina and Lars felt a burst of genuine hope. Now they wanted to go to Hungary, to see what it was like, maybe even try to escape—to start their lives together somewhere else.

WHEN IT FIRST FORMED, ON OCTOBER 7, 1949, THE GDR WAS FOR many something to dream about, an experiment in socialism pressed all the way up to the edge of the capitalist west.

The GDR emerged after the partition of Germany was agreed upon at Yalta at the conclusion of World War II. Originally, Germany was divided into four parts after the war, but this consolidated into a bifurcation between West (comprised of American, British, and French zones) and East (Soviet); the same was true of Berlin, divided into four but really only into two. After the war, East Germany was occupied by Soviet forces, with power progressively handed over to local Communist leadership. Russian language study was made mandatory in schools.

In the beginning, Berlin remained an open city despite its administrative division. But this proved short-lived. As early as 1948, the Soviets tried to throttle West Berlin, forging a blockade of through-roads; the Allied powers responded by airlifting food and fuel. On June 16, 1953, a workers' strike erupted in East Berlin, sparking protests against labor conditions. GDR police, aided by Soviet units, cracked down on the demonstrators in Stalinesque fashion—as many as ten thousand people were put in jail.

This was the first step toward the ruthless rule for which the GDR would become infamous. More immediately, it encouraged those who felt it was time to emigrate west. Across the GDR, citizens began to feel a pull—to West Berlin across the street, to West Germany just a short way away. The next years were filled with confusion, distrust, and fear. By the end of the 1950s, the stream of refugees from the GDR grew to as many as a thousand per day, and the government ratcheted up its rhetorical assault against the West—calling it the land of greedy capitalists, accusing it of harboring former Nazi officials who should have been purged. Once siblings, the two states increasingly became enemies. The story is tragic but familiar: division begets division. And as the states chafed, ordinary people got caught in the middle.

In her novel, *They Divided the Sky* (1963), Christa Wolf captures the mood in a story of star-crossed love between Rita, who chooses to stay in the Communist East, and Manfred, who flees west.

After Manfred moves to West Berlin, Rita goes and visits him in early August 1961. They embrace, both aware, somehow, of the moment's power, but unclear of what it means. Manfred has decided he will stay in the West, but Rita will not join him, as she cannot leave the homeland she also loves. Saying goodbye, they stand at a threshold in history far beyond their power to understand or control. "What they hadn't said yet, they would never be able to say. What they didn't know about each other yet, they would never discover. The only thing left was this pale, weightless moment, no longer coloured by hope and not yet discoloured by despair."

"At least they can't divide the sky," Manfred says hopefully.

On the night of August 12, 1961, in a desperate attempt to stop the flow of refugees headed west, GDR soldiers began the process of sealing off the state—militarizing its western border; and in Berlin, building a wall.

The Wall began with a simple strip of barbed wire, stealthily placed in the dead of night so as not to create a stir. The soldiers tasked with laying the barbed wire were unarmed. And the line was unaccompanied by any military infrastructure. And yet, when the sun rose, it cast its light upon a city divided. Overnight and without warning families were torn apart, people were barred from their places of work and the whole humming traffic of the city was forced to a halt.

The initial order for the Wall came from then Soviet leader Nikita Khrushchev. He had predicted that the Americans wouldn't react, and they didn't. In fact, what little resistance there was came from the East

Berliners. Some tried to force their way through the barbed wire while there was still a chance; others jumped out of windows that abutted the line before they were bricked up.

With time, bricked up they were—not just the windows of the adjacent buildings, but the whole linear division. Soon came steel and concrete, then a second wall—clearing out all buildings that lay between them, an empty stretch about one hundred meters wide that came to be known as the death strip, filled with mines and traps. Guards stood sentry in hundreds of watchtowers that studded the expanse, guaranteeing that would-be refugees would never even make it to the Wall, let alone cross it.

With the Wall in place, Christa Wolf's Rita realizes she will be alone without Manfred. "Rita went to bed. She lay with her arms folded under her head, staring at the ceiling. Completely still. She felt a deadly rigidity creep up inside her." Like her country, Rita too begins to internalize control. Shut out from the world around her, she shrinks into a carapace of sorrow and delusion, to the silent, sanctified chamber within.

Together, the Wall and the Inner German border (*Innerdeutsche Grenze*)—built up at the same time—were hugely successful in stemming the flow of refugees. Between 1949 and 1962, about 2.5 million people fled from the GDR. From 1962 onward, the number shrank to just a few thousand.

The totalizing power of the Wall is captured most clearly on GDR-issued maps. The Wall didn't just tear across the cartographic city, it literally deleted the other half of it—West Berlin streets went unnamed, its parks and administrative buildings vanished into a monochrome nothingness. It was as though the mapmakers had tipped over an inkwell, blotting out the entire western portion of the city into undifferentiated blackness. This fed the ideology of the state: if the West disappeared, maybe people would give up trying to go there. If the citizens couldn't see it, maybe they would forget it existed.

In this, the Wall and the Stasi worked in tandem. As the Stasi expanded, the Wall seemed to grow alongside it as though by political alchemy; just as the Wall helped the Stasi keep people in, the Stasi helped the Wall create a world in its image. Not just obdurate and brutish, the Wall was now all but invincible. It wasn't just something in the way, it was something you couldn't even get to if you tried.

For citizens of East Germany, escaping would soon become an unimaginable dream. The population of the GDR was as-if mummified—captured by a magic spell, where it would remain until something came along to snap it back to life.

NÉMETH'S CUTTING OF THE ELECTRICAL WIRING OF THE IRON Curtain, on May 2, 1989, was a message that traveled the globe. But it resonated especially powerfully in East Germany. And while for many citizens, like Regina and Lars, the news from Hungary offered a vision of hope, for Prime Minister Erich Honecker it was a nightmare.

The previous afternoon—May Day—had been a regal affair, celebrating Communism and its faithful. The Party organized a parade, larger than usual since this was a jubilee year, commemorating the fortieth anniversary of Communism in East Germany. And indeed, 1989 so far had gone to plan. A few months prior, Honecker had declared, "The Wall will still be standing in fifty, even a hundred years." Honecker stood triumphantly on the bandstand, flanked by generals and Party functionaries, soaking in the admiration of the passing crowds.

When the following day Honecker learned what Németh had done he was outraged. If the Iron Curtain opened, he knew that many of his citizens might try to escape. What good were his own fortifications if people could just leave another way? But Honecker also couldn't just close his own borders entirely and bar people from going on ordinary vacations around the Eastern Bloc. These summer travels were an important pressure valve. There was already a lot of built-up tension in the GDR. He didn't want the bubble to burst.

GDR leadership called up Ferenc Kárpáti, Németh's defense minister, demanding an explanation. Kárpáti gave the same line Németh had given Gorbachev—that the electric wiring had become too expensive to maintain; that their border with Austria would remain heavily controlled. Just because the current was cut, didn't mean anybody would be let out.

These answers did little to soften the shock in Berlin. And in fact, their concerns were borne out. Suddenly across the GDR, citizens began to wonder whether they might be able to escape. It was getting near summer, when citizens normally started applying for visas to go on holiday to destinations within the Eastern Bloc—to the shores of Lake Balaton in Hungary, for example, or the Black Sea coast of Bulgaria. Now they were looking farther afield.

Within days of hearing the news from Hungary, Regina and Lars began to plan. For a start, they sent a letter to a friend who had made it to the West and might be able to help out or offer advice. Since they couldn't speak directly over the phone or through letters, they arranged to meet up in Prague, just a few hours' drive from East Berlin—they could travel to socialist Czechoslovakia without difficulty—in early June to plot the escape.

Until then, they just tried to live their lives, tried not to think too hard about it. For Regina, the experience was nerve-racking, following her daily routine, walking about the city, taking classes—she was studying to get the same professional driver's certificate that Lars had. Her thoughts were an echo chamber. Was she being foolhardy taking such a gamble? Risking the life they had just embarked upon together for such a dangerous, flimsy dream? There was a lot that was good about her life in the GDR too. Was it worth giving it all away?

These were paranoid days. You had to keep constantly alert, attentive to how you looked and behaved, trying not to give anything away. Regina often found herself in tears from the pressure of it: all the things you know but can't say and all the things you don't know and can't talk about.

Lars's days also felt more oppressive than ever. Stuck as he was in his daily grind, driving up to, against, and along the Wall, but never through it. At least not yet.

Chapter Nine

Today, Berlin remains the city of the Wall, now reimagined as a sequence of public memorials. Some are bright and prominent, like the stretches of intact walling designed to re-create division and attract tourists—*this is what it looked like*. These are the famous bits, with loud graffiti displays commemorating 1989. Walking along the longest segment, the East Side Gallery along the Spree River, one confronts a medley of colorful murals, mostly from 2009, long after the Wall had fallen: the image of a Trabant, that famous East German car, crashing through the concrete; of Honecker and Khrushchev, socialist stalwarts, locked in an eternal kiss. Tourists flash peace signs and strike poses, and stalls peddle GDR- and Soviet-era kitsch.

Then there are more subtle reminders, found throughout the city, where the course of the Wall is marked by metallic strips embedded in the ground, the kind you might walk past and not notice, or trip over accidentally. Theirs is an imaginative domain. They give you pause to wonder what life would have been like in the divided city, when you couldn't pass from one side to the next.

One encounters in Berlin today a special quality to life, even in banalities. The city survived a kind of death, and thus its rebirth everywhere carries meaning—the erstwhile division carried forth now by the city's denizens and the memories they bear, by museums and displays, and the yearly commemorations by which the Wall is performed and remembered. The Wall is thus both always there and constantly being erased, a Möbius strip of historical experience.

I find it all very affecting, the fingernails of the past dug into the flesh of the present. The stickiness of lived time. Nowhere is this clearer than in the mountains of paper left behind by the Stasi—files upon files documenting how peoples' lives were picked apart by the state and its informants, now open to citizens interested in seeing their personal records. These are housed in an archive, a paper labyrinth, where the scars of these past injustices are daily revisited.

It is fall 2021 and I am in Berlin. I have come to the archive to find out what Stasi officials were looking for, especially the first days of May 1989, right after the news broke from Hungary. How did they react to would-be refugees planning secret trips south and what had they done to stop them?

The building, on Karl-Liebknecht Straße just north of Alexanderplatz, greets you with a wide, inscrutable face, its windows nearly opaque. A glass plate hangs over the entrance, designed as an awning in case of rain but, practically, a repository for bird droppings. Because of the sensitivity of the material, the directorate takes special interest in what I am looking for and how I might use it. Mika, a research assistant helping with translation, also signs documents—in case of misuse, we're both legally liable. The staff is well-intentioned, but the experience is intense. The old Stasi aura lingers somehow, a ghastly presence that clings to the halls like a film.

When we get settled, an archivist comes over with a glossary of Stasi key words and acronyms—a Rosetta stone to an antique and vanishing code. The first entry is *abfangen* (to intercept, as when they read people's mail before forwarding it); the next is *abhören* (which also means to intercept, but now with the added connotation of listening in). This latter entry is modified with helpful applications—"to bug a phone" (*ein Telefon abhören*); "to tap a room" (*einen Raum abhören*).

The files come in tattered blue and gray folders, some more plump than others. Everything is preserved: the to-do list of an officer scrawled in blue ink with a rough hand; cheap filing papers, translucent and brittle; a newspaper clipping here, a set of notes there. Some of the documents say *Streng Geheim!* (Top Secret) in screaming letters.

It doesn't take long to find what I am looking for: starting in May 1989, the number of East Germans trying their luck at the Hungarian border balloons. Nearly all were apprehended by the Hungarian guards. The reports are bleak: a group of friends apprehended just a few meters short of Austrian soil; a man deported hundreds of kilometers north to the GDR. All of this registered in a massive dossier, compiled by swift, dispassionate hands.

One file is just statistics: how many were caught, how many made it across, categorized by the districts of the Hungarian borderlands (Hegyeshalom, Kőszeg, Sopron, Szentgotthárd). The crudeness of the numbers and the grid in which they are framed give the appearance of an old-fashioned box score, as from a ball game long ago. In the numbers there are neither names nor faces. Just a win-loss column.

At first blush these files tell the story of a ruthless and well-oiled operation, coordinated between Stasi agents and their Hungarian counterparts. But with time, another kind of portrait emerges: of a Stasi that by 1989 was struggling to comprehend why so many people were trying to run away. This is manifest in the interrogation reports compiled later, once suspects were apprehended and brought back to the GDR to be examined. These are autopsies, in a way, test cases from which lessons might be gleaned.

M_____ was captured trying to flee to Austria via Hegyeshalom on May 16—just two weeks after Németh first cut the electric wiring of the Curtain. But unlike so many others, who were dissatisfied with the GDR, M_____ was a devoted citizen. As a kid he had been a socialist pioneer; later, a member of the Party-sanctioned Free German Youth (Freie Deutsche Jugend). He got good grades during high school, then went on to a top university. On March 15, 1989, he began work as an engineer. Two months later he was arrested in Hungary.

The Stasi questioned his school supervisors, who said he was a model student with an exemplary moral character. They went to his workplace to interview colleagues—fifteen in total—who spoke glowingly of his work ethic. They interviewed his father and his friends.

The dossier offers no verdict. M_____ lived a very private life; whatever discontent he felt, he kept to himself. This was surely infuriating to the Stasi. But it is hugely telling about the kind of place the GDR had become, so effective at driving people inward, away from the public sphere and into that private sanctum in which they cannot be found. That M_____'s intentions went unnoticed was thus not simply a failure of the system, but also, paradoxically, evidence of its success.

This kind of social atomization is a mainstay of authoritarian systems, a point Hannah Arendt makes in *Origins*. Her study focused on Hitler's Third Reich and Stalin's USSR, but its resonance with the GDR is immediately obvious. These are systems defined by extralegal violence and indoctrination, where state slogans are repeated by rote and citizens follow orders not out of any deep, abiding belief, but for fear of persecution. "The aim of [totalitarianism] has never been to instill convictions," Arendt writes, "but to destroy the capacity to form any."

In such conditions, the entire fabric of society unravels. Since people are isolated from one another—each existing in their own fearful pod—they stop sharing their experiences. This produces what Arendt calls *loneliness*, a special kind of solitude where you feel alone, even when surrounded by others.

For the Stasi, this was very much the point—to infiltrate social units and destroy the trust people had in each other, thereby ensuring no communal bond was strong enough to overwhelm the state. But it's clear that, by 1989, they had become victims of their own effectiveness. With time, people begin to unknow, unlearn, unobserve as an emotional response to state power. In such a system, people's thoughts become so guarded that even when they do report on one another, the information garnered is unreliable. And when people disappear totally inward, there is nothing to report at all.

In the case of M____, hours of investigation turned up more questions than answers. But starting in May 1989, the Stasi built up a strategy to defend against the onslaught of would-be refugees: being extra careful in vetting visa applications; homing in on signals that suggested people might try to flee; informing all operatives working along the southern border (the route people would take to Hungary, via Czechoslovakia), as well as the airports.

They also had to improve their investigative work, drawing up reports of those who managed to make it to the West and outlining why they were successful. They needed to map out new or unknown routes and target anyone helping people across, whom they labeled criminal smugglers (*kriminelle Menschenhändlerbanden*). They had to identify potential refugees and stop them.

AS CITIZENS WHO WOULD TRY TO ESCAPE THE GDR WOULD SOON learn, you couldn't just get past the territorial limit of East Germany. When you went abroad, certainly anywhere in the socialist East, the Stasi followed you there—even if Stasi officers themselves didn't have jurisdiction abroad—usually with the help of local agencies with whom they worked closely, in this case the Hungarian secret service.

Coordination worked like a link of chains. Ordinary Hungarian citizens were enlisted in the task of providing information to Hungarian officers, which was sent thereafter to the Stasi. This included people working in hotels, campsites, and other shops in tourist areas. They listened for stories of illicit travel, or critical remarks about the GDR and its leadership—overheard at dinners or other gatherings, the casual conversations of people who don't believe they are being surveilled.

Those first weeks of May 1989 were a catalogue of horrors, as thousands of East Germans walked blindly into capture, person after person, family after family, seeking to cross to the West, only to find the guards waiting for them at every turn. Here too, the story of M____ is illustrative. If anyone should have been able to make it, it would have been him.

As an engineer, M____ had reason to feel confident about his chances, even despite the tight web of security around the Iron Curtain. After all, he knew a thing or two about signal systems. He had spent three years, from 1981 to 1984, doing military service, for which he had been positioned at the Inner German border. He excelled in this training, and even won a medal for his service to the border guards—specifically for fence maintenance.

M____ had actually been considering trying to slip past the Iron Curtain for years, but never pursued it—we know this from his interrogation records. He was also an avid consumer of illicit West German media. One can imagine it would have been tantalizing to read those reports about the clipping of the electric border fence, wondering whether the opportunity was real, trying to calculate the risks.

A few days after reading the news, M____ learned his parents were planning a vacation to Hungary. He took this as a sign. They had intended to go in June, but M____ convinced them to go earlier. He was concerned that if they waited too long some of the Hungarian reforms might be reversed. Or, alternatively, that if Hungary pushed further reform, the GDR might get skittish and shut the border. Either way he wanted to get there quickly.

On May 12, M____ packed his bag. He knew exactly what to take. In addition to basic necessities, he brought a shovel, flashlight, binoculars, compass, and a tension gauge (which would be used to test if the electric fence was charged), stolen from his father's office, a chemistry lab. He also brought a wire cutter and extra wiring so he could repair whatever bits he cut and keep the signal intact.

Photographs of these items are taped into the Stasi file—black and white pictures, separated and labeled like evidence from a crime scene.

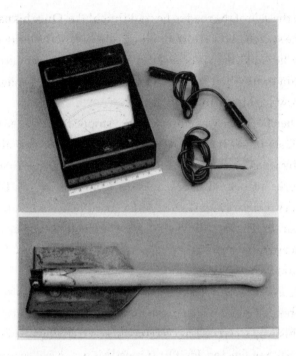

Looked at now, these images have a power to them, the embodiment of misplaced dreams. But there is an indeterminacy too. On first glance, it's not clear whether they are the tools of the refugee or the Stasi. It was a game with two sides, each emulating the other. This is part of the tragedy: to escape the Stasi, you first had to learn to think like them.

M＿＿＿ and his parents left their village outside Berlin at 5 a.m. on May 13 and headed south. They didn't have any trouble crossing from the GDR into Czechoslovakia. The authorities did only a cursory search of the car and didn't open M＿＿＿'s bag. If they had, they surely would have found its contents suspicious.

It was a family vacation. M＿＿＿'s parents didn't know his intentions. But as you read the interrogation transcripts, you can feel the awkwardness of this arrangement. M＿＿＿ wouldn't let his parents lift his bag, for example, lest they discover what was inside.

After a few days, M＿＿＿ took his leave. He told his parents he wanted to go to Lake Balaton on his own, that they should just drop him by the side of the road so he could hitchhike. Once his parents were gone, he switched course, thumbing a ride toward the border. He got as close as he could, then proceeded on foot, following a country road that took him partly there, then forging his own course through a heavily overgrown field, cutting inward.

When he felt he was close, M____ stopped and waited until it was dark. Then he set out, following a tree-lined path with dirt tracking made by jeeps or trucks. When he caught sight of the first stretch of fencing, he hid behind a tree to take stock of where he was. To the side of the road was a parking area for border guard vehicles, but this was presently vacant. He froze for a while, long enough for anyone who might have heard him to pass, then crept forward. It was only a few minutes to the first layer of fence.

M____ looked about, but felt the area wasn't right. It was too close to the border guard parking space and the shrubbery was thick, so he made his way slowly along the line. It was late when he found a suitable stretch of fencing. First he snipped his way past the first barrier— simple fencing, mostly designed to bar the passage of animals. This was

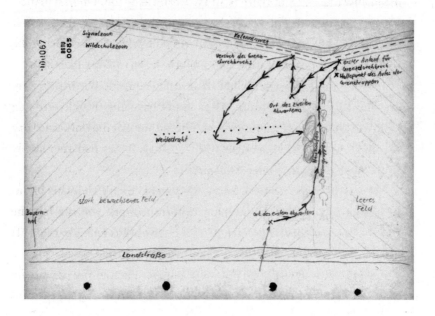

clean and efficient and made no noise. Then he approached the second layer, which carried a signal. Working fast, he set up his system, rigged the wire so it wouldn't trigger the alarm. Then he made his cut.

The plan failed. A siren went off and M_____ dashed back into the overgrowth and ran until he saw a row of haystacks, nestled against thick bushes, which he dove behind to hide. At roughly 2 a.m. on May 16, Hungarian guard dogs found him and he was arrested, handed over to the Stasi, and then taken back to the GDR. He would stay in prison until after the fall of the Wall.

———

IN EASTERN EUROPE, THE PAST DOESN'T LINGER, IT LURKS. JUST as the shadow of 1956 loomed over Hungary, so did 1968 in Prague and 1981 in Poland—always the possibility of violence, of Soviet tanks, of incommensurate force. There was no corner of the Eastern Bloc that violence had not touched. And in everyone's mind the fear remained. They didn't know when, or how, but they were sure, deep down, that it would happen again.

On June 4, 1989, the worst of these fears was confirmed—not by Soviet tanks, but Chinese ones, which rolled through Tiananmen Square in Beijing and crushed a student pro-democracy protest. This produced one of the most arresting images of the century. One man, unarmed but for plastic shopping bags, his white shirt billowing in the early summer breeze, standing before the tanks. A picture of human frailty before faceless power, its cold indomitability. We all felt a visceral shock when we first saw the image. But in the old Eastern Bloc, they felt something else too. That it could have been them.

Most of the leaders of the East were appalled by China's action. But not Honecker. In the days and weeks since Hungary had begun pulling up the electric wiring of the Iron Curtain, Honecker had spent his time glued to the television watching footage of Hungary's reckless reforms. He understood immediately that Hungary's actions posed an existential threat to his rule. After Tiananmen, Honecker addressed reporters.

The task of the government is to preserve law and order, he said. China should be lauded for its restraint. The evil came from outside provocateurs sent by the capitalist West. It is they who should be punished.

Citizens across the GDR read the news in dread. Honecker's ideological blindness was so strong and so deep. No one in the GDR doubted he could use violence too. For many of the would-be refugees, this moment was decisive in encouraging them to flee. If we don't leave now, they will do the same in East Germany, they thought. The tanks will come. They will shut the doors and let nobody out.

Chapter Ten

The Berlin Wall was not the only demarcation line of the GDR; far more expansive was the Inner German border—the stretch of the Iron Curtain that separated the two Germanies from each other. As in Berlin, people lived alongside that demarcation line too.

The village where Margret and Hermann Pfitzenreiter grew up was tiny, pressed all the way up against the border in the Eichsfeld region, pretty much as far west as you could physically be while still being in the East. As with anyone positioned so close to an international frontier, their lives were a parody of division: being so far west they could easily receive West German television signals, which kept them abreast of the news; but being in the borderlands, they were under constant surveillance, even more so than everyone else. Caught between East and West, they were stuck in a kind of political purgatory. Like they were born onto a bridge that didn't lead anywhere.

Growing up, Margret and Hermann experienced a level of state control that others would only encounter later, after the Stasi consolidated its power.

The Inner German border, like most borders, was less a line than a layering of lines—and between them, a seam zone—each with its own rules. Closest to the border there was a five-hundred-meter no-go area, and then farther into GDR territory, a controlled five-kilometer border strip in which people also lived. Hermann and Margret lived just outside this latter divisor, but could not cross it. In this way, their location was doubly paradoxical: in some sense they were already up against the border, but the people they bordered were also East German.

The policing of West German TV was especially rigorous in the borderlands. For Margret, one example from her childhood sticks out. There was a stop-motion animation program she liked called *Unser Sandmännchen* (*Our Little Sandman*, based on the Hans Christian Andersen character), a version of which played in both West and East. The shows were nearly identical but for one difference. In each episode a vehicle was introduced—a truck, a rocket, a bike. In the East, the vehicle entered on its own. But in the West, it arrived on a cloud.

At school each morning teachers would ask their pupils to describe what they had seen the night before. If a student mentioned the cloud, the teachers knew they had been illegally watching Western TV and their parents would be reported.

Margret never got caught. Her parents didn't even have to coach her how to respond. She just knew. Such was the internalization of authority in the GDR, the culture of caution unconsciously imparted to children by their frightened parents. As Margret grew older, the tightening of state control around her became harder to endure. In school, she refused to wear the class uniform or participate in socialist youth activities. This led to fights with her parents and school authorities and eventually the suspension of her studies.

Margret and Hermann Pfitzenreiter were just twenty-one years old when they got married in 1974. Hermann, a reserved, careful man; Margret, outgoing and headstrong. Their life together out in the borderlands was not easy but they made it work, with Margret constantly pushing the boundaries and Hermann pulling her back in.

Western TV remained a source of solace for Margret into adulthood. She became especially transfixed by debates in the Bundestag, the West German Parliament. Those politicians in their sharp suits, grandstanding, hectoring, debating ideas out in public. She was watching real democracy in action. Only a few kilometers away, on *that* side, those politicians could say whatever they wanted. But on *this* side, in the GDR, it was all lies all the time.

Sometimes, after Margret eventually graduated and found work as a teacher, she took sick days just to stay at home and watch.

Having access to Western TV was a blessing, but also a curse. You got a vision of the broader world, but you also saw what that world thought about you. Conversations you wished to be part of; stereotypes and false narratives you wanted to correct but couldn't. All you could do was sit, stuck, staring at TV shows documenting your stuckness.

———

THEMES OF ACCOMMODATION ARE A MAINSTAY IN EAST GERMAN literature—pre- and post-1989. In her recent essay collection, *Not a Novel* (2018), Jenny Erpenbeck discusses growing up in East Berlin close enough to the Wall that she could play in the cul-de-sac created by the streets it blocked off. "There is nothing better for a child than to grow up at the ends of the earth," she writes. "There's not much traffic there, so the asphalt is free for roller-skating."

The Wall was restricting, Erpenbeck observes. But it was also an opening. "As children in the East," she writes, "we could sometimes hear the sounds of the West Berlin subways through the ventilation grates as they passed underneath. . . . We heard the construction workers on the scaffolding in West Berlin hammering and drilling." Looking over the Wall at the facade of a building which displayed a giant clock, she writes: "Throughout all of my years in school, I read the time for my socialist life from this clock in the other world."

The Wall was a space of limitations but also contradictions. Sounds of things you could hear but not see; odors of things you could smell but not touch.

More than anything else, though, the *Wall* just *was*. Just like the Inner German border, these barriers were just something to get used to.

In 1987, Hermann Pfitzenreiter was permitted to travel to West Germany for his uncle's sixtieth birthday. Obtaining a visa to the West was challenging, but some exceptions were made for special occasions, provided you left the rest of your family in the GDR to ensure your return.

Hermann bought his train ticket well in advance. He exchanged money before boarding, then found his cabin and took his seat. He found himself fidgeting, unsure where to place his hands, still awed that this thing he had so long been dreaming about was finally happening. To go West, to come to the border—the same border he had lived beside his entire life—and finally cross it. The train was abustle with movement, so many restless travelers feeling the same power as Hermann.

With a whistle and a lurch they were on their way. But as they approached the border, the cabin fell silent. Hermann looked at his papers and filled with dread. Somehow the guards would find a problem and he wouldn't be able to continue on—he had heard stories of this, people removed from the train, even though their documents had been checked beforehand. Looking around he could tell everyone else was fearing this too.

When the train docked and the border guards split up, the cabin quickened with uncomfortable glances and shifting feet. Hermann steadied his breathing and kept his gaze downward. But then they crossed.

The trip itself was a blur, filled with visiting relatives, shopping trips, and excursions. So many *things*: swollen supermarkets with kaleidoscopic shelves; brands he had never seen before, products he had never even heard of. This was a universe apart from the barren shelves and drab, state-issued products he was used to in the GDR. Hermann could not eat. His mind was blank. That simple act of crossing from one side to the other, of passing the gates and breathing an air that felt fresh and new, stunned him. It revealed in a visceral way the nature of the prison he was living in.

On the way back, Hermann boarded a train in Frankfurt. He

entered his assigned cabin and took a seat. This time he felt more at ease. Certainly going *back* to the GDR wouldn't be as difficult. Then, just minutes before their departure an elderly woman entered their compartment. Hermann offered his seat, but she refused. Sit, she said. Everyone standing will be forced to leave.

Hermann slid over to make room anyway. When the train departed, there were four people on one side and three on the other.

At the border, passengers throughout the train prepared for checks. Items that were not allowed in the GDR, especially newspapers, were tossed out the window. Everyone did what they could to avoid drawing attention to themselves. Hermann was aware that there was one more person in his compartment than permitted, that this would create trouble. But he did his best to stay calm.

When the guard entered she stared at Hermann, wedged in the corner. *Out!* she screamed. At this point, the elderly woman rose. No, she said to the guard. First you will greet us politely, then you may carry on.

Livid, the guard threatened to throw her off the train. But the woman didn't budge. Instead, she pulled out a sheet of paper, authorized by the GDR government. She was a Holocaust survivor and had been invited to Buchenwald to attend a memorial service. This was the only train available, she explained. Then she told the guard to change her tone because it reminded her of what it felt like to stand before the Nazis.

As the elderly woman spoke, Hermann braced himself for the worst, for the guard to call to her superiors, to take names. He watched in astonishment as the guard continued her checks then disappeared wordlessly.

Hermann came home with gifts. Sweets for the children, shorts, an umbrella, and a tiny stuffed Alf—the American television character, popular in the West. But as he watched his children play with their spoils, he found himself returning to the elderly woman on the train: what she had said about tone, suggesting that the abuse of power might be a matter not of the rules but of how they were conveyed; how human relations contort to fit the uniform and office. The ability of that woman to stand up to authority was something Hermann never would have thought possible. She had put into words things he himself had been feeling about life in the GDR but had not known how to express.

Hermann vowed to find a way for Margret to go to the West too, to see it for herself. When, after trying several avenues, she finally did—also on account of a special occasion—her reaction too was visceral: her nerves were a wreck; she cried. She spent the days devouring newspapers, shocked at the things they were allowed to say. It was like being transported through time, back to her younger self first watching the Bundestag debates on TV. Yet here it was, now in living color. And the free world was bigger and bolder than she'd even imagined.

It would be another year before they heard the news from Hungary. But beginning in May 1989, Margret and Hermann began to talk about leaving—not to their children, and certainly not to anyone else—but quietly to each other, usually when they were driving, under the hum of the engine.

———

THROUGHOUT JUNE AND JULY 1989, FAMILIES ACROSS THE GDR began planning their escape.

After their brief trip to meet their friend in Prague, Regina and Lars returned to Berlin. Their plan was to meet again that August in Budapest, at which point their friend would take them to the Hungarian border. The friend had Western papers and a car, so he could transport their things across, then wait for them on the other side. But before this, Regina and Lars had to find a way to get out of the GDR. They had never taken a holiday to Hungary before, to do so now might appear suspicious to family and friends. Instead, they applied for Hungarian visas in secret and signed up for work at a youth summer camp in the GDR, which wouldn't raise eyebrows. They would send postcards as cover before heading south.

Still, plenty of things had to go right. Regina finished her professional driver training, but panicked when she learned she would not receive the diploma until that fall. She didn't want to leave without it; if she made it West, she would need the diploma to work. She couldn't just steal it—this would be found out. But nor could she easily copy it. In the GDR photocopiers were under strict supervision.

On the last day of class, Regina loitered until the premises emptied out, then took the school secretary aside and asked whether she might make a copy without telling her boss. This was a huge favor. If the secretary were to be caught, it would likely have cost her career. She looked at Regina, taken aback. She should have reported her then and there. But something in Regina's manner aroused her sympathy. Without speaking, the secretary went behind her desk and, looking furtively about, pulled Regina's file from the cabinet and walked over to the machine.

Sometimes you don't need revolution to bring about social change, just the slow disintegration of institutions, the simple loyalty of people to each other even if it means breaking the rules. In the grand scheme of things, a secretary agreeing to make a photocopy might seem a minor transgression. But for Regina, at that moment, it meant everything in the world.

Regina and Lars also needed a way of getting cash. Lars had a Lada—a Soviet car, common across the Eastern Bloc—which they could sell, but in the GDR there were no places for such transactions, only black market shops, which entailed risk. Lars spent some time poking about—going down to Leipzig and up to Rostock. With time he found takers—two men at a junkyard on the outskirts of Berlin. They made the exchange, then Regina and Lars piled into Regina's Trabant and drove home.

This was a huge relief. But two days later the doorbell rang and there were the two men who had bought their car, now in police uniforms. One of the policemen took out his book to register the crime. But he stopped. Looking back at their sallow, sunken faces, he took pity on them. They were just a couple of kids. So he offered them a deal: give us back the money and we will give you back the car. No record, no punishment.

Here again, the institutions were decaying. These men, whom

Regina and Lars did not know and would likely never see again, chose to betray their orders and do what they felt was right, even at their own personal risk. It is another great irony of the GDR, so good at driving people apart, that in doing so it sometimes brought them together.

For Margret and Hermann Pfitzenreiter, a principal source of anxiety pertained to packing—especially for Margret. Starting in July, she began setting an alarm for midnight, after the kids were asleep (and the neighbors wouldn't be watching), to get up and tiptoe about, deciding on what to take on their trip and where the rest should be hidden. She couldn't bear to simply leave things at the house. If they were caught, they would obviously lose everything. But so too if they made it across, as their house would be impounded and their belongings confiscated and sold off.

Margret had a friend who lived on a farm with a spacious barn, only a few minutes' walk away. She knew she could stow things there without her friend noticing. Margret started with their valuables, getting up that first night, sneaking over and burying things in the hay. With time, the items got larger and more unwieldy. Hermann was uncomfortable with this from the start. It's too risky, he told her. Someone will surely notice and report you. Once we're in the West we can buy new things, he said.

But Margret was adamant. She didn't want new things, she wanted *their* things. Of the items she hid under the hay she was most proud of their vinyls—the Bee Gees, Queen, Whitney Houston—all the newest tracks, impossible to find in the GDR but which they had bought bootleg during a trip to the USSR. Obviously such vinyls would be available in the West, but for Margret they were precious.

As the date of their departure got closer, there was one last thing to do—burn their contacts. If they did get caught, they wanted to make sure none of their friends or family members got punished by association. Margret spent days scouring the house, looking for contact information of any sort—on a letter or parcel; in an address or phone book. The most important ones they knew by heart; others they committed to memory. The rest they set on fire. Now they were ready to go.

Chapter Eleven

Politics is often like physics: for every force a counterforce, equal and opposite. Once East German citizens started making their way south by the thousands, so did the Stasi.

I am in the archives again, working through materials from June and July 1989. Stasi officials followed events in Hungary closely. In one of the folders is a photocopy of a Hungarian newspaper, dated June 27, the day Prime Minister Miklós Németh pushed through his second major border intervention, the staged fence cutting by Foreign Minister Gyula Horn and his Austrian counterpart, Alois Mock. The Stasi internal communiques express worries about this; that these small snips at the Iron Curtain might foretell a more expansive liberalization of the border regime.

A few days later, these fears proved warranted. On July 1, the Hungarian government announced that from that day forward, Hungarian border guards would stop marking the passports of GDR citizens who had been apprehended. Of course, in special circumstances they might be interrogated or detained—certainly repeat offenders—but most were to be simply turned away from the border. This was pursuant to a Hungarian government document, citing the Geneva Accords, which declared that all GDR citizens captured at the border might be considered for asylum if they claimed it.

On the outside this might have seemed like a small measure. For the Stasi, it was a crisis. To that point, while the Stasi had been actively attempting to stop East Germans from running away, the actual task of catching refugees largely fell to the Hungarians—there was a limit to what Stasi officers could legally do on foreign soil. But now, not only would the Stasi not be getting help from the Hungarians, they wouldn't even be getting information about which citizens had attempted to flee.

On July 6 came another piece of news: the West German embassy had become so full of refugees they planned to expand into another building to accommodate the arrivals. For the Stasi, these threats were existential: both the Hungarians and West Germans were now *helping* GDR refugees.

An angry debate erupted in the Ministry in East Berlin. The documents scrutinizing the Hungarian decision are now immortalized in the archives, slashed with angry underlining, bristling with notes. That day an internal memo was sent from the central Stasi headquarters to branches across the country desperately seeking advice—the last words *"Kurzfristige Meinungsäußerung übermittle"* (Report back immediately!) are circled in a deep, swooping blue.

The East German authorities needed a new apprehension strategy. If the Hungarians weren't going to cooperate, they would have to do it themselves. Their original plan had been to ramp up efforts to identify East Germans who might be headed south and catch them before they left the GDR. But now the Stasi understood these efforts wouldn't be enough. They would also need to radically increase the number of people catchers on Hungarian soil.

The problem was just beginning. The real crunch would come in August, vacation season. In 1988, an estimated eight hundred thousand East Germans traveled to Hungary. This summer, it might be many, many more. And so the race began. If GDR citizens were

traveling in huge numbers down to Hungary, Stasi officials would
have to go after them.

––––––––––

POLITICAL MOMENTS ARE OFTEN CHARACTERIZED BY SPECIFIC
spaces—places and their moods that capture the character of the era.
In the summer of 1989 in Hungary, more than anywhere else, these
places were campsites—sometimes built up with lavatories and kitch-
ens, other times little more than a peppering of tents splayed out in
not-so-neat rows—mainly along the placid shorelines of Lake Balaton.
Ordinarily such places are a refuge *from* politics. But at this precise
moment, they were the center of the political world.

Beginning almost immediately after the Wall went up, in 1961,
Lake Balaton became a popular meeting spot for German-German
reunions—East and West Germans getting together to enjoy each
other's company in a country they found mutually congenial. These
were not rule breakers, just vacationers eager to see loved ones who
lived at a distance.

Over the next decades, Lake Balaton became something of a
utopia—a place to escape the devastation of the Wall, to experience
family togetherness as it once had been. This idea of Balaton as a
reunion ground persisted into 1989, but by this point it had become
something else too: a meeting ground for would-be refugees—families
and young couples, trying to find a way to reunite in the west.

Katja and Oskar met in Kaluga, a city to the west of Moscow in the
Soviet Union, in April 1987, when they were seventeen. Both were on
school trips: he from the West and she from the East. But in the Soviet
Union, they were housed in the same accommodation. In the evenings,
students from different programs got together in the common spaces
of the building complex to drink and smoke cigarettes, talking late into
the night. When the trip was over, Katja and Oskar decided to stay in
touch as pen pals. For each it was exhilarating to write letters to someone *on the other side.*

Their missives were extensive, spilling out the details of their divided-yet-proximate lives usually over many pages, sometimes multiple times a week. Oskar was at that time doing compulsory service in the West German army. He found little meaning in this training and was attracted to the East with its socialist ideals. In the long evenings after military service, he put these thoughts and feelings into words.

Katja's situation was more complicated. She wanted to study medicine and did well enough on her exam to qualify for a university position, but her applications were rejected because her family wasn't close enough to the regime. When she was eighteen, she was called before a panel to decide her future. Her father drove her to school that day; usually Katja biked. She wore her nicest dress. In the car she told her father she wouldn't take any job where she would be forced to preach the gospel of the regime.

It was a large room and she was seated in front of a row of school authorities on the opposite side of a long table. They were there to tell her what options were available, offering her a range of mediocre positions, mostly in education. Katja looked back at her superiors and said no to everything they proposed. She knew this would mean trouble, but the system was so unfair—saying no felt like her only recourse.

Justice was swift and merciless. She was told to leave and not return. Now she was stuck working angry hours on a farm, amidst the mud and manure, in a valley east of Dresden. She didn't have a car to go to work, so she took her bicycle. But the terrain was hilly and the bike had no gears, so she often had to push it up steep inclines in the sweltering heat of summer, in the wind and rain.

Her correspondence with Oskar became a crescendo of bitter complaints. Katja knew she was treading dangerous ground. If the Stasi had read her letters, she would have been penalized. But she didn't care. She felt compelled to write down her thoughts lest she go mad. Also, because she felt Oskar would understand. His letters had become something to look forward to, the one thing the state hadn't taken away from her. One night after a letter from Oskar, Katja decided to take things forward. If you are so interested in the GDR, she wrote, come visit me.

Oskar traveled to Dresden in April 1988, accepting an invitation from Katja's grandfather. It would look less suspicious that way. At this point the young couple were beginning to fall in love, thrust together in the way of teenagers who felt the world was against them. Oskar spent a little less than a week on that first visit. Later they went to Lake Balaton with Katja's family. The following spring, 1989, they met in Prague, just the two of them. At one point, curled together, listening to Katja's woes, Oskar turned to her. Let's get married, he said. That way, I can get you out.

They made plans to meet again in Hungary that coming summer. Back home they continued writing letters, but Katja was less critical at this point. She no longer wrote about politics, or her anger at the GDR. She was careful. She didn't want to get caught. Now she had something to lose.

————

IF LAKE BALATON HAD FOR YEARS BEEN A HAPPY WONDERLAND for East-West reunions, this fairytale was quickly coming to an end. By late July of 1989, the lake had become the focus of the Stasi's extraterritorial operations. Like every other utopia—in Greek, it is the happy place (*eu*)-*topia*, but also the non-place (*u*)-*topia*—Lake Balaton was now also proving too good to be true.

Monika Tantzscher, a German scholar, refers to this migration of the Stasi to Lake Balaton as the "extended wall." In fact, Stasi operations in Hungary had been developing for years, mirroring the travels of East Germans after the building of the Wall. But that summer this accelerated. Now rather than respites from the GDR, the campsites in Hungary, and especially around Lake Balaton, became a continuation of surveillance-as-normal, exerting just as much pressure as back home—if not more.

The Stasi aim was to infiltrate the GDR traveler communities, to make friends, become confidants, to induce people to spill their plans and then ensnare them, and bring them back to the GDR. Many East Germans were totally unsuspecting. For them, the awakening would be abrupt and brutal, in some cases ending their holiday excursions before they even began. The people who let their guard down, who went to Hungary hoping to experience something like freedom, to be themselves among the people they loved, theirs were the lives most quickly and efficiently destroyed.

And still, the East Germans kept coming. If July was a month of packing and fretting, by early August they were on the road. The first border, with Czechoslovakia, was the easy one. They were still in the Eastern Bloc, after all. Most families passed this obstacle. They were careful not to carry anything that might set off alarms, such as letters or addresses in the West—these were transcribed into code or memorized. Maps were okay—everyone was camping—but compasses suggested navigating off the trail. And nothing too nostalgic. Photographs or items of childhood remembrance might suggest you are not coming back.

Hermann and Margret Pfitzenreiter's main concern was for their older son, L____. He was fifteen already and beginning to ask questions.

The night before they left, Margret had taken their television, the last item she wanted to stow away, to their neighbor's barn. She had labored to get it there, but finally it was buried among their other belongings. Until that point, the kids had not seemed to notice that anything was missing. But when they woke on the morning of their trip, the TV was glaringly absent. Margret explained that they had taken it to get fixed. It makes sense to do this before we go on holiday, she told them, so it will be ready when we get back.

This explanation seemed to satisfy their youngest son, U____. But they weren't sure about L____. Nothing was said and they all busied themselves with the normal routine of packing the car. They hadn't yet told the children they were going to Hungary—it was too much in the news. Instead they said they would be going on vacation to Berlin. This had worked for the weeks leading up to their trip. But once they were on the road, L_____ saw the road signs passing by and put it all together.

You don't go to Berlin via Dresden, he said. You're going to Hungary, trying to escape.

Margret looked over the back seat at her son. Yes, she said calmly. Now you need to be quiet.

From that moment on, no words were exchanged in the car.

They stopped in Dresden on the way down. They had to go to the bank—this was the last detail of planning to be taken care of before they left. They had some money saved up—about two thousand Ostmarks (the East German currency; a few hundred dollars' worth)—which they didn't want to leave, as it would be impounded. If they'd withdrawn this in the village, people would have been suspicious. But they also couldn't take it with them—the state wouldn't let you leave with too much currency. So they decided to go on a last Eastern spending spree, mostly for swimwear and other summer stuffs. It felt uncomfortable, spending so liberally money they had spent so long saving. But better that than giving it to the state.

The drive from Dresden to the GDR-Czechoslovakian border is a short one. Looking back into her son's face, Margret understood then that he had suspected them for some time. This almost brought her to tears: how much he had been holding in; the fear they each felt for each other.

At the GDR border, the guards asked for their passports and papers for the car. Then they walked around the back, just the usual checks. There were tents and other camping gear, as befit a family vacation. Anything that would have aroused suspicion was safely tucked away in the hay of their neighbor's barn. Their main concern was their children, that they might be taken out of the car, separated and questioned. Kids' reactions are very honest. They wouldn't have been able to lie.

But after a cursory inspection, the officers waved them through—

first the East Germans, then the Czechoslovakians. And just like that, they were on their way. The real issues of course were to come, after they crossed the next border and made their way toward the Iron Curtain. But for now, they had at least made it out of the GDR. Hermann let out a whoop as he stepped on the gas.

Next stop, Hungary.

PART III

BREACH!

Chapter Twelve

On July 31, 1989, Mária Filep set out by bus to visit the Hungarian-Austrian border. It was a long trip, nearly the entire width of the country, from her home city of Debrecen by the border of Romania, all the way across the Pannonian Plain to Sopron, tucked into a bend in the Iron Curtain.

She had never been before. Less a country than a capital and its hinterlands, Hungary is laid out like a wheel, with Budapest as its shimmering hub and roads splaying out like spokes from the center. It was expected for Hungarians of all stripes to visit the capital, but a trip from one periphery to another was more unusual.

Staring out the window as the wide agricultural flats of eastern Hungary transformed into the industrial heartland around the capital and finally to gentle hill country out west, Mária was filled with trepidation. She and Ferenc Mészáros—who had first come up with the idea of the picnic—had built a tight unit in Debrecen, supported by a small group of friends. But now she was traveling to Sopron to discuss the planning with members of their local MDF. Could these people be trusted? Given her disappointing experiences with MDF activists in the past, Mária had reservations.

The date of the picnic was August 19—just a few short weeks away.

Back in Debrecen, the past weeks had been intense. Mária had thrown herself headlong into the project, laboring long hours often by herself. After establishing contact with László Magas in Sopron on July 15—their first link to the borderlands—Mária had started making calls. On July 20, she established contact with the national headquarters of the border guards. Now that she and Ferenc had a section of the Curtain picked out, they could start to figure out what the border authorities might deem permissible. On July 22, Otto von Habsburg faxed to Mária the statement that he would deliver at the event.

While Mária worked the phone, Ferenc wrote the program and a companion text to be published beside it. These would be translated into several languages—English, German, Russian, French, Polish, Romanian, and Czech—a reflection of the Pan-European project they hoped to create.

As the summer progressed, the group of activists around Mária and Ferenc swelled. Some local journalists, including Gábor Túri, were given the responsibility of communicating with the media. Ákos Gali, president of the Debrecen MDF, agreed to sign their letters, providing an official air to their efforts. Lukács Szabó got donations for pork, paprika, soft drinks, and pledges for a pair of buses to transport people to the border. A friend of Mária's, Ákos Varga, designed the flyer. With his help they managed to print five thousand copies for free.

But this was about as much as they could do from Debrecen. Now it was time to coordinate things at the border. Hence the meeting in Sopron. Mária's hopes for the meeting were initially disappointed. Rather than finding people as motivated as she was, she found—as she would put it—a bunch of slackers.

The MDF in Sopron was skeptical of the plan. The work that needed doing was monumental given how much time remained. Mária soon found herself exasperated and could hear her voice growing unwelcoming and shrill. In the beginning, Magas—the leader of the Sopron MDF—remained silent, giving Mária space to outline the plan. But sensing the dissent in the room, he intervened. The picnic would give us the opportunity to work together as an opposition and show our strength, he said.

While Mária's Pan-European message was a good one, the activists from Sopron were more interested in the domestic side of the equation: promoting a democratic Hungary. Magas seized on this. Size is power, he said to the room. If we do this right, the event could be huge.

As Magas got involved, the air shifted. Soon other members started to voice support. Still, the main issue was left unresolved: they had to pick a site.

Magas knew the borderlands better than almost anyone. He was a professor of forestry at the local university and held permits that allowed him into areas still off-limits to ordinary citizens. He was also hugely disciplined—a marathon runner—and well regarded by the local authorities. He quickly put Mária at ease. We'll find a place, he assured her.

The following day, August 1, Magas and Mária drove together to a section of the woods that demarcated the beginning of the Iron Curtain. Then they cut inward, past the first line of Curtain defenses and into the seam zone between the Curtain and the border. Here, Magas' white Škoda acquired a phalanx of border police to accompany them through this restricted area.

Mária was enchanted. It was her first time in the borderlands, this forbidden wood, untouched for generations. Absent development, the western borderlands had become something of a wildlife reserve, flush with overgrowth and birdsong. They drove some ways along a dirt track intended for border guards and other security personnel, until there opened before them a field, Sopronpuszta, a wide, untrammeled expanse, out on the edge of nowhere, proximate to nothing but the frontier. It was *perfect*.

There were still issues to resolve. Since the Iron Curtain extended far into Hungarian soil, this meant that from the field in Hungary, Austrians could be neither seen nor heard. But Magas knew of a small gated crossing nearby and this gave him an idea. Perhaps they could find a way to open it. Trying to arrange for a delegation to come via the main crossing—on the road to the Austrian village of Klingenbach—would have been problematic, as it was many kilometers away. But opening this tiny, rusted, unused gate for a one-time-only crossing—this might be possible.

As soon as she was back in Debrecen, Mária was on the phone with their patron, Minister of State Imre Pozsgay, the only person she knew who might help them open that gate.

———

REVISITING HISTORY IS ALWAYS A PROCESS OF RECALIBRA-tion—of reconsidering what you thought you knew in light of what you didn't. But for events in living memory the process is especially tortuous.

When we try to envisage the politics of 1989, most of us conjure images of Gorbachev and Bush, staring each other down from opposite ends of an imaginary-but-world-sized table. The United States in this rendering is an avatar for freedom, beacon to revolutionaries around the world. And surely it also was. But seen from the ground in Hungary, in East Germany, in all the other satellites caught in the middle, it looked a bit different. While the US might have embodied broad ideals of freedom, it wasn't in any real sense an agent of change.

According to the US State Department, a neutral Hungary was only possible "in the long term." To some degree, this had been the US position all along. The image from the Cold War perhaps most imprinted on the American consciousness is that of Ronald Reagan's speech given on June 12, 1987, in West Berlin, before the backdrop of the Wall—a masterpiece of dramatic staging, positioned before the ominous concrete slabs, framed by guard towers. (With a line of sol-diers behind this, an invisible wall pushing back East Berliners who had gathered to listen.) In his address, Reagan uttered the now famous injunction: "Mr. Gorbachev, tear down this Wall!"

The speech played terrifically well in the US—its principal

audience—but its reception locally was muted. The hero in West Berlin was not Reagan but Gorbachev—the fervor for whom was tagged Gorbi-mania. East Berliners had long relinquished the idea that America would help them—at least since Kennedy's famous *Ich bin ein Berliner* speech in 1963, which decried the Wall but did little to challenge it. Like Kennedy, after his speech Reagan packed up and left.

And of course, despite Gorbachev's commitment to reform, the Soviet Union was interested in perpetuating the status quo above all else.

But this geopolitical stasis would soon be disrupted, due to the tide of East Germans flooding into Hungary—as many as fifty thousand would-be refugees already by midsummer, and this was before the high season. Most crossing attempts were stymied—95 percent, according to Hungarian records. But this volume was already more than the Hungarian border guards were equipped to handle. The potential for an international incident was considerable.

One day, the Hungarian prime minister, Miklós Németh, made a visit to Lake Balaton and observed the swollen campsites along its shores. Outside the West German Embassy in Budapest, he found himself stepping over the bodies of refugees on the pavement. This was becoming a crisis. No guidance was forthcoming from Washington or Moscow, so Németh tried a different approach: in late July he contacted the West German chancellor, Helmut Kohl, who was on holiday in the Austrian Alps. We need to do something about the refugees, Németh told him.

Kohl was noncommittal. We feel for the refugees, he said. But we don't want to see any bloodshed or be sucked into another great war on their behalf.

It soon became clear this problem was Hungary's to deal with. The obvious thing would have been to open the borders and let the refugees out. But this would have been a massive violation of the Warsaw Pact. Indeed, Németh's prior provocations at the Iron Curtain were tolerated only because the border itself remained heavily controlled. Opening it was out of the question.

The issue was also delicate internally, as Károly Grósz, a Party stalwart, stood with the other leaders of the Eastern Bloc and considered any support for the refugees treasonous. Grósz maintained a good deal of power in Hungary, as did the Worker's Guard, the Party's militia. As the situation grew more tense, reformers in government feared an anti-revolutionary backswing.

Hungary's position of tolerant inaction worked for a while. But with each passing day, resolving the refugee situation was getting harder to postpone.

———

OF THOSE EAST GERMANS WHO HAD CROSSED INTO HUNGARY intending to breach the Iron Curtain, most had a plan, or at least something resembling one. The Sobels, a family of four packed into a Trabant, were going to make it up as they went.

Walter had been talking about leaving for a while. At first Simone didn't believe him but tolerated his musings, the venting and frustrations of a man she loved. With time, she began to realize he was serious. He'd wanted to go to the West his whole life. Now was the time.

The trip to Hungary started off as a compromise. They would take a vacation first at Lake Balaton and then make up their minds. For as much as Walter had his eyes fixed on the future, Simone cast hers backward, on the life they had left behind, to which she wouldn't have minded returning. When they loaded the car to drive south, their lives were intact—they kept open their bank accounts, cleaned their house—just in case they decided to return.

Walter knew all the West German football clubs, the geography, even the names of the autobahns he dreamt of one day speeding down. He came from a large family, with dozens of cousins living in the West. They sent letters depicting their lives in unvarnished detail—not the vicious propaganda he received from GDR sources, but nor the all-too-sunny view he might have concocted on his own. Instead it was the

West with all its blemishes. A place where you had to work—hard, in an unrelenting way—but where you had a chance of something beautiful: freedom, a life unfettered by the state.

Like so many others who tried to escape, Walter had struggled in school. He got good *schulnoten*—school grades, the marks received in subjects like reading or math—but poor *kopfnoten*, a social grade written out by the headmaster, which evaluated your commitment to the socialist cause. This experience of being pushed down by the system contributed to a chip on his shoulder, which he nursed. He became outwardly defiant. When he graduated, he was given work as a metal smelter. More attractive careers were unavailable to him.

Walter and Simone came from altogether different worlds. Simone's father was a respected Party member and Simone had done well in school, eventually taking up work as a physiotherapist. Being with a man like Walter was a risk for her and positioned her against the current of the GDR. It also set her on her path to leave.

They had been extremely disciplined in the lead-up to their trip—more than most, because of Simone's father. Had he found out about their ambitions, he would certainly have informed the state.

They entered Hungary in early August but a vacation proved impossible. When they arrived at Lake Balaton, what they found was a space contaminated with Stasi. Walter and Simone took to covering their mouths when they spoke—this was Walter's idea, he'd learned it from footballers talking strategy on the pitch.

They also had to be careful talking in front of their two girls, just four and two years old. Who knew what they might blurt out? Since Simone wanted to keep open the prospect of returning to the GDR, anything overheard or jotted down would have been devastating. Although, given the sheer density of Stasi officials at their campsite, their license plate number was surely already recorded. They probably couldn't have gone back anyway.

The experience at Balaton was a nightmare for Simone, who'd

believed that taking a week of vacation first would calm her nerves for their trip. For Walter, it was a nightmare in a different way. Back home he hadn't thought much about the Stasi. As far as he was concerned, the GDR was already a prison—what harm could they do to him that they hadn't already done? But here, in Hungary, now that they could fill their lungs with the air of possibility, he found the presence of the Stasi rattling.

The whole climate was one of distrust and suspicion. Perversely, the stultifying society they'd fled in the GDR had followed them to Hungary. All the big questions of their lives could not be talked about. There was just a quiet passing of thoughts and unsaid things—the reading of facial expressions, the saying without saying. These classic marks of authoritarianism came with them like luggage.

They left the campsite just a few days after they arrived. Their first plan was to try the border with Yugoslavia, a straight shot south— Walter had heard the Yugoslav border was less harshly patrolled than the Austrian. The area was mostly vineyards, large stretches of land patrolled by farmers who had a reputation for benign neglect, an inclination to turn a blind eye, provided those who were transiting didn't do anything to upset the grapes.

On the road south, the Sobels came quickly upon the desired farm country, but it wasn't easy to find a place to cross. They drove around, lost in a web of small roads that seemingly led nowhere. Along the border they could see the barbed wire running through the thicket. Several times they drove right up against the line but thought the foliage too thick to try and cross. All they confronted was quiet, and the mocking, simplified certainty of the map.

After a sequence of dead ends, Walter decided to change strategy. Maybe he could find a guard who would take pity on them, someone they could bribe. He knew this was a risk—the Hungarians could send their details back to East Germany—but felt they had to take that chance. When they pulled up to a border crossing, Walter stuck a hundred Deutsche Marks—coveted West German currency; a generous amount—into his passport. The young Hungarian guard looked down kindly and spoke to them in rough, heavily accented German. I would let you pass, he told them, but I can't. My boss is sitting right behind me. He would never allow it.

Rather than report them or force them to reckon with the higher authorities, the young guard directed them to turn around discretely and drive away before anyone else noticed.

Walter was demoralized. When he could bring himself to look at Simone, he expected to find resignation, their defeat registered in her expression. Let's go back home, he expected her to say. And he would have been fine with it. He felt humiliated and maybe somewhere inside he wanted this too. But she didn't. Instead, she took hold of the map and silently, intently surveyed it.

Finally, she pointed at a little bend to the west. Let's try here, she said. Sopron.

She had never heard of the place before. But she'd always wanted to go to the nearby Neusiedlersee—Lake Fertő, in Hungarian. Maybe they could have a vacation after all. And so they set out, a new, quiet if resolute air in the car. Whereas in the beginning it was Walter who led Simone to overcome her nerves, now it was Simone who kept the ship afloat.

They drove north and then west, following the path of the sun. But they didn't make it far before their car was stopped by Hungarian guards at a makeshift checkpoint. This time the officers were not friendly. A man holding a Kalashnikov rifle reached into the car and pulled out the keys, telling them to get out and stand on the side of the road.

The interrogation was brusque. We're lost, Walter told them, just trying to meet up with my parents. We weren't trying to go anywhere near the border.

The guards were unconvinced. But once again they let the Sobel family go, their passports untouched. Just turn back, they said. Drive away and don't let us see you here again.

Simone was shaking. To have a gun pointed at her, the fear she felt for herself, her kids. Where the first experience at the border had produced feelings of disappointment, the second induced despair. When she emerged from her shock, she considered the road again, the trees, the horizon beyond. The thought came to her with perfect clarity: they had worked too hard to turn back now.

Walter asked what she thought they should do.

Let's go to Sopron, she said.

Chapter Thirteen

opron is a quaint, midsize city, surrounded by the rolling hills of Hungary's western borderlands. Like many places that stand at the end of one world and the beginning of another, it has a forgotten quality to it, all the more poignant on still, cloudless summer days.

In early August, the organizers' days were filled with letter writing and telephone calls, and the labor of preparing the grounds. Things were going well, at least on the Hungarian side. There would be a picnic, this at least they felt sure of. When Pozsgay learned from Mária about the closed crossing outside Sopronpuszta he gave his support to open the gate, but since their request pertained to a restricted part of the border, permission would require the signature of Balázs Nováky, commander of the border guards. This would take time.

In Sopron, Magas's first priority was to expand the field of organizers to include members from other opposition groups, notably the Free Democrats (Szabad Demokraták Szövetsége, SZDSZ) and Fidesz. Several local MDF figures took on prominent roles in the planning, among them László Nagy and János Rumpf, a forestry professor like Magas.

Magas and Rumpf were off work during the summer, so they took the lead on tasks that required daytime hours—getting legal permissions, mainly. László Nagy and most of the other organizers worked office jobs during the day, so they took on responsibilities in the evenings and on weekends—letter writing, producing posters and flyers, and generally helping to publicize the event.

Németh's performance in clipping the electric wiring of the Curtain had given the organizers the idea of letting people snip bits of it themselves and take them home as souvenirs.

Rumpf came up with the slogan *"Break it and Take it!"* The idea came from the apple trees that grew wild around the seam zone of the Curtain, an area he knew well from his forestry work. It was a common expression in Hungary that if you saw wild fruit you could "pick it and take it." They would invite guests to come to the picnic with wire cutters. Pál Csóka, another MDF member, forged the link between the Berlin Wall and Ceaușescu's violence against ethnic Hungarians in Romania with the line, *"Destroy the Wall instead of Villages!"*

On August 10, the various local political authorities—health officials, border guards, the city hall—met the organizers in Sopronpuszta to survey the site and agree to the conditions under which the event could proceed.

But a problem remained: the event was just over a week away and they still had invited no Austrian guests or found a way to bring them to the site. It didn't make sense to put the request in writing as they didn't have the time. Pál Csóka, it was decided, would cross into Austria and approach government offices in person.

On August 11, Csóka made his way to the office of Andreas Waha, mayor of Sankt Margarethen, the nearest town of any size across the border. Waha was not convinced of the plan. He was brusque and felt it was too late to be trying to execute such an ambitious endeavor. But Csóka was insistent. Look how far we've come, he said, spreading the materials they had created across the mayor's desk—maps, flyers (written in German), a tentative program.

The picnic won't be complete if it is just Hungarians, Csóka said. To celebrate brotherhood across the divide, we have to be there together.

The next day, Waha started making calls on the organizers' behalf.

Soon he was able to get in touch with the Austrian border guards to alert them to the plan. Placards were passed about in town, advertising the event.

Now that the Austrian side was moving, Mária redoubled her efforts to get permission from the Hungarians to open the gate. It had been some days since their first requests to the border guards. Letters were followed up by phone calls, which were followed up by letters.

———

I AM HAVING A BEER WITH LÁSZLÓ NAGY. IT IS AUTUMN 2019 AND we are at his favorite bar, a surprisingly respectable English pub in Sopron. He knows I have been taking trips to do interviews in the old GDR and is eager to talk about why life there was so different than in Hungary. He revisits the story of his father, a successful engineer despite being a dedicated anti-Communist.

You want to know why my father never got in trouble? László asks with a flourish. Because he was useful. So the authorities kept him around. That's the big difference, why Hungary succeeded and East Germany failed. In Hungary, if you provided value, you were tolerated. In East Germany, if you were disloyal, you were punished.

László is grandstanding, speaking loudly and gesticulating, even though it is early afternoon and the premises are otherwise vacant.

One of the challenges of your project, he says, is going to be to capture how crazy it was in those days. For us organizers, we understood there were some reformers in government who believed the same things we did—about democracy, about freedom. But that's all. The rest was darkness.

The problem, László continues, was that we never knew anything *for certain*—what the authorities were thinking, what they might do to us. Even Németh barely knew anything and he was prime minister! What could we know?

I'm impressed you didn't end up in prison, I tell him.

László shrugs. It wasn't East Germany, he says.

László wasn't the only one to home in on the differences between Hungary and the GDR—another was political philosopher Hannah Arendt, who traces this divergence of paths back to the Hungarian uprising of 1956. For her, Hungary was a major bright spot in postwar Europe and a clue as to how totalitarianism ends.

In her first reissuing of *The Origins of Totalitarianism*, in 1958, Arendt included a substantive conclusion, "Reflections on the Hungarian Revolution." By 1967, this chapter was gone. It was too different in tone from the rest of the book; it painted a picture of hope. I hadn't read this chapter before embarking on this project—it was difficult to track down, as the 1958 book is out of print. But it rewarded every effort.

In Hungary, Arendt diagnosed the factors propitious for revolutionary change: a Soviet regime relaxing controls (the thaw of Khrushchev following the death of Stalin in 1953), coupled with an internal reform movement within the government (led by Imre Nagy). These conditions provided just enough room for students to believe that change might be possible—to envisage freedom, to think about it, dream about it. This was unimaginable in a place like the GDR, the state most tightly held in Soviet grip.

Change happens slowly in politics. Until it happens quickly.

In 1989, the groundwork for revolution had been laid and conditions in Hungary were ripe once again: a Soviet regime loosening controls (now under Gorbachev), alongside a split in the local Party (led by Németh). Such conditions were absent in the GDR, where Erich Honecker stood atop a unified regime, and attempts at dissent were ruthlessly suppressed.

In the pub, László opens his satchel and pulls out some files. This is customary in our conversations. László is the unofficial archivist for the picnic and the curator of whatever documents he has been able to get his hands on. The files hold a jumble of maps, often hand drawn, newspaper clippings in various languages, lots of signed and stamped briefs churned out by the bureaucratic establishment. It was a wild time, those mid-August days just before the picnic, and the papers reflect this.

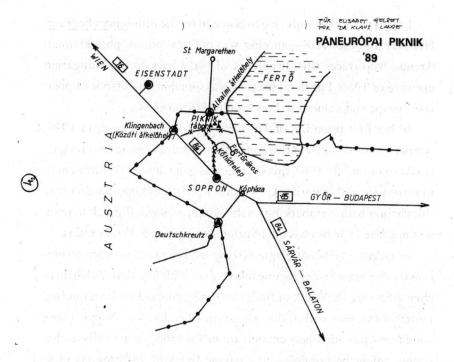

Looking now through these files, László and I are piecing together the exact sequence of events. One of the last permissions they received, in a process that stretched out to the absolute end, regarded sanitation. They couldn't throw an event like this without having places for people to use the toilet. We had to do everything from scratch, László exclaims. We had to learn how to build latrines!

He brandishes the permit stamped by the health inspectors, procured just days before the event.

László's collection is amazing. I take pages of notes. But what strikes me later, after departing the pub, is something the archive cannot reveal: the universe of actions happening behind the scenes. For every official government permission, there were so many steps taken in private. A shadow archive of secret decisions, beyond what the organizers could possibly have known or understood. Indeed, though it was true that many in the Communist Party opposed their actions, there was always someone, somewhere, willing to help them out. And while for the organizers the state was something terrifying, a live wire that could destroy their plans, in fact state officials were largely on their side—especially at the top.

Like Pozsgay, Németh was optimistic about the picnic when he heard about it—although he didn't think much of it. He saw it as another opportunity to test Gorbachev, another provocation at the Iron Curtain—just as the May 2 and June 27 events had been.

Pozsgay saw the potential for something bigger. By early August, he began to wonder whether the picnic might even represent a solution to the problem of the refugees. Németh supported Pozsgay's involvement but didn't want any documentation—that way if the situation blew up it couldn't be traced back to them. Other reformers in government had stronger reservations. The defense minister, Ferenc Kárpáti, would have been happy to see the picnic more tightly controlled or even shut down.

But Pozsgay wanted to make sure it succeeded. He understood the picnic could be disastrous. But it had the chance of being something great too.

NOT EVERYONE WHO TRIED TO FLEE DID SO ON PURPOSE.

Oskar and Katja met up again in Budapest in August 1989—he coming from the West, she coming from the East. Their plan was to get married, as they had discussed that spring in Prague. But they wanted to talk this through when they were together, this momentous decision.

Lovers generally prefer not to dwell on matters of legality or logistics. But in this case law charted the way forward. Oskar, as a West German, *could* make Katja his wife. It would just take some paperwork. The idea filled Katja with trepidation—they hadn't known each other that long. But Oskar had it worked out. They would submit their application in September when they got back from vacation. No special papers were needed in the West, but to the GDR, they would have to prove they were a couple—marrying for love, not simply escape. For this it would help to have proof they were traveling together. If everything went through, they would marry in 1990. They would be twenty-one.

Oskar wanted to know what a wedding would look like in the East—it would have to be held in the GDR or the authorities might get suspicious. They talked about who they would invite. Katja started to think about her dress.

They were in love and on vacation and didn't want to consider politics—but it was unavoidable with all the photos of East Germans trying to breach the Iron Curtain splashed across the papers. And then there was the reburial of Imre Nagy that had happened in June, just a few months prior. When Oskar told Katja about it, she immediately wanted to see the new grave. In East Germany, Nagy was known in a storybook sort of way.

One day they made their way to the back of the vast cemetery on Budapest's outskirts. It was scorching out and the walk was long, but before they knew it they had stumbled headlong into a sea of flowers and flags in Hungary's distinctive green, white, and red that graced the grave of this revered revolutionary.

Being there in the cemetery, Katja quickly understood how far Hungary had progressed. This kind of complex freedom—to mourn the dead of your choosing, even someone the state condemned—was not something she thought would ever come to East Germany. Not in her lifetime, not for another hundred years. Katja looked around for police, certain that someone was watching her.

That trip to the cemetery frightened Katja. But it also fueled her curiosity. Suddenly, the borderlands became alluring. Oskar had a car so they decided to go see what it was like over there by the border, to check it out. They had no intent to cross—that would have put all their plans in jeopardy. But one day, while driving around, they ended up in the open country of the western borderlands, by the city of Kőszeg. There was a church, visible out in the distance. Let's go see it, Katja said. She found the road on the map, directing Oskar as he drove.

Katja hadn't realized how close they were to the Iron Curtain, which wasn't marked. She also didn't expect to find a checkpoint suddenly popping up, as if out of nowhere. On the map, this was just a normal road, the kind that Hungarians might take every day and never think about. And anyway, it was parallel to the border—not headed toward it.

But it was close; too close. An officer with a gun stepped in front of their car, barring passage. They were ordered to pull over, to stay seated. A sequence of young officers examined the car; Oskar was asked for his passport and registration. All of this checked out—the car and its driver were West German. For a small breathless moment it seemed this might be it—no more questions and they'd be through. But then one of the boys came by and wanted to see Katja's passport too.

We're just tourists, Oskar explained, pointing toward the church atop the hill at the end of the road. The official was unimpressed. He told Katja to get out of the car. Suddenly there she was, East German again, and scared. We have no interest in crossing, she said, hearing her own desperation. We will get married.

Just don't write anything down, she pleaded. If you do, we will lose everything—our future together, *everything.*

The officer took it all—their names, passport numbers, home addresses. Turn around, he said curtly. I don't want to see you in my district ever again.

Once Katja had gotten back into the car, the officer came over to the window, looked down at their blanched, sunken faces. Listen, he said. If you want to escape, go farther north, near Sopron. It's easier there.

Back on the road, Katja flushed with doubt. What if those officials contacted the East German authorities? From their point of view, she shouldn't have been traveling so close to the border. And the fact that she was in a West German car would have told them everything they needed to know. That certainty she had felt just moments earlier, sitting in the car beside Oskar, navigating the map; that feeling of freedom in Hungary so sweet to the taste, the future they envisioned. All of this had evaporated.

Katja felt sick to her stomach. Not just because it was she who had chosen the road, steering them so close to a place that would have been forbidden in the GDR. But also because she'd been forced to face the limitations of her station. This was not a checkpoint for everyone. Hungarians could go freely down this road. So could Oskar. It was only a checkpoint for her, for people like her.

Sitting there in the car, looking at Oskar, she knew then that she could never go back to East Germany. The holiday was over. Now there was only one direction for them to go.

Sopron.

Chapter Fourteen

Mária's resting face is almost expressionless. The first time I met her, what struck me most was that behind the stolid countenance was a spirit so fearless.

More than anyone else in the planning, Mária dealt directly with people in positions of power. First Pozsgay and Habsburg, later Nováky and other border guards—men with authority and guns, who had for decades held the country in the tightest grip. Yet here she was, a fair, rosy-cheeked young woman from Debrecen, armed with a telephone, calling about a picnic. We want to open the border for a special crossing, she demanded. And what's left of the Curtain, we want to cut that too.

Her officemate, Márta, chronicled those days of planning with a mix of terror and awe. "God must be with her," she wrote in her diary.

Mária had a refrain she liked to repeat: If the Communists can do it, why can't we? Many in her circle found this irksome. After all, there were only a handful of activists, up against thousands upon thousands of Communists. But Mária pressed forward.

Where did this confidence come from? During our time together I have asked this question so often, in various ways, that finally she's become bored by my wonder. It's part of organizing, she says.

But no one else did it, I insist. *You* did.

If you want a house, you have to build a foundation, she says.

She is steadfast in not taking more credit. For her it was natural to be opposed to the regime. She grew up in a family that had suffered at the hands of Communists, so she felt opposition was a duty.

And in 1989, the foundations she had built were blossoming. Every day more invitations went out, asking people to RSVP by August 15. Soon responses started streaming in. When she lists the various embassies they invited, I am incredulous. Even the Soviets? I ask.

She looks at me at some length through the thick glasses she now wears, until the edges of her lips curl into something of a smirk. Of course, she says. But we were happy they didn't come. We thought they might show up in tanks.

The very qualities that made Mária such a good organizer also created trouble with her team. At the outset, in Debrecen, Ferenc felt she was bossing him around. At her first meeting in Sopron, the men found her jarring. As August progressed, temperatures rose and tempers flared. Increasingly, activists on both sides of the country had disparaging things to say about her. She was always on the attack, they felt, with vast swings in mood. In their telling, those days sound like a party, a bunch of good-time guys dreading the moment that she would come and wreck their fun. They used to joke that the reason they had come this far was because the border guards were scared of her too.

You know, Ferenc once reflected to me in a moment of candor, she was exactly the type of person we needed. Otherwise, nothing would've happened.

It wasn't easy being a woman leading a group of men—then, as now.

Mária did not let criticism thwart her plan. The last important detail that needed attention was permission to open the border crossing. She kept up the pressure and finally, after so much stalling, the bureaucratic engine lurched into action, like a deus ex machina, swooping in at the last moment.

Maybe God was on their side after all. Or at least someone high up.

It was August 17, just two days before the picnic, when the organizers hand delivered a letter to the Hungarian customs headquarters
showing they had all the necessary stamps to secure permission to open
the gate. Meeting with representatives from both sides, they agreed to
the following: the crossing connecting Sopron and Sankt Margarethen
would be opened for three hours, from 3 to 6 p.m., August 19, so Austrians could enter Hungary if they had a valid passport and permit. Five
guards would be stationed at the border to facilitate the crossing. The
key to the lock had long been lost, so they had to find a way to open it.
But the stars were aligned.

———

AS THE DATE OF THE PICNIC APPROACHED, CONCERN IN BUDAPEST
was considerable. Government officials knew some East Germans
might make a break for it. But how many? And at what cost?

With each passing day the crisis was getting worse. It was also
becoming public, as major newspapers, notably the *Bild Zeitung*, a West
German tabloid, were running sensational articles about East Germans getting caught and brought back to the GDR. Soon there was
outrage sufficient to mobilize the support of West German politicians,
notably Hans-Dietrich Genscher, minister of foreign affairs.

Pozsgay especially was becoming a bit spooked by the situation.
Inside government, he was the picnic's main proponent. But as the
event neared, there was a lot of gossip swirling around the capital that
Soviet forces might leave their garrison—less than half an hour away—
and go to the border.

The events of 1956 were on everyone's mind. In the beginning,
Soviet troops didn't react to the uprising. Until one day, they did.

News from Moscow amplified concerns. Gorbachev was facing
trouble at home, including from within the politburo. Criticism had
for months been steady but usually kept out of the public eye. By midsummer it had even made it onto TV, rowdy images of officials pointing
their fingers at Gorbachev and shouting. A coup didn't seem far-fetched.

Hungarian officials monitored activity at the Soviet base nearby. At several points, Pozsgay tried to contact the local Soviet command personally, but couldn't get a straight answer. After one of those unhelpful phone calls, Pozsgay turned to his deputy, László Vass, and told him he should attend the picnic on his behalf. His own presence, Pozsgay felt, would give the event too much of an official endorsement, precisely what the government was trying to avoid. Shortly, Otto von Habsburg, a diplomat and vice president of the European Parliament, made a similar decision. He would send his daughter, Walburga.

Vass was sensitive to the risk. He had recently been invited to the Soviet Union to give lectures about the reforms underway in Hungary. The invitation had been Gorbachev's idea. During that trip, Vass spoke to people across the Soviet government, many of whom were openly critical of reform, even making scathing remarks directed at Gorbachev. Previously, this would have been unheard of; it was evidence of how fragile the circumstances had become.

A few days before the event, Vass received a short note from Pozsgay. If the Soviets move, there will be no picnic. That's all it said.

SOMETIMES THE SMALLEST POLICIES HAVE THE BIGGEST CONSE-quences. In early August 1989, the Hungarian government made the decision to open up the camping grounds in the border areas to East German refugees (who had previously been banned from anywhere remotely close to the border). Practically, this meant that the camps outside Fertőrákos, on Lake Fertő—the very lake that had meant so much to László Magas growing up—were now available to them. This decision had a massive impact on the lives of the would-be crossers. Suddenly they weren't just in the broad area of the border, they were right next to it.

An unlikely actor stepped in: Ágnes Baltigh—Tante (Aunt) as the Germans called her—a Hungarian woman in her early sixties, who had decided to take a job at a campsite beside Lake Fertő to supplement her pension.

It seemed a nice way to ride out the summer, to be out in nature and find interesting people to talk to. Her days were mostly uneventful until the East Germans started coming. Ágnes was the only camp attendant who spoke German. Certainly there were reasons for the East Germans to be guarded around her—as they were around everyone—but there was something about her, an openness to her smile, that many felt they could trust.

Ágnes was born in Sopron in 1926, to a country in shambles, decimated by the First World War and then carved to bits at Trianon. On December 6, 1944, when she was eighteen, Sopron was bombed and she fled to Germany with her father. It was an impossible situation. They went westward, because they thought the Germans were less terrifying than the Russians—as she puts it, the Russians killed everyone; the Germans put some in prison. She survived as a prisoner until after the war.

These were traumatic years, bouncing between camps, often at the edge of starvation. And she had fled Nazi-occupied Hungary, only to return to find her house taken over by Soviet soldiers. She was forced to live in the cellar. Because her father was an anti-Communist, he wasn't allowed to return.

Ágnes lost a lot in those years as a refugee. But she came back to Hungary with a deep sympathy for the suffering of the dispossessed. And now she spoke German.

It didn't take long in August 1989 for her to realize that something at the campsite was off. She knew there were Stasi officials poking around the camp—you could tell by their ill-fitting dress, the way they stalked about. The ordinary East Germans were behaving strangely too, removing identifying numbers from their cars and parking in hard-to-get-to locations, such as in heavy shrubbery. None of them seemed interested in spending time at the lake. Some cars were abandoned for long stretches and everyone spent the days looking around nervously.

Ágnes soon started chatting with people at the camp, trying to understand what was happening. One day, a family approached her.

They stood together looking out across the lake. The man pointed to a church in the distance, over in Austria. Tomorrow we are going to swim there, he said.

Ágnes was taken aback. That's impossible, she said. There are soldiers on motor boats, you'll never make it.

Ágnes had spent quite some time observing the lake and she knew about the watchtowers, the soldiers who spied there. The man hadn't anticipated this. They had only heard that the Iron Curtain wasn't operating any more. They assumed it would be true here too. So what *can* we do? He asked.

Ágnes didn't know, but she told them she would look into it. There had to be some way across, a road or path, something through the woods. That night she went home and asked a friend. But no luck. The next morning, she approached the family. Wait, she told them. I'll find something. Give me a few more days.

Meanwhile, as Ágnes was looking into leads, more and more people started coming.

Back in the car after their harrowing experience with the border guards, Walter and Simone Sobel steeled themselves. They had no precise plans, only to make their way in the direction of Sopron. Most pressing was the question of the children, their two precious girls in the back seat. Simone did everything she could to think of anything else.

Walter did the opposite: the kids were the whole point, the only thing that made sense of this ordeal. He didn't want them to have to grow up in the GDR, where they would be forced to toe the party line or be thrust outside the system as he had been. More than anything else, he was doing this for them.

After driving for some time they decided to pull into a campsite outside Fertőrákos. They were relieved to have a place to sleep for the night. But what they found there was arresting—even more so than the camp at Balaton had been. Before them stretched a wasteland of empty cars and tents, teeming with Stasi. And even though there were so many people, no one was talking.

The next morning, Walter went to a bakery in town to buy bread. When he was alone in the store, the woman behind the counter addressed him directly: Are you looking to flee? She told him she knew a way across, through the high reeds on the edge of the lake. She would take them, but for a price.

Walter thanked the woman but didn't say more. Back at the camp-site he paced about uncomfortably. Some people were escaping, or at least trying to. He could tell because each day more cars and tents were abandoned. The people you saw one day simply weren't around the next. Had they succeeded in crossing the border? Had they been picked up by the Stasi and deported? It was impossible to know. Walter found this maddening. He was angsty, eager to try something, but didn't know how.

With each passing hour the idea of crawling through the reeds grew more attractive. But his thoughts returned to his kids. They were so little. What if one of them coughed or cried out?

Nasty rumors swirled around the campsite of people getting caught. In the woods, in the reeds, everywhere. There was talk of jail-ing and deportation. Even shooting. Soon this gossip overwhelmed reality—it was the only thing people spoke about publicly, the rest of their thoughts kept inside. The Sobels spent a week in limbo, vacillating between hope and dread.

The Stasi circled their tent like wolves, lending the camp an oth-erworldly feel, like a way station at the end of the earth. Walter and Simone had heard of a kindly camp attendant to whom some of the others had spoken to. But they were scared to go to her. It seemed too risky.

As the days passed, Walter became increasingly agitated, his nights sleepless, his thoughts careening around a circular track. And as Walter wound himself up, Simone grew quieter, did her best to tune everything out, to behave even-keeled, so as not to raise panic in the kids. Their travels had already taken a toll. Their youngest had developed a fever; her eczema was flaring up.

And in the back of Walter's mind was the woman at the bakery. When he went back to her a few days later she informed him she was organizing a crossing in a few days' time. Walter didn't know if this could be trusted, if it was possible, or wise, or even a trap. Soon they would have to decide.

It was at about this time that another couple came into the camp. Their faces were heavy from travel, drained of color, but something about them seemed kindred, so Walter went up to speak to them. Their names were Hermann and Margret Pfitzenreiter.

Hermann and Margret's road had been treacherous. The previous night they had tried the border, near the tripartite frontier of Czecho-slovakia, Hungary, and Austria. But they were quickly caught, pulled over, told to get out of the car. Then their nightmare: they were isolated from their children, who were interrogated separately.

They were detained for hours. Hermann and Margret sat silently apart, paralyzed by fear, there in a darkness punctuated by the scald-ing brightness of flashlights and cars. They were forced to sit for long stretches, then interrogated and left to wait before being questioned by someone new. It was a torturous game, with the guards building up pressure, asking the same questions over and over, waiting for some-one to slip.

Finally the verdict: their documents—passports, car registration, everything—would be sent to the GDR authorities. Now they could never go back. Margret and Hermann got back into the car and drove off in a pensive, fearful silence. At this point they just wanted to find a place to spend the night. They knew there would be campsites around Lake Fertő, so they headed there.

It was dark when they pulled into the camp, that graveyard of aban-doned Trabants. But presiding over this horrorscape was Aunt Ágnes, face aglow, tired but happy. She had spent the previous night fixed to the radio. Finally the story came: the night before, twenty-four East Ger-mans had illegally crossed the border into Austria from Fertőrákos. Her plan had worked.

It didn't take long for the word to spread—to the Sobels, the Pfit-zenreiters, to everyone. The next day, August 17, Ágnes came around. She had found someone who could take them to the other side, through the vineyards, she told them. This was to happen the following evening. Until then, there was nothing to do but wait.

Chapter Fifteen

Early morning, August 17, 1989, Ferenc Mészáros arrived in Sopronpuszta. It was his first time out to the borderlands. The air was crisp, not yet muggy, and filled with birdsong. And yet, the place irked him. Whereas Mária had looked upon a glimmering sea of potential, Ferenc saw nothing but a grassy expanse on a narrow road past an active military prison, nowhere near ready for a party of the size they had envisaged.

The picnic ground was on the site of the Iron Curtain, slowly being dismantled since Németh's intervention on May 2. The field itself looked something as Ferenc had imagined, with a giant patrol tower and the leftover stretches of barbed wire. But it was still just an empty lot, in the middle of nowhere, far from the border—which was about two kilometers away—and surrounded by woods.

He had known it wouldn't be quite the theatrical setting he had first envisioned, with Austrians and Hungarians gathered together with only the barbed wire between them, sharing sausages and beer across the line. Still, this would take some getting used to.

There were also soldiers walking around—at Mária's behest—to help erect tents. Ferenc had an inherent distrust of soldiers, struggles with authority having dogged him his whole life. Thinking of the military prison made him shudder.

Mária couldn't be there because of her commitments to the other reform-minded group she was involved with, the Common Fate Camp—she wouldn't arrive until the morning of the picnic. But she kept on top of logistics. At the moment she was incensed at people who had declined their invitations—not just Habsburg and Pozsgay, but now also Zoltán Bíró, head of the MDF in Budapest. He felt that as an opposition group, the MDF was already walking a tightrope in Hungary. He wanted nothing to do with an event that had the potential to be volatile.

The previous winter, when opposition groups had been first allowed to form, Party head Károly Grósz had threatened that if even one car got vandalized during opposition demonstrations, the police would shut them down. Bíró was concerned.

To hell with him, Mária thought as she crumpled up his letter.

Mária had also met with renowned Hungarian poet, Géza Szőcs. He would attend, he told her, but not read. Szőcs was an exiled dissident born into the Hungarian minority in Romania. He felt that reading poetry at the event might have been risky.

Szőcs was Mária's favorite poet. The persecution of Hungarians in Romania was the cause that first spurred her to activism. Szőcs's poetry sang of the horrors of Trianon, which Mária revisited daily. I tracked down a copy of one of his collections. I had never heard the name Szőcs before, but it came up in many of my conversations with the Hungarian activists. Perusing the pages, it wasn't hard to see why.

Szőcs details the frustrations of life under Soviet occupation, how Communist rule had taken away people's freedoms—not just in the individualistic sense we imagine in the West, but also in broader societal terms, the freedom to celebrate national traditions. In one poem, "Underground" (1983), Szőcs decries the disappearance of Hungarian culture under Ceaușescu. "The folk songs are changing costumes / into warrants for arrest."

Szőcs was also interested in problems of authority. The state takes many guises; as do institutions of rule. This was especially true in the Hungarian lands, tread upon by great powers and their ideological machinations throughout the twentieth century: imperialism, Nazism, Communism. When Hungarians think of politics and history, it is this experience that comes to mind: their bodies ravaged, their lands pillaged, the ever-present fear that it may someday happen again.

In "What I Want to Be When I Grow Up" (1988), Szőcs writes about the cyclical nature of war and struggle. The poem begins:

> Dedicated to my grandfather's bronze bust that was melted down
> with others after the war for the casting of a large statue of Stalin

Every Hungarian could feel the weight of this history. In the poem, Szőcs dreams of one day becoming a soldier for his people, "But also a monument / continuity cast in bronze," all the while knowing that this too might one day be melted and remolded into something else.

These themes—of hope and constraint, of repetition and redemption—are common in Hungarian literature, the feeling of a life written upon by history. In his memoir *A Guest in My Own Country*, György Konrád puts the point succinctly: "At twelve I survived National Socialism; at fifteen I saw Communism take over. Communism and I grew old together. . . . I spent the best years of my life in the shadow of its stupidity."

Such themes were motivating for all the organizers, but especially Ferenc. They were what got him interested in politics in the first place, and what inspired his dream of the picnic. Working now, out in the field at Sopronpuszta, Ferenc soon forgot his misgivings about the site, and started thinking again about that dream of transformative change. The thousands of people that would soon gather together at the Iron Curtain, each making their tiny snip.

Ferenc had only been at the picnic grounds a few hours that first day before he found himself surrounded by other activists who had come to share in the labor. Chief among these was János Rumpf. Together they built a stage, picnic tables, a kitchen area, and most important, the toilets—putting the finishing touches on work that Rumpf and his students had started a few days prior.

Looking around during breaks from hammering and sawing, Rumpf fixed upon the out-of-use watchtower, a ruin looming above them. Rumpf wanted people to go up there, to reclaim it as their own. But it was a creaky behemoth. He put up a sign that read "Enter at your own risk."

The labor was enormous, but the men worked well side by side. Several last minute crises presented themselves, but they were taken in stride. One of these arrived in the person of Péter Horváth, who showed up at the picnic grounds in a fury. As it turned out, the stretch of barbed wire they'd gotten permission to clip abutted a state-owned farm, directed by Horváth, who had requested to preserve the perimeter around his territory for a wildlife reserve. The area between the Iron Curtain and the border was the most untrammeled in the whole country.

To resolve the dispute, the organizers summoned the border guards to broker a deal. They agreed finally that only a two-meter stretch of the Curtain would be cut, and that after the picnic the organizers would put it back.

The irony is inescapable: in the end the state was willing to move on but a private citizen was not. And those most determined to tear down the barrier were now pledging to rebuild it.

The health authorities arrived to check on the facilities. There was some nervousness among the organizers about whether what they had built would be deemed sufficient for their purposes. But these inspections too came and went.

For the most part, things were settling into place. And there was an exciting new development: after toiling for so long in obscurity, suddenly reporters began to show up. And not just a few. One film crew came all the way from New Zealand. Soon it seemed as though the entire world had a presence at the border.

László Magas had been handling journalists' requests and was now leading them about, helping evaluate the lighting, showing them where to stand. As a leading organizer, Magas was also the object of their attention, if reluctantly, standing for one interview after another in the unforgiving heat. Unlike Mária, who was bubbly and direct with journalists, Magas was shy. He wore a suit and tie to look nice for the cameras. He stood upright, tight-limbed, shifting about uncomfortably, waiting for questions to be asked, then responding dryly, often with few words.

Magas was visibly relieved when the workday came to its close. Now they had just to go back to their respective beds and mattresses and cars and tents and try to get some sleep. The next days would be a whirlwind.

———

NOT ALL HOURS ARE THE SAME LENGTH. AT LEAST IT FEELS THAT way when you are waiting. There comes a point when you will believe anything—ghosts, mirages, miracles—if it will break the stasis. It was like this in the camp. As it was around Hungary, and indeed the whole Eastern Bloc. Waiting was a mainstay of those years, a common feature of their humor.

A joke made its way around the campsite outside Fertőrákos. A train is moving through the vast Soviet steppe, when suddenly it screeches to a halt. People sit about, confused, first for hours then days. Finally, a man leans from the window and calls to a passing shepherd. "What's happening?" he asks.

"They are exchanging parts of the engine," the shepherd replies.

The man is exasperated. "What's taking so long?"

"They are exchanging them for vodka."

There is a special character to jokes about waiting in the old Eastern Bloc, a mix of time sputtering to a standstill, alongside the near certainty that what you are waiting for will never arrive.

The Pfitzenreiters and the Sobels spent August 17 milling about, sweeping out their tents and brushing the car seats, washing clothes. All the things you do to make an inhospitable place livable, even one you are desperate to leave.

At one point Hermann struck up a conversation with Ágnes about the refugee smuggler she had found, who was due to lead them across the following evening, the 18th. The man wasn't asking for money. But Ágnes had offered him dibs on everything the refugees abandoned—suitcases, car seats, binoculars—all the little things of value that were nonetheless too heavy to be carried any farther.

There is something poetic to this contract, forged amid the wreckage of this campsite on the edge of the world: the smuggler would be paid only in remainders, the residue of past lives.

Crossing the border illegally was a big decision; there was a lot to think about. The Sobels: Walter, pacing around, pugnacious if skittish; Simone, cautious and inward-looking. The Pfitzenreiters: Hermann, calculating the risks as though they were measured along the length of his arm; Margret, chomping at the bit.

Time inched forward. At one point, Ágnes sauntered over to Margret and asked if she spoke Italian. Ágnes had been hoping for a chance to practice. Margret didn't.

No Italians ever come here, Ágnes said with a sigh. Then she trundled away.

For the East Germans, social encounters tended to take place in a slender orbit around family tents, especially those with kids' play spaces. There was something inherently trustworthy about families with children. If you were willing to risk your life for their future, there was something in your moral fabric that could be counted on.

In the case of the Pfitzenreiters and Sobels, it wasn't a perfect match, as the Sobels' girls were young, just two and four; the Pfitzenreiter's boys were fifteen and eight. And L_____, the Pfitzenreiter's eldest son, had anyway found a group of older boys to tag along with. Their names were Stephan and Andreas Nagler—big, athletic kids who'd grown up

on a poultry farm in Saxony, in the southeastern corner of the GDR—
and Heiko, Stephan's friend.

Stephan and Andreas had come with their father, one of the only
people in camp who wasn't either a would-be refugee or Stasi. This
made him instantly suspect. While everyone else was talking on the
hush, or not talking at all, the elder Nagler was making wisecracks.
"Tomorrow, West Germany?" he'd quip to people standing around the
kiosk. Pretty soon people started to avoid him.

When they arrived, the Nagler boys had no real plans to run away.
Or at least nothing outside of testosterone-infused make-believe. The
night before their trip, Stephan got on his motorcycle and sped down
to the local disco. Cocky and drunk, he told everyone he wasn't coming
back. When challenged, he promised one of the local boys the keys to
his bike. Take it, he said. I won't need it.

This was all talk. They certainly didn't have any plans. But now in the
camp, basically alone—their father didn't attend to their whereabouts;
their mother had stayed home to look after the ducks and geese—they
quickly caught a case of border fever. They went out to the lake with binoculars and lay about in the reeds. They play-acted that someone would
try to make it across the line and the others would try and stop them.

The game was fun, until one evening, they were out in the lake, past
the reeds, far—dangerously far—from shore. They were being dead
quiet, standing in the shallow water, not even whispering, egging each
other on with their eyes, to inch, to drift, just a bit farther out. Then
suddenly a group of men a few short meters away made a break for it.

The boys were shocked, realizing instantly that they were caught
in the middle of something—who would believe they were just playing? They sped for the shore, fast as they could, ran until they reached
the campsite, then collapsed, utterly stunned. Their bodies were cut up
from racing through the high grass, the color drawn from their faces.
They spent the next hours expecting to be hunted down by soldiers.
They rehearsed what they would say.

They never heard what happened to those men they had seen, but after that they didn't go back to the lake. It felt easier to stay at camp, a playground of picked-apart cars and torn-up tents. One night they even found an abandoned caravan, which they decided to commandeer and turn into a fort.

Soon they found themselves competing with some local Roma who had come to scavenge for abandoned goods, often grabbing tents wholesale, throwing them onto the tops of cars and driving away. The boys would wake early to poke about among the ruins and play with whatever had been left behind. Such were their environs, whole worlds existing one moment and vanishing the next.

One day, when prowling around the campsite, the boys met a West German named Norbert. They had lain low for a few days since their scare. But this man, the smell of mischief that wafted off him, was too good to resist. He had been a mercenary in the French Army, a foreign legionnaire. He lived in his car, alongside items of unimaginable pedigree: Ballantine's from Scotland; Gauloises from France. He had West German cash.

The boys bobbed around him excitedly, reveling in his stories of combat; his evocative scars; the knife he carried, giant and sharp. To them, he was Sylvester Stallone. Their own Rambo. They called him the Wessi (the Westerner) and Staatsfiend (enemy of the state).

That afternoon, Andreas saw him at the kiosk. He had gone to buy some food, but there was nothing left. Forget it, Norbert told him. I'll take you to town and get you something to eat.

This was August 17, two days before the picnic. Andreas dashed off to find Stephan and Heiko. He ran so fast he tripped over the tent cords and fell flat on his face. When he'd gathered the boys, Norbert was waiting by his car. Hop in, he said. Let's go for a ride.

Norbert drove fast and reeked of whisky. He took them to a hotel, one of the nicer ones, the kind that as GDR citizens they would never have imagined entering. But Norbert was a West German. He passed some Deutsche Marks to the concierge and before they knew it they were waited on by the entire staff.

Stephan and Andreas wandered about the halls, starstruck. They felt like kings.

Later, now back at the camp, Norbert approached them. Tomorrow, he said, I'll take you to the border.

Chapter Sixteen

All I remember is the waiting, Annette says. It was a hot, late morning, and Frank had disappeared into the cornfields.

Annette and I are sitting in a large pavilion room in Sopron in August 2019, outside the book display of a local historian, Wolfgang Bachkönig. She is telling me about the moment when Frank went to see the border. It was August 18, and they were on the road that leads to Sopron. Not quite there. But Frank wanted to see what it looked like.

He didn't tell me where he was going, she says. He just went.

Annette was in the car, sitting in the passenger seat. They had just driven all the way from Bulgaria where they had been vacationing, and before that, from the GDR. After a few hours of driving, they had reached a quaint stretch of farmland beside a town called Fertőrákos and pulled over. Frank spread their map out on the hood of the car to see how close they were to the border.

Annette put her feet up on the dashboard and watched him through the windshield. Then she drifted off into thought. Before she knew it, he had disappeared into the cornstalks. She didn't go after him. She couldn't just leave the car. At that moment it was her only possession in the world. And so she waited, looking out at the wall of corn.

First it was an hour, then two. With time, her doubts grew. He had been caught, perhaps; or gotten through. Either way, an eerie feeling grew inside her that he wasn't coming back. So she sat, penniless, loveless, abandoned like the Trabants that were scattered about the countryside. She felt she understood in that moment what it meant to be truly alone.

Now Annette wants to keep going with the story, but I am stuck on this image of her waiting. It is something I have heard many times in different guises from the East Germans I have spoken to, an essential part of the refugee experience; the corollary of uncertainty. Because it is not just ordinary waiting, but the kind that comes from being precarious, adrift in the world, without a place to call home or a community to rely upon.

In times of political crisis, if you feel oppressed, treated unjustly, forced to live in fear of the law, solidarity is one of the things that sustains you. The feeling that even if the world is against you, at least there are people you can lean on and trust and love—people who you will fight and die for and who will fight and die for you.

Solidarity. Precisely the kind of bond that authoritarian governments seek to destroy. This is what Hannah Arendt meant when she wrote about loneliness in *Origins*, when the state drives people apart, robbing them of the one thing they need to keep their sanity—the love and trust and loyalty of others. Once people are isolated they stop sharing their experiences, they lose the sense that they are part of a common world. This, Arendt writes, is "among the most radical and desperate experiences of man."

For Annette, there in the car, what she lost in that moment was precisely this feeling, the belief that whatever else might happen, she and Frank were in this terrifying circumstance together. They had each given the other something to believe in. And then, all of that was gone.

Thinking this, watching the light thicken around her and the horizons constrict, Annette found herself in tears. And then, just as suddenly as he had disappeared, Frank returned, parting the corn and emerging from the hot and buzzing din. She ran to him and threw her arms around his neck.

Frank had made it to the first run of barbed wire before he'd turned back. He had to see it, to touch it. But crossing it was something they would do together.

Ever since they'd heard about the picnic, shortly after their arrival in Hungary, this had been the plan. Before heading to the borderlands, Annette and Frank had spent a night in Budapest. The embassy was full, but they heard about a place in Budapest that was sheltering refugees—a Catholic church in the Zugliget neighborhood, up in the hills on the west side of the Danube River, with tent facilities administered by a humanitarian organization, the Order of Malta. In the days before the picnic, the church had become a hugely important hub of information.

When Annette and Frank arrived, the grounds were spilling over with East Germans. It was exciting, but they were only there for a few minutes before a man came over and snapped their photo.

They looked at each other in horror. They knew right away that this man was Stasi. That now there would be a record of them at this refugee sanctuary. The photo was taken from close range. Until that point they had not committed themselves to trying to cross. But there was no chance they were going back to the GDR now.

Annette and Frank struggled to get their bearings. It was a chaotic space. Church helpers were distributing information about the border and paperwork for becoming a refugee. Later the pastor summoned the newcomers into a circle and spoke to them directly. He had one piece of advice: go to Sopron.

There will be an event at the border, he said. A picnic. Go mix with the crowd. See what happens.

AS ANNETTE AND FRANK MADE THEIR WAY WEST TOWARD Sopron, a little farther down the road, Katja and Oskar were making their way north, to the same destination.

They had taken a few days to regroup after their run-in with the authorities. Their plans—the wedding, their life together in the West—all of that seemed impossible now. All of a sudden they saw the world for what it was, its colors less luxuriant, its smells flat and drab. Nevertheless, they decided to go to Sopron, to try their chances one last time. It was not a long drive from where they had been caught, outside Kőszeg. And they had a West German car. Oskar could get close to the border in ways others couldn't. He could even cross back and forth. He was confident something would work out.

Katja's faith was different. Its contours were moral. The Hungarian people didn't want to hurt her, she felt. Yes, they had guns. But they didn't want to use them. It was the opposite of what she felt about the GDR. No one had faith in the Stasi.

It didn't make sense for a person in her position to be so trusting; Katja knew this. But there was something about the Hungarian mentality she felt she understood. They were gregarious, in an in-your-face sort of way. They wouldn't use violence to avoid confrontation—the way Germans might—or hew closely to the letter of the law. They wanted to negotiate, to hustle and barter. Katja felt she could talk to these people, even when staring down the wrong end of a gun.

When they arrived in Sopron, the sight that greeted them was startling. Everywhere around them were Trabants, abandoned. Seeing those jettisoned cars, left willy-nilly on roadsides and on the shoulders of highways, made tangible something Katja previously could not identify or understand. More than risking your life or rotting in jail or any other abstraction, leaving behind a car was simply unimaginable. She appreciated this in a way that no one who grew up outside East Germany possibly could. You invested your life savings trying to get one; you waited and waited.

It was at that moment she felt she understood the pull of freedom, its enormity and force. And the border too. What powerful thing might lie beyond? Something strong enough to yank people away from their lives, their plans, the structure of their world. Suddenly Katja didn't just want to look at the border. She wanted to cross it.

They drove to the village of Fertőrákos, where they heard there might be a place to sleep. Katja felt deeply uncomfortable, not just from fear, but from the sense of moral responsibility she felt toward the people whose world she had stepped into. These locals never asked for their streets to be overrun by people like her, trailed by the full force of state security. She felt like she was something terrible, a pestilence, a plague; that she would bring them peril. This is what it felt like, being from the GDR.

There in Fertőrákos, Katja resolved not to talk to anyone. She was an invisible woman, or rather, a woman willing herself to become invisible. Still, they needed a place to sleep. They set out to find one. Ideally, a campsite.

———

WHILE THE ORGANIZERS WERE PUTTING THE FINISHING touches on the picnic grounds, at the campsite outside Fertőrákos everyone paced about anxiously. It was August 18. That evening, many of the refugees planned to meet with Aunt Ágnes and the smuggler who would take them along the shadowy perimeter of the lake, then through the woods to the West.

Hermann Pfitzenreiter woke early and peeked his head cautiously out of the tent. Each morning the scene was different than the one he'd observed before heading to bed the night before. Cars were dismantled or had disappeared; tents were picked apart or stolen outright. And every day, new vehicles pulled in. He went to get breakfast at the central kiosk and there, waiting in the queue, he met Norbert, the West German, who said he was taking people across the border. He asked Hermann if he wanted to come.

Hermann had heard about Norbert from his son, who had been hanging out with the older Nagler boys. Normally—but what was even normal anymore, out here in a place like this—Hermann would have told someone like this to shoo away. But this time, trepidatious about crossing with Ágnes's man, a total stranger, Hermann drew closer.

Come by our tent, he said. Let's talk about it.

Something about Norbert checked out, this vigilante, scarred and stinking of whisky. In another setting, his recklessness would have been the reason not to trust him. But Hermann didn't see it that way, not in this campsite-qua-carnival, this lawless, upside-down place. The fact that Norbert was only in it for the thrills was precisely what made him reliable. Norbert was an adventurer, not a profiteer. And at that moment this was exactly what they needed.

The campsite was in so many ways a *state of exception*, an undefined space, outside of conventional law or norms. Places like these can beget the most inhuman violence. But sometimes the exception engenders something else, a space for action—as Hannah Arendt might say—and politics. Something new and strange.

In the campsite outside Fertőrákos, this is manifest most clearly in the transformation of Hermann—a careful man, seemingly ill-suited for such an environment. Yet something about the campsite nourished him, showed him things he otherwise might have missed.

Walking back to the tent, Hermann found a Stasi agent lurking about, taking notes. Hermann had witnessed a scene like this a dozen times, but this time he had a lift to his step.

Rather than seeing menace, Hermann perceived something different: cowardice. And this time, rather than turn his eyes or retreat, he walked up to him.

Sir, Hermann said sharply.

The man looked up, but didn't reply. Unfazed, Hermann took another step forward, and the man skulked back. Hermann advanced again and the man shrunk farther away, then again, until finally the agent ducked into his caravan.

Hermann stepped up to the door. The windows were darkened so he could not look inside. *Come out*, he demanded. When the man didn't respond, he banged on the window.

And just like that, Hermann didn't feel paralyzed by fear anymore. This feeling had been growing inside for some days, especially as he had the experience of talking to others—to Walter and Simone Sobel, to Ágnes and the Nagler boys. It had happened imperceptibly, but somehow, out there in the land of deserted tents and disassembled cars, he had found a community to draw strength from.

Solidarity. For the first time in Hermann's life, in all of their lives, the tables had turned. It was they who had the numbers, who could gather and talk and share their feelings—what they had not done for a generation, and still couldn't back in the GDR, but which was suddenly possible out here, on the Hungarian frontier. Community. Exactly what Hannah Arendt had diagnosed as the precursor to revolution in Hungary in 1956.

That Stasi agent, alone in his caravan, may have had authority. But he had no power. Hermann and the rest of them—the outcasts, gathered together, unarmed and with children—had no authority. But in that moment, they had power. All that Stasi man could do was scurry back behind his tinted windows.

In fact, the whole Stasi apparatus was reeling—they felt their mission in Hungary was compromised by the behavior of the West German Embassy and the Malteser International (the noted humanitarian organization of the Order of Malta), which they accused of inspiring GDR citizens to break the law. They knew they had to find a way to sabotage this behavior. A document dated August 18 details a propaganda campaign that would spread misleading reports across Hungary that GDR citizens would *not* be recognized as refugees or be legally resettled in the West (despite everything they might have heard).

The GDR Red Cross was to disseminate this message, deliberately to undercut the progress of other humanitarian organizations, like Malteser International. Moreover, starting in August the Stasi began focusing their information-gathering campaign on the Zugliget Catholic church in Budapest where the Order of Malta volunteers were helping out refugees—the very place where Annette and Frank learned about the picnic.

On one trip to the Stasi Records Archive, in November 2021, I visit their image library, located in the main building in Lichtenberg. There I come across pictures taken by the Stasi at a press conference held by the Order of Malta on the steps outside the church.

One sequence of images depicts a young East German boy, no more than six years old, looking wide-eyed at the video camera of a West German journalist. It is surely bigger and fancier than any camera this boy has ever seen. The journalist basks in the attention; a cigarette dangles from his lips. In the background, a set of older people, perhaps the boy's parents, smile gaily.

It is easy to get carried away by the tenderness of the image, the curiosity and wonder in the boy's eyes. The intermixing of East and West, so effortless and natural. And then you remember who it was taking the pictures: a Stasi official pretending to blend in, taking notes, so that these lives can be captured and destroyed.

It is the same place, precisely, that Annette and Frank had been photographed; the same day too. Maybe even by the same operative.

This mix of scare tactics and misinformation is familiar. But in the Stasi communiqués of this period, a new voice had begun to emerge. It was not contrite, at least not yet, but it appeared to recognize that fearmongering might not be sufficient. That summer they also started spreading rumors that refugees wouldn't be punished if they wanted to return to the GDR—even after they had been captured or fled to the West. This was a new, complicated, multisided game, where the aim wasn't simply to intimidate people into staying in the GDR, but also to lure them back.

The form of these communiqués was the same as before—the brittle paper, the cheap ink, the angry underlining. But the genre had shifted. It was no longer a set of orders, but a plea. Looked at now, they seem desperate and sad. Also too late, as by this point, the tide had shifted. Not just Hermann, but thousands of others in Berlin, in Budapest, and out in the campsites, had started believing in themselves again. The fear they felt was no longer debilitating.

That afternoon, Norbert stopped by the Pfitzenreiter's tent. It was quickly decided that rather than follow Ágnes's lead that night, they would go with Norbert the following morning. When Norbert departed, Hermann and Margret sat together quietly. They told Ágnes they would wait one more day.

Chapter Seventeen

When Mária Filep pulled into the field in Sopronpuszta, early morning, August 19, it was her first time back to the borderlands. She stepped out of her car, tired from travel, and surveyed the sky. It's a good day for wearing a hat, she thought. The forecast predicted thunder showers later in the day.

Approaching the picnic grounds she felt a flutter of nerves. There it all was in front of her, everything she had worked so hard for, suddenly real. The grassy plot was already filled with tents, scattered about like polychromatic mushrooms; a vast field designated for parking was already filling up with cars. Even from afar, it was clear the event would be huge. For a moment, the sight took Mária's breath away. The open field, immersed in a still-sleeping stillness, yet bursting with possibility.

Amid this mess of quiet clutter, Ferenc emerged from his tent and walked toward her. They smiled at each other. Here they were in Sopronpuszta, together.

Mária made her way to the border. The guards had clipped the old lock on the gate, replacing it with a new one to be ceremonially opened that afternoon. They had cleared the path to accommodate traffic, no easy feat as it hadn't been used in forty years.

In addition to the Austrian delegation coming to Hungary, the organizers also planned for Hungarian delegates to cross over to Austria. Mária had spent time over the last days finalizing this list, making sure no one was left off. She handed it over now.

Many of the officers, including those of high rank—major generals and colonels—knew Mária, or felt they did, after so much telephone communication. In fact just the day before, she had called the regional command office frantically, double-checking that they hadn't changed their minds about opening the border. Meeting now in person was a casual, even jovial affair.

Back at the picnic grounds, soldiers were helping with finishing touches. One of the artists, the singer Tamás Kobzos Kiss, had arrived from Győr and was checking out the stage. People were showing up by the busload.

At about noon, a light drizzle started to fall. The organizers gathered and started making their way over to the Lövér Hotel, a few kilometers away. This was a formal venue, suitable for a press conference, after which the festivities would begin.

At the hotel they were directed to the terrace, shielded from the elements by an awning, where they stood in a line; Ferenc to Mária's right, László Nagy, wearing his best bow tie, to her left. László would act as their interpreter, as he spoke German and English. On his other side was Magas. In front of them was a smattering of recording devices and a reflector, and beyond this an audience of international journalists, as well as some Hungarian reporters and notable guests.

Ferenc opened the press conference by telling the origin story of the picnic. Mária and Magas added details about the program. The remarks were to be followed by a trip to the border for the ceremonial crossing of the Hungarian and Austrian delegates at 3 p.m., after which everyone would adjourn to the picnic grounds for food, music, and the ceremonial snipping of the Iron Curtain. At 5 p.m. there would be speeches, with a special statement written by Ferenc to be read out in eight different languages.

The press briefing went well. But the timing was off. Walburga von Habsburg hadn't arrived yet. Neither had László Vass, Pozsgay's deputy. It was nearly three o'clock already, so they decided to go ahead without them, wrapping up the proceedings and making their way to the border.

ON THE MORNING OF AUGUST 19, PEOPLE ACROSS THE CAMPSITE outside Fertőrákos woke up anxiously. Walter Sobel stretched, cracked his knuckles, then took a walk around the grounds. He knew about Ágnes's trail, about Norbert too. But he was filled with doubt. He plodded about gloomily, until a spot of color caught his eye. It was a poster

nailed to a tree. The language was Hungarian, but the headline was easy enough to make out: *Páneurópai Piknik*.

The words jumped with possibility. Soon he saw posters everywhere—tacked to trees, flying about in the air, falling underfoot. A few hours later, around 10 a.m., Walter saw the flyer again, this time in German, advertising the *Paneuropäisches Picknick*. It showed a map of the borderlands, and an entreaty: *"Baue Ab Und Nimm Mit"* it said. Dismantle the Iron Curtain, it said, and take it with you.

Suddenly everyone in the camp started talking. Would the border open? Was this their chance?

Walter ran back to show the flyer to Simone. Get dressed, he said. We're going.

They put on as many layers as they could, beginning with two pairs of underwear, despite the rising heat. Everything they couldn't wear would be left behind.

Not everyone was excited about the news. The elder Nagler was crestfallen. He had known his older son Stephan would want to rush the border, but now he feared Andreas would too. What will I tell their mother? he groaned aloud to anyone who passed by.

Hermann Pfitzenreiter had woken up early to head out with Norbert to survey the borderlands. When he was leaving, Hermann noticed that the caravan of the Stasi man who had tormented them was gone. Hermann didn't see the flyer. Margret did. Clutching one that had all but fallen into her hands, she thrilled with excitement.

Now that people were speaking openly, they were also organizing. Word spread that trying to get there by car would be risky, as East German cars might be barred access. So a large group gathered to go by foot—it wasn't far, five kilometers or so.

Margret would wait for Hermann. She busied herself taking care of the boys and attending to their things. But as the campsite emptied out, she grew increasingly nervous.

The Sobels wanted to join the throng, but their kids were so little—how could they protect them from being trampled or crushed? Walter and Simone were talking it out when they heard a honk on the side of the road. A man in a car with Austrian plates had pulled up beside them. Need a ride? he offered with a sunny grin.

It was a time of impossible things—of *exception*—an upending of normalcy that extended across the border into Austria. The man said he'd heard about the picnic on the radio and wanted to help out. There wasn't enough room for everyone. Simone and the girls accepted the ride. Walter would go by foot with the rest.

Simone and the girls got to the picnic grounds before everyone else. When they arrived, the scene was not promising: a drizzle-soaked field covered in tents and cars but no food or music and mostly without people. The organizers and many others had already gone to the Lövér Hotel for the press conference. All that was left was a scattering of East Germans, angsty and confused.

Simone pressed the girls against her legs. Where was the border? The map on the flyer wasn't easy to read.

Annette and Frank had the same impression. They hadn't seen the flyers, because they hadn't been at the campsite; they'd slept in their car. They found the picnic grounds following the instructions given to them by the pastor in Budapest.

It was unsettling, but as the place swelled with people, Annette forgot her misgivings. Looking around, a feeling of kinship grew in her. These people, East Germans, were all after the same thing. This might well be hell, she thought. But we are in it together.

As the crowd continued to grow, many decided to walk toward the border.

Simone, nervously scanning about, finally saw what she was looking for: the crown of Walter's head craning above the crowd. Together, within the moving mass of bodies, they made their advance over fields, gullies, and muddy stretches of road. The rain had slowed somewhat. The air was now humid and heavy.

Meanwhile, Hermann returned to the camp with Norbert. Margret was upset. She handed him the flyer. We need to go, she said. Something's happening at the border *right now*.

Hermann was incredulous. Look around, she said. Everyone is gone.

They all piled into Norbert's car and sped to the grounds, but when they arrived the field was all but empty. Margret kicked the ground and cursed. We blew it, she said.

Then another dark thought flashed across her mind. In their haste, they had forgotten a pair of pants that belonged to their son. Before they left the GDR, Margret had sewed one hundred Deutsche Marks into the inseam where the guards would not look. This money was all they had, and Margret didn't want to leave without it. We have to go back to the camp, she said.

You shouldn't do that, Norbert said.

But then Margret's panic seemed to reach him and something changed in his demeanor.

Go to the border, he said. I'll go back and get your things.

In a trip already filled with guardian angels, Norbert was perhaps the most unexpected.

Meanwhile, about a kilometer up the road, the crowd pushed ahead. As they walked, they started to assume a formation. There were many children in the group, some really young, like the Sobel girls. The adults moved to the front and sides, flanking the children, pressing them into the middle in case the scene became violent.

When a helicopter passed overhead, parents tucked their kids under their arms and tried to fold over them in case gunfire rained down from above. But nothing but the propeller sounded around them. As they continued on, the formation grew tighter, moved together like a single organism.

The border took them by surprise. As the road had been at an incline, it was hard to see what would come at its crest. Those at the front saw soldiers, men in blaring white uniforms. Five men stood before the gate; there may have been others farther along, it was hard to tell.

Then they started to run, in unison, as out of an explosion. Annette had gotten separated from Frank in the scrum and found herself at the front of the line. She saw the guards, there before her, their weapons glinting in the sun. She tried to look away, to take her mind to other things. It was hot, and she was thirsty.

The last meters felt endless. Annette sprinted toward the gate, crashed into it with all her might and the force of those beside her. She felt the compression, the firmness of the wooden crossbars, the sweaty oneness of their bodies. Then she heard a bang: loud, very close, as though someone had opened fire. This is it, she thought, this is how it ends.

When the gate gave, she pushed through and kept running. She couldn't bring herself to stop. But when she did, she found herself before a wall of people. Not the ragtag gathering she had just been a part of, but others. Austrian guards, Red Cross volunteers, journalists snapping pictures, a crowd of onlookers.

The bang she had heard was the sound of a man opening a bottle of champagne, one of the Austrian delegates on his way to the picnic.

He came over to her. You made it, he said. You are in Austria. *You're free.*

A few feet behind her was Walter, clutching his youngest daughter. Finally you will meet Grandma, he said through his tears.

The stream of East Germans continued for several minutes. When the last bodies dashed through, a heated argument erupted among the guards.

Far back, the Pfitzenreiters were still making their way forward. When they saw the border, they started running, ever faster when they saw the arguing guards, panicked the border might now shut. There was so much noise and screaming and honking. Margret felt her knees buckle.

The gate was still open but obstructed by so many bodies. Tempers were high. One boy was held in the arms of an officer, writhing, crying, calling for help.

The moment they pushed through, Margret let out a wail. All that pressure that had built up in her all those months, from that first

moment she began stashing things in her friend's barn, through all those hours in the car, the hours in the camp, even this morning waiting for Hermann by the tent. All that control, everything she'd kept inside, now came belting out of her.

Margret fell to the ground, exhausted. When she looked up, there before her, beneath a sign that read "Welcome to Austria," were her two beautiful sons, standing beside the Sobels, their arms wrapped around each other. They had made it. They had *all* made it. They were free.

Most of the refugees had already passed at this point. Whatever commotion remained was among Hungarians—officials debating what to do, and the organizers looking on in disbelief.

Among the last straggling East Germans were the Naglers. When Stephan had first reached the border, he dashed across only to see that his friend Heiko hadn't followed.

Standing about ten meters past the gate, he beckoned to him to come. He didn't. So Stephan crossed back into Hungary. Heiko was standing beside Andreas and their father.

Come on, Stephan said. *Let's go.*

Heiko looked away. No, he replied. I'll stay.

Fine, Stephan said. I'll go alone. Then he turned to run back to the West. He had almost made it across when Andreas called out. *Big one*, he said. I'll come with you.

Big one. Andreas was only a few years younger, but so much a child.

Looking back, Stephan was suddenly doubtful. No, he said. Go back to Mom. She needs you.

Andreas didn't listen. He walked over to his brother and tucked under his shoulder. Then they walked across the border together, penniless, paperless, to a freedom close enough to touch, and yet still impossible to imagine.

———

WHEN MÁRIA AND FERENC AND MAGAS AND EVERYONE ELSE from the press conference finally made it to the border, the setting they encountered was bewildering. The gate, unused for so long, was all but knocked off its hinges. And the roadway it had barricaded, severed in half for longer than anyone could remember, was now unified as a trampled slick of mud. It was there, standing in stunned silence, that they learned what had happened.

Mária walked up to the gate. She had spent so much time looking at her side, the last outpost of Hungarian soil before the frontier, that she had never stopped to peer at what lay beyond. The border for her, as for everyone else, had been the wall of her world. Now it was a portal to a new one. The foliage was wild, leafy branches reaching to meet overhead, like fingers intertwined. A white billboard etched with red letters screamed: *Achtung Staatsgrenze* (Attention State Border).

The scene was utter chaos: East Germans celebrating on the other side of the line; Hungarian officers in heated conversation; Austrians walking into Hungary, Hungarians crossing into Austria; journalists snapping photos. Árpád Bella, the commanding officer, came over to where Mária and Magas were standing. *Who's in charge of this event?* he

demanded. He was rattled by the whole affair, concerned that he might be punished for it.

Mária darted away. She had a picnic to attend to, after all. The Hungarian delegates were due to be sent over to Sankt Margarethen where the mayor, Andreas Waha, would welcome them, alongside a local band. But of course this plan had been scuttled. When Waha heard the news of the breach he started frantically calling local inns to see if they might offer food and accommodation for the refugees. He also phoned the West German Embassy, which arranged transportation to Vienna.

After the last bodies trickled through and things had settled a bit, the organizers asked the border guards to close the gate so they could reopen it in front of the cameras. Magas held one side of the gate, Mária the other, smiling brilliantly. Afterward, she crossed the border herself, taking a step into Austria for the first time, then hopping back, her light blue summer dress swaying, as in a kind of dance. Hungary–Austria, East–West.

Now it was time to party. The picnic grounds, when the organizers returned, were a scene to behold: not just tents and cars but a mob of people—singing, dancing, merrymaking—as many as twenty thousand in total.

It was as irreverent as the organizers had hoped. A brass band boomed across the field. Goulash cooked in giant pots over open flames; beer and wine were there for the taking. People danced around a bonfire. Other dancers, professionals in folk garb, evoked a distant and originary scene: grandmothers mixing their spicy stews, grandfathers tilling the fields—which in the midst of so much that was tremendous and wild and new, leant an air of surreality to the proceedings.

The weather didn't hold. Just as the program was set to begin it started to rain.

"For all our friends in Europe!" Ferenc bellowed above the din. "The only chance for worldwide peace . . . is the demolition of barbed wires and cultural barriers."

He invited everyone to gather not just this year, but every year to share in their dream of a united, peaceful, and free Europe. "The next century cannot be an age of war and hatred," he continued. "Europe has to become a home for all the peoples inhabiting it: a land of pure human relationships, ignoring differences of nationality and ideology."

The writer György Konrád spoke, as did Walburga von Habsburg and László Vass, alongside others. A letter from László Tőkés, a dissident Hungarian pastor from Transylvania, was read out by Lukács Szabó, an MDF member from Debrecen, who had smuggled it out of Romania.

Konrád's speech was a barn burner. "Why are we freer today than we were two years ago?" he asked. "Because we dared to open our mouths. Not so that we can shout, but so that we can earnestly, until the end of our days, say our thoughts." No autocrat in Hungarian history escaped his scorn. "We have had enough of paternal overlords," Konrád declared. "Enough of Franz Joszef, of father Horthy, father Rákosi, father Kádár!"

László Vass spoke on behalf of Imre Pozsgay. "Let borders be the stage for the peaceful and joyous meeting of peoples," he read, "not for states to imprison their citizens . . . or to stamp out other peoples' desire for freedom."

Vass read the words of their powerful patron with gusto. But when he finished, there on the grandstand, looking down upon the rain-damp crowd, Vass found himself overcome with emotion. In closing, he added his own words. *Hungary tomorrow*, he said, *will be different than it was yesterday.*

The organizers milled about during the speeches; there was a lot to talk about. So many things could have gone horribly wrong. Thinking about it then, running through scenarios, they were overwhelmed by the good fortune of it all, the beauty.

Not everyone was celebrating. Péter Horváth, the landowner who had wanted to turn the seam zone of the Iron Curtain into a wildlife reserve, showed up irate. They had agreed that only two meters of wire would be cut. But by the time he arrived, so many thousands of people had cut snippets you would have to walk kilometers to find any fencing. He stayed a few minutes before driving away.

Amid the rejoicing, there were fears too. Who knew how the hostile forces of the neighborhood—Ceaușescu's Romania, for example, or the hardliners in Moscow—might yet react? At one point László turned to Konrád. Do you think we'll end up in jail? he asked.

Konrád cracked a mischievous smile. This time, he said, I think maybe we'll make it.

They both started to laugh. There were a lot of qualifiers in that remark. The conditional, uncertain, Hungarian life.

The party lasted until finally the storm clouds that had been steadily gathering overhead released their water and doused the rapturous crowd. People danced around the fire until eventually it sputtered out. With time, even the hardiest picnickers started to turn in. Locals went home; the rest took to their tents or curled into buses or cars to sleep for the night.

BACK AT THE BORDER, WALTER SOBEL LEANED AGAINST THE broad trunk of a tree, trying to catch his breath. It had been some time since they had crossed, or maybe only a few minutes, and he was still clutching his young daughter. Walter had been crying and now she was crying too. There was so much noise, the excited screams, the pops of champagne.

Their elder daughter held tight to Simone's legs. What's happening? she asked repeatedly.

The Sobels were off to the side, where the chaos of bodies met the overgrown fringes of the forest. Looking about, Simone felt everything around her was happening in slow motion. All those celebrating bodies, she wanted to join them, to share in their euphoria. But she couldn't.

She was transfixed. All she could see was the path ahead. That old life was gone now—the GDR, Hungary, all of it. The film reel had rolled on and entered a new scene. You could not rewind to the old one. You just had to hold it in your memory and try not to let go. Such was her introduction to freedom: a state of shock, of magical out-of-placeness.

Walter Sobel took out some Ostmarks and threw them in the air. He was in the *real* world now. There was no need for things without value, those Eastern scraps.

All around people were bursting into tears, kissing the ground, calling out to freedom. Andreas Nagler found himself thinking about the Western brands he had heard of and wanted to try—Coca-Cola, especially, and Mars bars. He wondered what they would tell their mother. He bemoaned the loss of a pair of binoculars he had salvaged from an abandoned tent but had left behind at the campsite.

He looked back across the border, the comfort of family receding into the distance, replaced by this motley gathering of strangers, now somehow also kin. Andreas certainly would never have crossed without a strong protective shell around him—not just his brother, Stephan, but also the Sobels and Pfitzenreiters, and all the random people from the camp, some he knew by name, but many others too, people they had swum beside, or stood next to in the kiosk queue. And of course, Norbert, who connected these strangers with the bond of trust.

Just as Jean-Jacques Rousseau had said about the legislator, that good laws come from the outside, so it is sometimes with community. This band of refugees needed someone to bring them together. Norbert was the perfect outsider—neither citizen nor Stasi; not Eastern but also not really Western, at least not in any ordinary way. No one knew exactly where he was from. This was his magic.

For both Nagler boys, it was comforting to not go alone, blind, into this unknown world. But as they looked around, let their eyes grow accustomed to their new surroundings, it came to them: Freedom wasn't the end of their path, but the beginning. It was shapeless, identity-less, something that had to be molded. If it was to have mean-ing, it would have to come from them.

Soon it was time to depart, first to Sankt Margarethen—most people went by foot, as it was only a few kilometers away—and then on to Vienna, in buses furnished by the West German Embassy. The Pfitzenreiters and Sobels were offered a ride to Sankt Margarethen by an Austrian man. Both families piled into his small car; Hermann and Margret sat in the open trunk.

When the buses to Vienna arrived, most people boarded imme-diately. Margret and Hermann stayed back. They were waiting to see if Norbert would show up. They'd left it that he would go back to the camp to bring their belongings, including their secret stash of Deutsche Marks. But as the premises around them started to empty and the rains picked up, they gave up. Maybe something had happened to him. Or maybe he'd just made off with their things. They boarded the last bus.

It was late evening when they arrived at the West German Embassy in Vienna. They were tired and soaked and the building was packed with bodies—at least five hundred according to Hermann's count. Upon arrival, their youngest son broke into tears. He mourned the loss of his most treasured possession, his Alf doll, the very one that Hermann had brought home from his first trip West, and which he had slept beside all those rocky nights at the camp. He had held out hope that Norbert might bring it along with their luggage, but recognized now that it was probably lost forever.

At one point, standing about in the crowded embassy chamber, waiting for their name to be called, Hermann saw something that enraged him—it was the Stasi officer who had been lurking outside their tent at the campsite.

You, he called out, and started for him. Before he could say more the man pushed his way through the swamp of bodies and disappeared. Hermann glared at the man as he stole away.

They waited a long time, hours it felt. And while the staff was processing documents as fast as it could, the room stayed crowded with new bodies constantly streaming in. Finally, over the intercom came the call: *Family Pfitzenreiter, please come to the front.*

Hermann hopped to his feet, papers in hand. But when he approached the passport desk, he was rerouted to the front of the building.

He went outside onto the steps of the embassy, where he was greeted by flashbulbs. It was a mob scene—so many people had arrived, curious to see what was happening. Journalists were desperate for pictures, but found few opportunities since the East Germans weren't allowed outside. Embassy staff were concerned the refugees might be abducted by Stasi officers trolling about. Hermann was flanked by security guards.

There before him, blinking in the bursts of light, was Norbert, with his wide, imperfectly toothed smile, his breath of whisky and tar. And the Pfitzenreiter's luggage.

Hermann took the bags, looked upon the man who had helped them so much. There were so many things he wanted to say just then, but he couldn't find the words. He flushed, amid the chaos and clamor. Let us find a way to repay you, he said.

Norbert waved his hand dismissively, then cracked a smile. I helped myself to the gas from your car, he said.

Norbert had tried to return to the border, but by the time he had arrived, the gates had shut. The only way to catch up with the Pfitzenreiter's was to go all the way to Vienna. He explained this, then with little more than a nod, he disappeared back into his car and zoomed away, leaving only his memory and a faint aroma of peat.

When Hermann returned with their luggage, a single, joyful syllable issued from across the room: *Alf!*

Late that evening the embassy put out a call on Austrian public radio for volunteers willing to drive the refugees to the train station. It wasn't far, but they didn't feel comfortable having the refugees walk, even with escorts. They felt cars with local plates were safer.

When their names were called the various families were paired with volunteers. The Sobels were transported by an older couple; they sat in the back, the girls on their laps. When they had packed in, the elderly driver looked back with a glimmer in his eye. Do you want to see Vienna? he asked.

Walter and Simone looked wide-eyed out the window. Vienna, this beautiful city they were convinced they would never visit, now passed before them in all its twinkling grandeur. It was like being in a fairytale. And at the station, a magical, unmarked train, waited just for them. It was to make only one stop: Gießen, West Germany, the refugee processing center.

West Germany. The place on earth they most wanted to go, where they had traveled so many times in their minds but never been. West Germany, where they would soon call home.

PART IV

THE ROAD
TO BERLIN

Chapter Eighteen

These days, Árpád Bella lives in Csapod, a village not far from Sopron, in the house where he was born nearly eight decades earlier. He is elderly and negotiating illness—his hope now, he tells me when we first meet, is that he will die in the same house in which he was born. The house was built at the end of the Austro-Hungarian Empire, which withstood Nazism and Soviet occupation, and now stands in a free, open, and unified Europe.

Bella is conscious of the historical nature of the picnic, but unsure of his place in it. He was the commanding officer who oversaw the breach, but doesn't see himself as a hero or one who acted bravely. He had no choice, he tells me—what monster could use force to stop people like these? When I ask him what went through his mind as the mass of East Germans approached, his answer is straightforward. These were not enemies, he says. They had children.

The picnic was massive. And in fact, the story was bigger than anyone knew—an estimated six hundred East Germans made it across the border that day, maybe as many as a thousand. There is no official count.

For Bella, once the first rush was permitted, it was only fair to allow the others. But as his shift was ending that night, he was informed by his superiors that he would stand trial for insubordination. He spent the next hours anxiously reliving the breach.

He is there, standing at the border, strolling about with the boys, chatting. They are wearing short-brimmed caps and crisp white gloves that look resplendent in the sunlight. They carry pistols. They are responsible for checking passports.

There is some tension in the air. They know they should be on the lookout in case any East Germans try to escape. The border is the border, after all.

A large group of Hungarian delegates start to gather nearby, preparing to make their trip into Austria. They are easy to identify because they are carrying Hungarian flags.

Then comes the horde, a gathering swell of stamping and shouting that he hears before he sees. He can tell immediately these are East Germans. It's the look: all those bright colors, neon yellows and blues. The hair, long and shaggy, especially on the men.

Bella runs to the emergency phone at the border to call for orders. He cannot connect. He is frazzled. They were told some refugees might show up, a handful maybe. But nothing like this.

As the crowd gets closer, Bella starts to bark orders, telling them to stop. But no one listens. The group is determined. And now it is moving very fast. Bella feels for the edge of his gun. He is supposed to shoot in the air at this point. To warn them. But he doesn't. The group is too big. He stands aside as the great human wave crashes against the locked gate, shakes it until it opens, falls to safety on the other side.

Bella looks around this way and that, tries to keep his composure. The smell of the dust and dirt and sweat rises around him. He is not immune to the euphoria about him. But quickly the shadow creeps in. Bella is a lieutenant colonel. He has worked hard to attain this post. He will receive a good pension. Or at least he would have. Now he isn't so sure. Was it wrong, standing aside as he did? After spending so many years defending his country, had he now betrayed it? This is new emotional territory.

I felt alone out there, he tells me now. This was not a decision I should have had to make.

We have been sitting together for several hours at this point. He is elderly and his words come slowly. His critique is aimed at his superiors, the immediate ones in Sopron, but also those higher up. He is angry that he was left out there on the line without clear orders, while they covered their necks; angry that he was plucked from the familiar hierarchy, the security of being a link in a long and sturdy chain.

Until then everything had gone to plan. He had discussed matters with his counterpart in Austria, Johann Göltl. As agreed upon, they had replaced the old, rusted lock on the gate with a new one, to be opened with fanfare.

How ironic this seems now: the shiny little lock installed for a photograph was impractical for holding back a mass; the old sturdy one, keyless, sealed shut, would have been fit for this challenge, which in its forty-year existence it never had to face.

When Bella revisits the moment, a shadow crosses his face. I am sympathetic to the quandary. What do you do when you lose faith in the moral force of the law? How do you weigh the demands of conscience against personal risks, when the ramification of your actions might hurt the ones you love? These are the questions Bella grappled with out there in the field, as the edifice of state seemed poised to crumble around him. They are the same questions we ask today.

In the Netherlands, where I live, I teach a course called contemporary political philosophy. I always begin my lectures with the case of Adolf Eichmann as recounted by Hannah Arendt. The story is as timely as it is timeless. It also frames the relationship between morality and law.

Eichmann was a Nazi, responsible for the deportation of Jews to extermination camps. After the war he fled to Argentina where he was captured by the Israeli Mossad in 1960 and forced to stand trial at the Beth Hamishpath (House of Justice) in Jerusalem. Hannah Arendt, a Jewish émigré as well as a philosopher, was present in the courtroom, covering the story for the New Yorker.

At the trial, Eichmann disappointed the Israeli prosecutors. He was not the incarnation of evil that so many had envisaged. Instead, he was a man of stammering, obstinate ordinariness. It is this quality that Arendt captured in her oft-cited phrase, the banality of evil. But more interesting than his mediocrity, was the logic of his defense. He was innocent, he believed, for the simple reason that he followed the law. Eichmann, in his account, was doing what was right. His was a call of citizenship, of obligation. "He did his *duty*," Arendt tells us. "He not only obeyed *orders*, he also obeyed the *law*."

I always stop at this part of the text and ask the class to think through the anecdote. How many times have you followed the rules without thinking? I ask. Or assumed, if someone broke the law, they did something wrong? Associating *law* and *right* is natural—this is how we are taught to think. But to know whether the law is just, this requires us to think outside of the language that the law provides. We must first decide what the law *should* be. We must think in the language of justice. This is where political philosophy comes in.

Eichmann's example is a potent one. Men like him dominate the story of the history of violence. But there are also people like Bella. He too had the law behind him and the machinery of violence in his hands. But he decided not to use it. Why did he have the wherewithal to do what Eichmann couldn't? And what does this say about the system of which he was a part?

Within minutes, the first breach was over, and there were new issues to address. On the other side of the gate, a vast queue of Austrians had begun to form, due east to the picnic area on the Hungarian side. Bella busied himself with the task of checking passports, crossing names off a list. The flow of East Germans had not abated.

When László Vass, Pozsgay's deputy, made it to the border he went over to speak to Bella. What he found was an agitated man, his mind caught in a loop, thinking and rethinking about what happened. If I had used force, it would have caused panic, maybe even bloodshed, Bella all but yelled.

It's not fair, Bella continued. I will be blamed for this.

Vass assured him he would do his best to make sure he wouldn't be punished.

Bella was inconsolable. You aren't my supervisor, he replied angrily. What will happen when you go back to Budapest? Who will protect me then?

Vass tried to calm him down. Come by the picnic later, he said. Join me for a beer.

Bella stamped away. After the picnic, Vass went to Lake Balaton for vacation with his family. When he reported the details back to Pozsgay and Németh, they were pleased with how it had gone.

But of course none of this helped Bella. After he was discharged from his duties at the border, he trudged home to face his wife. How could he explain what had happened? The fears he might be fined or imprisoned. That the salary they depended on might be taken away. The feeling that he might have disgraced the nation that he so loved.

He stopped at the door. This was their anniversary, no less. The home he would enter would be filled with family and friends, baked goods and gifts. It was meant to be one of his happiest days. For now, Bella had to fight back tears.

FREEDOM CANNOT BE FLICKED ON OR OFF WITH A SWITCH. SYStems don't just turn over and change. Offices remain staffed with the same bodies as before. Petty rivalries and internecine battles only harden with adversity. The old uncertainties give way to the new. And all the people caught in between remain in that space of in-betweenness. It takes time to find a way through.

What's interesting from the outside is how such people get unstuck, how those caught in the gears find their way out—if, that is, they ever do. And to imagine all the other eventualities that could have obtained but didn't: words unsaid, maps unfollowed, paths untaken.

It wasn't just Árpád Bella who spent the next days riven with anxiety. So did people across Hungary, and especially the East Germans. Not everyone made it across at the picnic. For those who hadn't, things were about to get harder.

Katja and Oskar had seen the flyer, but they didn't trust it. They had arrived in Fertőrákos the day before and ended up at the campsite. For Oskar, as a West German, the experience was sickening. All those belongings people had left behind, now just ugly, expensive litter. When he saw the leaflet, there amid the garbage, he thought it might be a trap so he dismissed it. So did Katja, but for different reasons. As a GDR citizen she felt she wouldn't belong. It's celebrating Europe, she said to Oskar. It isn't for people like me.

They felt the commotion about them, families packing up, children scurrying about. But they let it pass. Still, by late afternoon they started to wonder if they had made the right call. The camp had all but emptied out. They went to the car, thinking they might have a look. Nearby a couple, a bit older with an adolescent daughter, were also hemming and hawing. They decided to go together.

Driving in their separate cars, they made their way onto the main road connecting Sopron and Fertőrákos, before veering onto a small side road toward Sopronpuszta. It was not paved, just a dirt track skirting a prison. It had been raining and the scene unfolding before them made Oskar uneasy. Rather than encounter a stream of merry picnicgoers, they found the opposite: a chaos of people dashing the other way.

The light was poor. Storm clouds blotted out the sky, which was already obscured by the foliage. It was hard to make sense of anything between the swipes of the windshield wipers. Was the picnic over, were these people returning home? They didn't dare open the window and ask. Oskar tried to push forward, but his tires couldn't get traction in the mud so he steered over to the side. The other couple approached. We're going to try to cross through the woods, they said.

Katja and Oskar stared at each other wordlessly. Katja didn't like the idea of going through the woods without Oskar. But it didn't make sense for him to go with her, because if he was caught, he might be kicked out of the country. If this happened, it would leave Katja alone in Hungary without anyone to support her. The seconds felt like minutes, cloistered in the car, in the rain. Katja decided she would go with the other couple. If she made it to Austria, Oskar would take her things and go meet her—Katja would call his parents, that's how he would know. If she was captured, he would be there in Hungary to get her out.

Oskar walked Katja to the edge of woods, stood with her on the muddy road, awash in the rain and the traffic of departing bodies. Then they split up: she, into the enveloping darkness alongside the other couple; he, back to the camp.

Katja stared at the curtain of trees. She had never been to the woods at night. She felt exposed, the light of the passing cars flashing over her. They walked in silence. Shortly the commotion of the road faded into a strange and ghostlike din. The forest was dense and they had to pick their way carefully over exposed roots and fallen branches. After some time the woods gave way to a clearing and they found themselves inside a cornfield. It felt good to be back beneath the graying sky, but they grew concerned they had been heading the wrong direction. The rain was steady and visibility limited. They pushed ahead until they saw a watchtower and stopped in their tracks.

Standing, huddled together against the rain, they fell into a frightened stillness. The sounds around them were spooky and indistinct, sometimes near, sometimes far, circling around, closing in. They could see the lights of cars in the distance. When the sky began to clear the noises got louder, the barking of commands by officers, nearby yet invisible.

Hours passed. First in the rain, then when this ceased, beneath a brilliant, starry sky. They had thought to cross in the night, but now their confidence waivered. They were scared to move forward with such little light. So they stayed, paralyzed, shivering. Unsure of what to do or where to go, they decided to do nothing. To just wait until dawn. To see what, if anything, the new day might bring.

OTHERS MISSED THE PICNIC TOO. WHILE KATJA SPENT THE NIGHT out in the cornfields, Bernd and Marlies Grunert spent the evening in their tent. The campsite outside Fertőrákos was ever desolate. That hellscape of rust and detritus was hardly a place to travel with their two young daughters, just four and seven. They had been in Hungary for only a few days, but it felt like a lifetime.

When they'd arrived in Hungary, Bernd had thought to go first to the West German Embassy in Budapest. But they had called some friends in Bremen, West Germany, who told them the border was open. Marlies wanted to go for it. Bernd wasn't so sure, but agreed to give it a try. It was some days later, on August 19, that they saw the flyer for the picnic. Bernd was instantly suspicious. They had already been caught by Hungarian guards once on their trip; he didn't want to risk getting caught again. And he thought he had seen some military vehicles outside the campsite. They would wait this one out.

That evening, Marlies went to use the phone at a kiosk in town to call their friend in Bremen. When the line connected, her friend cried into the receiver. *You made it!*

Marlies instantly understood the mistake they had made in not trying the border. Holding on to the receiver, she collapsed into tears.

By nightfall the winds rose, portending a terrible storm. Marlies tried to clear her mind but couldn't. Dreams of making it to the West had been part of her relationship with Bernd for years. They used to conjure up fantasies of daring escapes. One recurring vision involved floating across the Baltic on a mattress—like a flying carpet, except drifting across a pale and choppy sea.

Dreams like this were commonplace for the East Germans, especially after the construction of the Wall. In Christa Wolf's novel *They Divided the Sky*, Manfred tells Rita of a dream he had. "We're both sitting in a small wet boat and floating down the streets of a city. It's raining and raining. The streets are empty, the water is rising. The churches and trees and houses are going under in the flood. Just the two of us are rocking on the waves, all alone in a very fragile boat." The voyage would be treacherous, the dream implied. But if the water rose high enough, it might carry them to freedom.

For Marlies, now, there was only the rain.

When they had first hopped in the car and crossed out of the GDR, she had felt a huge relief. *Ein großer Stein ist uns vom Herzen gefallen*, she felt. It was like a big stone had fallen off their hearts. But now at the camp it didn't feel that way anymore. Marlies felt lost and vulnerable, as did so many others across the land: East Germans stranded in the woods or marooned in their tents; Hungarians of all stripes wondering what was happening to their country, what the next days might bring.

Marlies lay awake as thunder crashed overhead and rain shook the thin walls of their tent. She was frightened and miserable, sitting with her stone.

Chapter Nineteen

The morning after the picnic, August 20, was a national holiday in Hungary. The organizers met for lunch at the Lövér Hotel, where the whole adventure had begun just twenty-four hours earlier. Many showed up after a night of restive sleep.

The lunch was intended as an informal press conference, so there were toasts. One MDF member remarked boldly that history had been written in Sopronpuszta, and everyone applauded. But it was a nervous applause. A state official was present, Lajos Farkas, from military secret service, as was protocol. László Nagy took a seat beside him to see if he had any insight into what might happen to them. In the manner common to state officials at that time, Farkas's response was both matter-of-fact and hopelessly vague.

You will get a threatening letter tomorrow from Budapest, he said. If things go in your direction, you'll disregard it. If the politics turns against you, the punishment will be ruthless.

These words reflected a common strategy at the time. The higher-ups were also watching to see what direction the political winds would blow.

Despite the circumstances, the lunch at the Lövér Hotel struck a celebratory tone. Photos were taken, the organizers put their signa-

tures to a document for posterity, and there was even some laughter. But the uneasiness remained.

Returning home, László Nagy was stopped on the stairway by his mother. László was back living in the house where he grew up. His mother occupied the ground floor and he lived above with his wife, also a member of the MDF, and their young kids. His mother had so far tolerated their political activism. But after the picnic, her mood changed.

I won't look after the kids anymore if you two go to political events, she said to László as he was coming in. From now on, one of you must stay here.

If something were to happen to you, if you were to die, she continued, they would be orphans.

We're on the right side of history, László replied.

László's mother remembered 1956 vividly. The boys in Budapest thought this way too, she said.

———

OSKAR AWOKE EARLY THAT MORNING FROM WHAT HAD BEEN A cold, damp night in his tent. He called his parents to see if they had heard from Katja. They hadn't. He tried again a few hours later. He scoured the local papers, drove through Sopron and Fertőrákos. Nothing. Then he returned to the camp, heavy with regret. What had he done, allowing her to go through the woods without him?

When Oskar heard about the breach, new fears set in. How would the government react? What if they ordered crackdowns? Things change quickly in times of upheaval. The more he learned, the more concerned he became.

He called home again. Now his parents were worried sick for this young woman, their would-be daughter-in-law, gone without a trace.

When earlier that spring Oskar had told them this was the girl he wanted to marry, they went to Dresden to meet her. If Katja made it to West Germany, she wouldn't be able to visit her parents anymore. During their visit, Oskar's parents promised to take care of her, to treat her like a daughter. But this seemed like ancient history now.

That same morning, Katja awoke at dawn stranded in the cornfield, drenched to the bone. She was filled with regret too. It was obvious they had missed something big with the picnic. At least there would have been other people to take cover beside; other bodies struggling against the same current.

Now as the light was cracking through, Katja and the family she was traveling with fixed their attention on the watchtower they had stopped beside. They wanted to be completely sure it was empty before advancing. But as they waited, they worked themselves into paralysis, holding out for the perfect moment of clarity, which of course never came.

They also started coming up with justifications for not moving. Katja remembered hearing that this day was a national holiday. It's better to wait until it gets dark, she whispered to the others. That way the guards will get drunk and forget about us.

They didn't have much food, just a small box of fruit juice and a candy bar, and limited water. They tried to conserve their energy. They spent the next hours lying about, talking in hushed snatches.

Katja stayed focused. Growing up in the GDR prepared her for this, somehow. Being suspicious of everything, careful all the time. And all that waiting. Those times when you heard that a shipment of bananas or oranges had come from Cuba. You would queue for hours just to taste their sweetness. You learned how to control your appetites. This was a skill she put to use here, out in their tiny island in a sea of corn.

They spent much of their time tracking the sounds of soldiers, listening to the birds swooping past and the wind rustling the stalks. From their vantage, all they could see was the sky.

When evening came, they built up the courage to go for it. But nightfall was disorienting. The sounds changed. They recognized the regular steps of soldiers. But there were irregular steps too, sometimes accompanied by distant shouting, the screeching of car wheels. Perhaps the fields were filled with refugees like them, lots of lonely islands, an archipelago in a faceless ocean. Perhaps these were the sounds of people getting caught.

As the sky darkened, their paranoia grew. But they couldn't wait another day. They didn't have enough food or water. Up above them the moon began to show. They started walking. Their progress was slow, but they set off no alarms, drew no attention from any soldiers nearby. Soon a fence became visible in the distance, a track where the soldiers would walk, and between them a wall of bushes, several meters thick.

Katja's heart sank. They weren't prepared for this. They had wire clippers, but the bushes were deep and sharp—blackberry, she thought, covered in spines. They would have needed a machete. In her despair, she found herself revisiting the fairytale about Dornröschen, sleeping beauty, locked up in a castle, surrounded by rose bushes. When princes on white horses came to save her, one after another they died, cut up by the thorns.

The story made so much sense to Katja just then. Those princes, pursuing their impossible dream, there on the other side of the monstrous hedge. The princess too, caught under a spell, waiting for something, somehow, to come and save her.

Standing there before this uncrossable wall of bramble, Katja felt the immenseness of the world. This wasn't the man-made fencing she had prepared for, but the work of a higher power, godlike and immutable. They approached with their clippers but almost immediately found themselves stuck amid the thorns, only to be discovered there by a guard who had been waiting for them.

The officer was young, just a bit older than Katja. Back at the base, little more than a shack by the edge of the woods, he confiscated their wire cutters, tossed them atop a pile of others. He gave them tea and bread. Shortly a car arrived and they were taken to a prison. This was how the fairytale ended—in a cold cell with other women, all with stories like her own, and nothing to do but bide their time. Hoping just to make it out again, to not be abused. To be free, or at least as free as they had been just a few hours prior, before everything they had worked so hard to achieve had been taken from their grasp.

Outside the chamber she could hear the sound of feet, of officers barking orders. Katja didn't know where she was. Since they had not driven far, she suspected she might have been taken to the military prison they had seen the night before, just beside the place where Oskar said goodbye. Occasionally, someone would be summoned from the room. It was impossible to know where they had been taken, since no one ever came back.

Katja went over to the mother and daughter she had been traveling with. They agreed that whatever happened, however long it took, they would wait for each other on the other side. Solidarity is important in prison too; maybe especially so.

It was hours before Katja's name was called, at which point she was taken to a private room to be interrogated. After she entered, the door shut behind her and suddenly she was alone with an officer, older, with marks on his lapel that signified authority. Katja tensed up. Soldiers took many forms—the sadistic, the lonely, the mad. She was told to wait as he pulled her file, directed to sit upon a metal chair, positioned before a metal desk. There was no other furniture in the room. She ran her fingers through her hair, matted, gnarled, bearing still the odor of the wild. Her trousers were sweaty against her legs.

The officer came over and sat on the desk before her. This is the second time you've been caught, he said. If it happens again, you will get in a lot of trouble.

He looked down at Katja, his expression grave. I will mark down this transgression, he told her. A record of your actions will be sent to the authorities in Berlin.

Katja looked around the room as the man spoke. She had never been in a prison before. She found herself focusing on his words, which were gentle on the ears, German, but softened by Hungarian, its tonality and lilt. I can let you go this time, he said. But next time you'll be deported.

Then the officer stood, indicating she should leave. Katja rose and turned to the door. She felt grateful and relieved. Looking back, she saw the man's face differently. What had seemed like anger now looked like fatigue. Perhaps he had been there the whole night too.

Thank you, Katja said.

Be careful out there, he replied.

Katja stepped outside into an air impossibly sweet. The other couple was already outside, standing in front of the car they had abandoned the night before. They drove back to the camp to find Oskar sitting cross-legged before their tent, his face drawn after his wakeful night. He ran to her.

Oskar resolved at that moment that next time he would go with her into the woods. That he would never let her out of his sight again. Oskar had just come out of military training in West Germany. He knew a thing or two about how to navigate rugged terrain.

Katja went into the tent to get some rest. While she slept, Oskar set about finding a route to the border. This wasn't hard. People were talking openly now. There was a woman organizing things. Her name was Ágnes.

The trail to the border departed from behind a small restaurant called Diana—fittingly, as in Roman mythology, Diana (Artemis) is the goddess of moonlight and trees and the protector of young women. This was the same route Ágnes had been directing people toward for days.

By early evening, August 21, a group had gathered in the restaurant's parking lot, among them Bernd and Marlies Grunert and their two young daughters. Standing at the forest's edge, breathing in the cool woodsy air, looking at the collection of strangers around her, Katja felt a burst of energy. A new sense of kinship too. Previously she felt ashamed at her passport, but now she understood that she was not just *East* German. She was *German*. That this passage was her right. That it was her due.

Katja began seeing Germanness all around her. Everyone taking time to park properly—cars they would shortly abandon. One man prudently putting on trousers for the woods. These were people in the process of becoming German—a single, irreducible identity they'd never fully had or felt, but which they were doing their best to bring about.

Though they started walking as one big group, this didn't last. Oskar felt uncomfortable with the noise they were making. He wanted to hang back. Shortly he pulled Katja off the main trail down an incline to a slender path by a river. You always go to the lowest spot if you want to avoid being seen, he told her.

Back on the main trail, the others moved quickly ahead, almost at a trot. Some of the couples were carrying children, sometimes having given them sedatives lest they cry out. Bernd Grunert held their youngest daughter, C_____, four, in his arms. Their eldest, S_____, seven, walked beside them. Once she fell. Marlies swooped over to pull her up. You need to keep going, she told her firmly. You need to be quick and quiet, and you cannot cry.

If the soldiers hear you, they will take you away from us, she said.

Down below, by the water, the noise of so much movement up on the main trail made Oskar balk. He and Katja stopped and waited. Soon the forest quieted to just the sound of their own feet crunching through twigs and leaves. They spent the next plodding hours in silence. Oskar remained worried that there might be enhanced security now, after the breach. Every once in a while they stopped to listen for soldiers. Katja focused on the sounds of the woods, quiet, uninterrupted. Even the birds were sleeping.

She felt safer this time. She knew from her experience that the Hungarian guards didn't patrol the deep interior of the forest. They mostly stayed near the border. This was not a search operation like when the Nazis were hunting for Jews, she thought. The Hungarians weren't eager to do their job; they were hoping they didn't have to.

Then Katja and Oskar heard a loud crash and froze.

Up ahead, on the main trail, the Grunerts alongside several other families had come upon a watchtower and started running. Maybe they could catch the guards by surprise. Bernd carried C_____; Marlies held fast to S_____'s hand.

The tower was unmanned. Underneath there was a stretch of barbed wire with a hole cut through it. Working quickly, they passed the kids through.

Hearing voices in the distance, they stopped. It was still so dark, it was impossible to see who was coming. The noises grew closer, feet crashing through the woods. Bernd clenched his fists. There were some seconds of commotion and shapeless sound before they could make sense of what they were hearing. The voices were speaking German. The people greeting them were wearing street clothes, carrying home-made signs. *Welcome to Austria*, a man called out.

Suddenly so many emotions that Bernd and Marlies had blocked out came rushing up. Lifting the children up into their arms, they cried with joy.

Katja and Oskar, well back and down in the gully, couldn't make out any words, just noise. Were people getting caught? Should they turn back? It was hard to know what to do. They stayed put until the woods returned to stillness. Then they walked until they came to a stretch of cleared-out land; in the middle stood a watchtower.

Katja held tightly onto Oskar. This comforted him. The warmth of her touch after the long night of self-reproach. When, after some time, they felt confident that the tower was empty, they moved swiftly beneath it, merging onto a foot-trampled path. They groped their way forward, until finally there was a fence, and over to the side a hole cut through the wiring, stretched out at the sides.

Oskar and Katja climbed through and started running. The terrain was easy, as the forest gave way to a field. And there in the center was a stone with an *M* painted on one side and an *Ö* on the other. Now they were laughing, and kissing, and crying. It was a border marker. They had reached Austria, Österreich, past Magyarország, Hungary.

Katja collapsed to the ground, overcome with emotion—not just relief and joy, but also gratitude. All those people who'd come before, their feet stamping down their earth to forge a path, their fingers plying apart the fence. It was an escape that all of them, these myriad strangers, performed together, united somehow as a single body, seeking home.

And if her first breath was one of freedom, it was this second one, of solidarity, that was perhaps most sweet. The feeling that however you crossed the border, you didn't do it alone.

Chapter Twenty

Political circumstances look different depending on where you sit. While Árpád Bella awaited to hear if he would be punished, and the picnic organizers suffered restive nights, the reformers in government—especially Németh and Pozsgay—viewed the breach with a mixture of relief and awe. Relief that so many East Germans had been let out, helping lessen the crisis on their hands. Awe that the event had gone off without bloodshed.

They had spent the evening of the picnic assembled in Németh's office, studiously attuned to secret service reports on the Soviet headquarters, just twenty-five kilometers from the border in Fertőd, to see if anyone had stirred. They hadn't. The first great breach of the Iron Curtain, and Moscow *didn't even react*. GDR premier Erich Honecker was outraged. He demanded of the Hungarian ambassador in East Berlin that all GDR citizens be promptly and forcibly returned. But of course this had no effect. If Gorbachev was silent, there wasn't much Honecker could do.

Németh and Pozsgay were elated, but the reprieve proved short-lived. On August 21, an East German man was killed trying to flee through the woods outside Kőszeg. His name was Kurt Werner Schulz. He had been with his wife and six-year-old son. The details surrounding the death are hazy. At the border the family had been stopped by a guard. It was dark and the two men couldn't communicate—the guard barked orders in Hungarian. Schulz approached and the young soldier panicked.

Schulz died on the same night that Katja and Oskar and Bernd and Marlies and so many others made it across.

Németh was rattled. This was the situation he had feared all along—an innocent refugee killed by Hungarian hands. *We* didn't kill him, he told me the first time we met. It was June 2019, and we only had an hour together, so we mostly covered the basics. But about Schulz, Németh wanted to talk. It was a subject he brought up unprompted, a record he wanted to set straight.

Prior to the death of Schulz, Németh had thought it prudent to slow things down after the picnic. No reason to force Gorbachev's hand. But this now changed. More than 150,000 East Germans remained on Hungarian soil. It was too dangerous for them to keep trying to cross the border haphazardly. The risk of further deaths was too high. Something had to be done. It was time to open the border and let everyone out.

The following morning, August 22, Németh arranged a meeting of his inner circle of confidants—especially Foreign Minister Gyula Horn and Interior Minister István Horváth. The first step was to set up an investigation into Schulz's death. If in fact it was an accident—which indeed it proved to be—then he wanted this verified and publicized. Second, he had to get in touch with West German chancellor Helmut Kohl to see if West Germany would help with the refugees.

If we are going to open the border, Németh thought, then West Germany had better be ready.

———

BACK AT THE BORDER, KATJA AND OSKAR LAY SPLAYED OUT ON the ground, catching their breath. It was early morning, August 22, the sky was still dark. Oskar sat up. I need to go back, he said.

He reached for Katja's hand, warm in the predawn chill. Our

things, he said. The car. It's all in Hungary. My passport too. I need to get a Hungarian exit stamp.

I know, Katja replied.

She looked about with a feeling of glossy ease, only vaguely aware of the scratches and mosquito bites she'd acquired overnight in the woods.

Oskar would accompany Katja to Mörbisch, the nearest Austrian village, but didn't want to wait too long, in case a new shift of border guards came in. They also had to figure out how he would find his way back to the hole in the fence. Katja felt around her pockets and found some paper napkins. The moon was bright enough that if they tore them into pieces they could work as markers. So there was Katja, living another fairytale, Hansel and Gretel leaving their trail of bread crumbs.

Mörbisch wasn't far away. They had only walked a few minutes before they came upon a paved road, then streetlights. At the Red Cross tent, Katja was given a cot. The scene was chaotic, with doctors milling about alongside Austrian military officials, and of course all the refugees. Katja was so tired she could hardly appreciate her new surroundings, not even the ointment an attendant had brought to rub over her bitten up arms.

Oskar came to her side. They kissed quickly. Katja watched as Oskar departed, then shut her eyes, imagining his course back to the spot in the clearing.

The light was coming up, so Oskar's step was clipped. The pieces of napkin were still there. When he came to the edge of the woods, he ran into some Austrian soldiers. What do you think you're doing? one asked. You can't go there.

Oskar explained his predicament. One of the officers lifted his eyebrows and whistled. They conferred a moment among themselves then decided to let Oskar pass. They were mostly there to maintain order, they told him; stopping someone from crossing the border wasn't their job.

The officer gave Oskar a knowing smile. You were the ones who left the trail of tissues, he said. Very smart.

Back in the woods, back through the hole, back beneath the watchtower, Oskar made his way swiftly. He wanted to make sure that the Hungarian guards didn't try to make an example of him. After all, stopping someone from trying to cross the border *was* their job.

The passage was uneventful until Oskar heard footsteps rushing in his direction. He crouched behind a tree. But as they got closer, Oskar could tell this wasn't a Hungarian security detail, but another wave of East Germans. Be more quiet, he told them. Then he directed them where to go.

Before they passed, Oskar added: listen, if you make it to the Red Cross in Mörbisch, you'll find a girl there named Katja. Tell her I made it back.

The East Germans looked at Oskar curiously, clearly trying to comprehend what he could possibly be doing crossing the Iron Curtain the *other* way, but they assented. And so the solidarity chain continued. It was light by the time Oskar made it to the parking lot beside the Diana restaurant, his car exactly where it had been left, just a few hours before. He went back to the campsite and found his tent, packed up quickly, then hit the road.

Just as Katja had found her freedom the moment she crossed that border stone painted with an *M* and *Ö*, Oskar felt it while approaching the Hungarian frontier at the regular crossing point, Klingenbach, slipping easily into a short queue of cars and passing a gate where he was greeted with a wave and the prized stamp showing he had exited Hungary legally.

And so, Austria once again. Oskar gave a loving smack to the dashboard, then stepped on the gas. Now it was time to get Katja to Vienna, to West Germany. To a new life and whatever lay beyond.

WHILE OSKAR WAS MAKING HIS WAY BACK, KATJA FOUND herself flitting in and out of sleep. The tent was noisy. Sitting up, looking around, she mused at how people simply came and went as they pleased, could walk into town with no one ordering them not to or demanding they fill out paperwork.

Freedom in this guise was simply the absence of authority, no one telling you what to do.

At one point a young Austrian soldier came over and struck up a conversation. What stuck with Katja was the easiness of the exchange. It was the first time in her life she was not scared of speaking to a man in uniform. This was freedom too. Not just the absence of authority. But something different: the sense that the law wouldn't be arbitrarily thrust upon you.

Katja got up, wanting a wash. The Red Cross facilities had no water, but a local volunteer invited her back to her house to take a shower. And it was here, at this kind woman's house, that Katja's life in the West truly began. Walking into the bathroom, she gasped. It was as big as a ballroom, she felt. The water gushed from the tap.

Katja took her time. She washed her hair then washed it again, and fitted herself into secondhand trousers and a polo shirt provided by the Red Cross. She strode back outside with a sheen of newness, having shed something of her former self like a desiccated, outer skin.

When Oskar arrived, he found her lying on her stomach, feet in the air, devouring a newspaper. When she looked up at him, her smile was light. Look at this, she said pointing toward an article she was reading. You'll never believe the things these people are allowed to say.

But Oskar could believe it. This was the West he knew, the world he had wanted to show her for so long.

An Austrian photojournalist asked Oskar if he would show him where they'd crossed the border. Katja wanted to keep reading, so Oskar escorted the journalist on his own to their trail of tissues, a few of which remained. He pointed him toward the hole in the fence. But this time, now in the broad light of day, Oskar discovered something new. There wasn't just one hole, but many, several meters apart. And while the first might have been cut by refugees, the rest seemed to follow a scheme: evenly spaced out, almost metrically so; the sharp edges of the wires tucked in so no one would get hurt.

These holes had not been not cut haphazardly by East Germans, but by Austrians, ordinary civilians just trying to help out.

Listening to Oskar tell this story today, my thoughts return to Adolf Eichmann. We are enthralled by tales of monsters. But sometimes politics is forged by people on the opposite end of the moral spectrum: people concerned with doing what is right, what is good, who don't need anyone to tell them what that looks like.

Something can also be said of the Hungarian guards here. They probably didn't cut these holes. But nor did they patch them up. Instead, they chose to look away. This is a moral stand too.

There in the borderlands, politics was an elaborate charade: states and civilians pretending to be on opposite sides of a line, when in fact they were all, in different ways, standing together across it. It could have been war by another name, but instead it was something else. An expression of the responsibility we feel toward people we do not know and may never meet, yet feel deeply for all the same.

Martin Luther King Jr. famously remarked that the moral arc of the universe bends toward justice. I prefer to think of morality as a giant tapestry. In some stretches the ties are thin, the fabric all but bare; in others the weave is thick and textured, composed of a million tiny threads, each on its own too weak to hold the weight of our responsibilities, but together strong enough to buttress the world.

BACK IN BUDAPEST, NÉMETH BEGAN FORMULATING A PLAN. THE urgency he felt wasn't just because of the death of Schulz, but also because of another looming crisis. Starting on August 22, the vaunted Worker's Guard (Munkásőrség)—the armed wing of the Communist Party controlled by hardliners—began setting up checkpoints in the borderlands, stopping all cars with GDR plates, especially those on the road leading toward Sopron.

And so, just days after the Iron Curtain was breached, revanchist elements within Hungary had formed a new border, this time on Hungarian soil. Not only would they try to bar people from getting out, they wanted to make sure would-be refugees never reached the border in the first place.

On August 23, they began a terror campaign, shooting into the air and detaining East Germans in makeshift camps. Citizens in the town of Kópháza not far from Sopron reported not being able to sleep because of shooting that went on through the night. The Worker's Guard was behaving in the way that a lot of Communist institutions did in those days—showing up late and unprepared for a party that was already over. But they were dangerous all the same.

Comprised of civilians sworn to protect the Party, the Worker's Guard was instituted as a conservative force after 1956 to make sure that students or opposition groups didn't attempt to rise up again. These were not simple thugs. Guardsmen went for trainings and wore uniforms. From time to time they would parade through the streets to show off their arms.

Part of the reason the Guard was so dangerous was its nebulous positioning vis-à-vis the state. Indeed, in the aftermath of the picnic, it was neither the government nor the Party headquarters in Budapest that had issued the command to wreak havoc in the borderlands. Instead, the order came from regional Party offices in the border-adjacent counties of Győr, Sopron, and Vas. The Guard's unique position meant it was as threatening to the state as it was to the populace.

After the picnic, the two forestry professors, László Magas and János Rumpf spent their nights helping lingering groups of East Germans cross the border. But as they would soon learn, these days the woods were filled with horrors. One night, a young East German boy got separated from his parents and cried out. Some local farmers heard the noise and ran to help, but soon found themselves face to face with guardsmen.

Magas witnessed the standoff. The next morning, he put in a call to Pozsgay—he still had access to his private line. When Pozsgay heard what was happening he arranged that TV crews go to Kópháza to bring the situation to light. In the broadcast—a twenty-five-minute documentary—the reporter remarked that she had only witnessed circumstances like this before in conflict zones. Magas was interviewed; behind him a guardsman stood about idly, clutching a machine gun.

The image brought so much to bear at once: crumbling state institutions matched by heterogeneous pockets of power; the fact that there was always, simmering just beneath the surface, the possibility of violence. All those armed men, clinging to a past that was disintegrating before their eyes.

The broadcast brought the desired response: outrage at the Worker's Guard, who were ordered by the government to stand down. But the rift had been forged. Who knew how far the Guard might take this, what they might do to regroup, or whether they might even appeal to an authority higher up for help.

These were deeply unstable times.

Chapter Twenty-One

Regina Webert wanted to get a Big Mac. Hungary had the first McDonald's in the Eastern Bloc, a small franchise in central Budapest. It was hugely popular—a touch of the West situated in the East. She and her husband, Lars, knew they should have headed straight for the border. As it was, they were late getting to Hungary from the GDR youth camp where they had spent the first part of their summer. But they went to the McDonald's first. Regina had heard stories about the buns, how fluffy they were. On the way they got a copy of the *Bild Zeitung*—the *Bild*—a West German tabloid.

Eating a Big Mac with the *Bild*—this was everything they had imagined of the West. It was as though they were already there. It was August 22, their first day in Hungary, and the paper's headline told of the shooting of Kurt Werner Schulz.

The following afternoon, as previously arranged, Regina and Lars met their friend who had made it west—he had West German papers and so could cross back and forth. They would travel to the border in his car, a Ford with West German plates.

Just as the *Bild* had foretold, the situation in Sopron was unnerving. Within the course of a few days the border had changed from a quiet, well-guarded place to a strip of terror and vigilantism. The city was teeming with officers of various stripes—not just the ordinary security personnel of the borderlands, but now the Worker's Guard militiamen too—many with large guns.

Regina and Lars avoided making eye contact with anyone as they passed. It didn't feel safe to be there, even just sitting in the car. Their friend wanted to drive around and scope out the area but didn't think it wise for them to come along, so he dropped them off at a bathhouse outside the city where they could wash. Later, he took them to a hiding spot he had found in the periphery between the city and the woods— actually a garbage pit, a place no one would think to look—then pointed them in the direction of the border.

They would wait until evening before trying to cross. Over the next hours, the stench grew oppressive. As did their paranoia. Every time Regina heard the sound of a passing car, her heart thumped so loud she was sure all of Sopron could hear it. They were so close she could feel the proximity of the border almost as an aura. But also the fear. What if they were too late? She had her whole life ahead of her. Regina sank into a miserable silence.

Feeling paralyzed, caught in limbo, coming so close to your dreams only to have them vanish before your eyes—these are hallmarks of the refugee experience. And for every great success comes its mirror image in tragedy.

It was June 1940 when Hannah Arendt, who had just fled the internment camp at Gurs in Nazi-occupied France, made her way to Lourdes to find her friend Walter Benjamin, also a philosopher and Jewish émigré. Benjamin was en route to Marseille where he would arrange papers to flee France via Spain to Lisbon, Portugal, and there hope to board a ship to the United States. At Lourdes, Arendt and Benjamin spent two weeks together, playing chess. They had no official business; they were there just to keep each other company. Arendt feared for Benjamin's mental health. He was crippled by fear of crossing the border, of being caught and taken to the Gestapo.

"The complete uncertainty about what the next day and even the

next hour will bring," Benjamin wrote to a friend on August 2, 1940,
"has dominated my existence."

Benjamin possessed a Spanish transit visa to Portugal, but the
only way he could cross the French-Spanish border was via a smug-
gling path through the Pyrenees. Like so many refugees in that era, he
was known to carry large doses of morphine around in the event he
was captured—that way he could take his own life before the Nazis did.

It was in this period that Benjamin wrote his last, unfinished work,
"Theses on the Philosophy of History," written on torn sheets of paper
and the backs of envelopes, whatever scraps he could find.

In the essay, taking inspiration from the *Angelus Novus*, a painting
by Paul Klee, Benjamin invokes the figure of an angel who is looking
back upon the detritus of history. "His face is turned toward the past,"
Benjamin writes, where he looks upon a "catastrophe which keeps piling
wreckage upon wreckage." The angel would like to help, to fix things, but
cannot because he is being thrust into the future by a powerful storm.

The despair written onto the visage of the *Angelus Novus* speaks to
millennia of oppression and devastation—with fascism just the newest
chapter. But Benjamin's portrait is also intimate. When the angel looks
back at a past he cannot change, thrust toward a future he cannot see
or comprehend, we can find something of Benjamin's positionality as
a would-be border crosser too.

Benjamin's fears of being caught, deported, interned, are part of
the refugee experience across the ages. They remain present in African
accounts of crossing the Mediterranean; in Central American accounts
of crossing the Sonoran Desert. The concerns are timeless. The fear of
not making it, alongside uncertainty of what might await you if you do.

When I try to think through the fears these refugees endure, it is to
this image, the *Angelus Novus*, that I most often return. The liminality
of his positioning; the desperation it engenders.

After months of anxious waiting, on September 25, 1940, Benjamin traversed the Pyrenees arriving to the Spanish border town of
Portbou only to find out that the Spanish government would no longer

honor transit visas. All refugees would be returned to France. That night, Walter Benjamin ingested a fatal dose of morphine.

The following morning, the Spanish border officials had a change of heart, deciding to let the refugees through. Tragedy is not just terrible and cruel, it is also arbitrary. As Arendt puts it in an essay on Benjamin, "Only on that particular day was the catastrophe possible." Had he waited just a few hours longer, he might have made it to freedom.

Regina and Lars set out at nightfall: through the woods, past the barbed wire and guard posts, and finally the mad dash to whatever lay on the other side.

How can one express this feeling—that first gasp of freedom? I meet Regina in 2018 at the Berlin Wall Foundation (Berliner Mauer Stiftung) in Mitte, central Berlin. When I ask her this, she takes some time in answering, fumbled about with words to try and give the emotion its shape.

The familiar German idioms didn't work. It wasn't like a big rock fell off her heart, but something stronger, more transcendental. What finally came to mind was a passage from a fairytale: *The Frog King* (*Der Froschkönig*). Toward the end, the king has been transformed back into a human. He is seated in his carriage beside his attendant, Heinrich, when suddenly he hears a large crash. The King screams that the wagon is breaking. No, Heinrich responds. It's just my heart.

Heinrich, der Wagen bricht!
Nein, das ist das Band von meinem Herzen.

Heinrich is so relieved the king is safe from the evil spell that his heart audibly breaks. This, for Regina, is what it felt like to leave the GDR, to make it across the border alive. Not the lifting of a weight, but of an enchantment.

It was early morning when they got to the first village, Sankt Margarethen. Regina and Lars went to wash off at a public water pump, which let out a horrible squeak. At the sound, some windows opened and faces peaked out. Soon they found themselves surrounded by children. A couple invited them in to bathe and eat some breakfast. It all felt so beautiful, so simple and gay, and most remarkable of all, so ordinary. In Austria too, it seemed, people cooked with water.

———————

THOSE FIRST DAYS AFTER THE PICNIC—THE DEATH AT THE BORder, the militias terrorizing the streets, along with the continued flight of East Germans—put the Hungarian state on high alert. On August 25, Németh, accompanied by his foreign minister, Gyula Horn, flew to meet West German chancellor Helmut Kohl and his foreign minister, Hans-Dietrich Genscher, at Castle Gymnich outside Bonn. The meeting was held in secret. It was just the four ministers, without aides.

Németh didn't waste any time. Hungary will break from the Warsaw Pact and open its borders as a sovereign nation, he said.

Kohl was in a state of disbelief. The fate of his national brethren in East Germany was a point of great concern for him; as was the still nascent dream of one day reunifying—an eventuality that opening the border might hugely accelerate. What does Hungary want in return? he wanted to know.

Németh demurred. They had separately discussed a large loan that would help Hungary get on its feet during the eventual transition—as much as 500 million Deutsche Marks (or 250 million US dollars), which Hungary desperately needed. But Németh wanted to delay this funding. As far as he was concerned, the matter of the refugees was a humanitarian issue and separate from Hungary's sovereign future. Also, he didn't want to be accused of exchanging people for cash.

The other issue Kohl raised was about Gorbachev. Kohl was skeptical that Németh would do something so garish as to open his borders against the will of the Soviet ruler. How can you be sure Moscow won't react violently? he asked.

We are past the days of intervention, Németh replied coolly.

Kohl was an accomplished statesman and a seasoned cold warrior. Németh was new on the scene, still less than a year in office. Kohl didn't feel confident in his young counterpart's assessment. He agreed that West Germany would prepare for the influx of refugees, but left the meeting concerned. Of course Kohl knew that Gorbachev had made overtures toward leaving the satellite states to themselves. But if Németh's judgment was off, the move could spark a deadly conflagration.

Kohl wasn't the only one concerned. Back in Budapest, Németh felt tension throughout the halls of government. His principal political rival, Károly Grósz, was against opening Hungary's borders. Németh feared he might attempt a coup—the rumors that had percolated throughout the summer returned with renewed vigor. According to one report, Grósz had tasked his advisors with soliciting advice and logistical support from foreign allies, notably in Yugoslavia.

A few days after his return, Németh received a letter from a friend in Parliament. It was in a sealed envelope with another envelope inside on which was scrawled the words: "Take what is written inside very seriously." The letter chronicled a series of meetings Grósz had been conducting outside the capital, encouraging supporters to rise up against state institutions under Németh's control, specifically the energy supply system, which would spark mayhem and discredit the government.

Németh was now caught between competing imperatives: to speed things up and open the border while he still could; also to slow things down to give West Germany time to prepare. The days were moving quickly.

Soon, security concerns hit closer to home. As head of state, Németh and his family were living in an elegant, hilly neighborhood on the west side of the Danube. His two sons were attending elementary school. Németh had previously gotten reports that Stasi agents had been spotted around the neighborhood. This was to be expected in those days—the boys were escorted to and from school by a security detail. But one day in early September, Németh came into the office to find an envelope on his desk. In it were black and white photographs of his sons taken at close range.

This was the last push Németh needed. The tension in the country was too much. It was time to open the border.

On September 8, Németh called a meeting to formalize the plan. The border would be open, they decided, at precisely midnight, September 11, at all crossings connecting Austria and Hungary. Gyula Horn, the minister of foreign affairs, issued the announcement.

Czechoslovakia, the intermediary state between Hungary and East Germany and a staunch proponent of the Warsaw Pact, responded immediately with a counter move: from that point forward it would shut its border with Hungary to GDR citizens. All remaining refugees on Czechoslovakian soil would be detained or deported. This move complicated matters in the long term, but for the moment the pieces were in place. One issue remained: Németh's government still didn't know how to communicate the message to the refugees. Why would they trust the Hungarian announcement? The refugees were scared, the shadow of the Stasi great.

One of the suggestions bandied around during meetings involved sending Hungarian officials into the campsites to spread rumors that they would be dismantled; that anyone who stayed would be sent home. Németh dismissed these ideas. Just open the border, he said. People will know what to do.

Chapter Twenty-Two

Whatever concerns the reformers in government had about getting the word out were quickly allayed. By afternoon, September 10, thousands of refugees were heading westward. Legalizing crossings, however, didn't eliminate risk. The fear of the Stasi remained ever present, and justifiably so.

Uwe Bergander was camping on the western shore of Lake Balaton with his girlfriend, Anja. He woke early, stretched his arms, and went over to his car, a bright green Volkswagen Golf, a hunched little vehicle that in its shape and color resembled a frog. It was West German, a rarity in the GDR. He touched the front lights affectionately. Now it's time to take you back to where you're from, he thought.

This was not Uwe's first go around. He had first traveled to Lake Balaton earlier that summer, in June. But when he showed up at one of the campsites, he immediately started to second guess things. Uwe had heard rumors that there were Stasi "people catchers" in Hungary that would trick East German citizens, capture them, and deport them back to the GDR. It wasn't long before he packed up and went back home.

Months later Uwe was ready to try again. He drove with Anja to Hungary on September 4, one of the last days that travel south was still possible, before the GDR clamped down on border crossings, and Czechoslovakia shut people in. On their trip down they had been extra careful, avoiding the big camping grounds because they were full of Stasi, sleeping instead beside Uwe's car, the little green frog. The one luxury they afforded themselves was a meal at the McDonald's in Budapest, sitting at a street-side table, the sounds of city life bustling around them.

Conversation was halting. Uwe felt uncomfortable in such a crowded place, Germans and Hungarians intermingling around them. But the experience was revelatory. Uwe overheard talk about breaches at the border, about the Pan-European Picnic. And indeed, it was there, as they were leaving, that an exciting rumor swept past their ears: the Hungarian government would shortly open its borders.

On September 10, Uwe and Anja drove from Lake Balaton to the outskirts of Sopron, at which point they found a quiet area to pull over. It was afternoon, and they parked beside a cut tree upon which they spread out a lunch as though it were a table. They ate, lay about, and even went to dip their feet into a nearby creek. But mostly they stayed next to the car, listening to the radio. They were waiting to hear official news about the border opening.

It wasn't until early evening that the announcement came through. The border would open at the stroke of midnight, September 11. Uwe and Anja got back into the car and headed west.

They hadn't been driving long before a car pulled in front of them and slowed to a stop. It was a narrow country road and they couldn't easily pass, so Uwe pulled up too. But he was immediately suspicious. Three men emerged and walked toward them. Uwe felt sure they were Stasi. Their car had Austrian plates, but their faces were aggressive, and even though they were wearing Western-style outfits, the fit was imperfect, which only made them look more Eastern.

The men came to the window claiming to be from the Red Cross. Follow us, they said. We'll show you how to get to the border.

Uwe's palms grew sweaty. All those doubts that had been festering suddenly rose up. Uwe knew they wouldn't be heading anywhere good. He followed the other car, feeling hopeless. But in his panic, Uwe realized that he had been driving slower than the car in front of them, which had gotten quite a bit ahead. Sensing the opportunity, Uwe slammed on the brakes, swung the car around, and headed the other direction.

It was only seconds before the other car noticed, spun around to chase them in swirls of dust and screeching wheels. The other car quickly gained ground. Uwe drove as fast as he could, fingers clenched tightly around the wheel, pushing his foot as hard as he could upon the pedal. Soon they could see before them the intersection of their small road with a westbound highway.

In moments they were upon it, the only question was how to merge with the speeding traffic without causing an accident or slowing enough to let their pursuers catch up. Fast approaching the lane, Uwe waved frantically out of the window. *Please let us in*, he hollered.

They were just a few meters away when the car in front of them eased up to allow them through. Then with a slick turn, they were suddenly not a solitary car, but just one among others, all heading west, honking, brights flashing, illuminating the darkening sky.

The queue went on for kilometers, eventually grinding to a halt. Uwe and Anja could faintly see the other car, the faux-Austrians that had chased them, stuck some ways behind. But now they didn't care. They were not alone anymore.

At five minutes to midnight, the cars before them started moving. First in fits and starts, then accelerating. And then, in a flash, around them rose the sounds of merriment: people screaming, singing, waving flags, and honking. For each new car that crossed the line, a new shout. And for those few seconds of passage, the whole earth shook with the sounds of joy.

Over to the side of the road in Austria was a pavilion teeming with activity. A tent gave out water and T-shirts. There were toilets that smelled clean and new. Uwe and Anja got out to look around, whereupon a woman, an Austrian, floated toward them like an apparition in the flickering of the passing lights. She took a ring from her finger and gave it to Anja. It will bring you good luck, she said. Then they were crying and embracing and saying thank you, amid this wonderful, happy, jubilant din.

Then they were getting back in the car, driving slowly past the celebrating masses, until suddenly they were driving fast, so fast, on the Austrian highway, feeling dizzy from the speed, now surrounded by other cars, not East Germans, but drivers having nothing to do with the border or the GDR, or any other part of the world Uwe and Anja were leaving behind, just people living their lives.

And it was then, driving his fast little frog in Austria, that Uwe understood what freedom meant: he had nowhere special to go, but also nothing stopping him from getting there.

IT WASN'T JUST PEOPLE ON THE HIGHWAY TO AUSTRIA WHO understood that something extraordinary had happened that night. People all across the East knew it. On September 11, 1989, the Hun-

garian border was open for good. The Iron Curtain in Hungary had officially fallen.

The next day, Németh was visited by a senior member of the East German politburo, who had come to demand that the border be shut. You cannot do this, he insisted. These are *our* citizens.

Yes, Németh replied, but it's *our* border.

Their conversation grew heated. Németh asked the man to leave his office.

The man did, but stopped at the threshold, hat in hand, not moving. There was something pitiful about his face. You're humiliating me, he said, making me go home empty-handed. At least give us permission to come into the camps and convince our citizens to come home.

What specific agreement the man sought, Németh never learned. He just said no.

That same day, the politburo met in East Berlin. Honecker drafted a letter to Gorbachev demanding action against Hungary's irresponsible behavior. The Soviet response was terse: this is an East German-Hungarian issue, it said.

This was a nightmare for GDR authorities. Apprehensions continued in Czechoslovakia, where East Germans were stranded. But increasingly a new strategy was needed, focusing on citizens still in the GDR. Indeed, unrest had suddenly begun to emerge, the first public disorder in a generation. Collective action began on September 4, following a Monday prayer at the Nikolaikirche in Leipzig, when about 1,200 gathered to demonstrate against travel restrictions. In an act of unimaginable daring, the crowd began to chant, "We want out!"

Such rebellion was unprecedented in East Germany. In a speech the following day at the West German Bundestag, Kohl invoked these brave individuals in Leipzig and the inspiration they took from the recent breaches of the Iron Curtain. "They have seen the pictures from Hungary," he declared, alluding to the images that people across the GDR would have been able to access, mostly from West German TV.

The following Monday, September 11, right after Hungary's

border opening, there was another attempted gathering outside the church in Leipzig, but this time the police closed off the premises. Many were arrested.

As was evident to everyone, the battle ahead would be bitter. But the changes afoot were impossible to deny. Within days of Németh's decision, as many as thirty thousand GDR refugees had settled in West Germany (plus countless others who did not register), a flow that continued unabated. The two states, separate for so long, increasingly appeared to have their fates intertwined. The inevitable questions followed: Was reunification possible? If so, how and when? And, closer to home, was this something to be afraid of? Myriad newspaper articles stoked the debate. With each new protest in the GDR, the questions became more urgent.

IN THE BEGINNING, THE EAST GERMAN REFUGEES MOSTLY FOL-lowed a similar path when they crossed from Hungary into Austria. From the border, first to Sankt Margarethen or Mörbisch. Then on to Vienna, usually by bus; after long waits at the embassy they were transferred to special trains that took them to Gießen, in central West Germany, where they were to be processed. Following September 11, most refugees skipped the first steps and went straight to Gießen by car. Thereafter, their roads diverged.

The Pfitzenreiters, the Sobels, and the Naglers boarded the same train to Gießen, where they received West German passports and two hundred Deutsche Marks—an astounding sum given what they had been used to in the GDR. When they walked out of the processing office, they bore different identities than when they had entered—they were now *West German.*

Bernd and Marlies Grunert took some time before going to Gießen, heading first to their friends in Bremen. Annette and Frank first visited family across the border, in the Austrian hamlet of Rust. Regina and Lars skipped Gießen entirely. Their goal was to go back to Berlin—West Berlin, this time. *Ich bin ein Berliner*, Regina proudly told the embassy worker in Vienna, using the same phrase as John F. Kennedy in 1963.

Since the road to Berlin traveled through the GDR, their only option was to fly. Regina had never been on a plane before. Flying into Berlin, soaring above the divided city, this was a new experience in every way. After they landed and checked into Marienfelde, a refugee camp where they would stay until they got themselves settled, Regina and Lars went immediately to the Wall, to see how it looked from the other side. Just to stand in awe at this edifice that had once held sway over their lives, but which now stood inert before them—no longer almighty, just brutal and strange.

For all the refugees, life in the West would take some time to get used to—and indeed, West Germans would take some time to get used to them. Everything was in flux. And while the story of East Germans fleeing westward via Hungary was the dominant storyline of the summer, sometimes the flow went the other way too. One figure of the growing demonstrations in East Germany was a Hungarian pastor named Zoltán Balog. That September, he took up a position in the Nikolaikirche in Leipzig.

Balog had a complicated relationship with the Hungarian authorities. Communist states were secular and tended to be hostile to church activity. Balog was not outwardly political, or at least hadn't been until that summer when the mass of East German refugees came through his parish outside Budapest. His church had doubled as a campsite in those days, as had so many others.

Since he spoke German, he had a lot of contact with the refugees. In his sermons, he spoke about peace—peace in the teachings of Jesus, peace between people, but also, increasingly, peace between East and West. These words were not traditional church fodder. His sermons became very popular.

Balog also performed baptisms. East Germany was even more anti-religious than Hungary, but West Germany was Christian. Many refugees felt that their physical journey westward was also a spiritual one. Balog's baptisms became a rite of purification—a cleansing of Communism. Balog was doing so many baptisms in those days he started grouping people together and washing them down with a hose—it was summer, after all.

The last night he performed this rite was September 10, just before the border opening. He went to the campsite beside Lake Fertő as a representative of the church and comforted the refugees before their journey. You're German, he told them. You're going home.

Balog felt giddy, out there by the border, partaking of the same infectious spirit as Aunt Ágnes, as Norbert, as so many others who helped the East Germans find their way across the line. After the opening, he moved to the East German city of Leipzig. When he got there, the churches were already swelling with energy. Soon he was giving sermons at the Nikolaikirche. He spoke about the changes in Hungary, things many East Germans still found unfathomable. He didn't mention the border or the refugees—he would have been arrested on the spot. But he did speak indirectly about politics. His message was conciliatory: stay here, he said. Fight to make the GDR a better place.

East Germany and Hungary will go into the free world together, he told them.

Balog's words resonated. Increasingly, Stasi officers with guns were lining the walls of the church. On September 18, for the third consecutive Monday, protestors gathered outside the grounds, facing down the police barricades. The demonstration was short-lived and many were arrested. But there was a shift: rather than focus on travel to the West—as per the previous chants of "We want out!"—this time the crowd focused on reform within the GDR. "We're staying here!" they chanted.

The shift is an important one. It suggests that these brave citizens saw the state as vulnerable. Far from a behemoth that had to be escaped at all costs, it was now something different: a homeland that could be reclaimed.

The state did not agree. On September 21, the government refused to formally recognize the newly formed opposition movement, the New Forum (Neues Forum). The following day, Honecker sent a message to all GDR administrative units to end any further demonstrations, saying they were "hostile" and "counterrevolutionary" and must be "nipped in the bud."

But state officials underestimated the extent of these developments. On September 25, at the next Monday gathering outside the church in Leipzig, as many as eight thousand people showed up. And Stasi efforts to infiltrate the demonstrations led to a counterproductive outcome. There were so many Stasi officials present that they made the Leipzig rallies appear larger than they actually were, emboldening resistance, rather than crushing it.

On September 27, the government of Czechoslovakia stated publicly that it would not open the borders to let out the East Germans trapped on their soil. There would be no "Hungary solution," they declared. But a few days later, following pressure from both Moscow and Bonn, a settlement was reached: special sealed trains would transport East Germans to West Germany.

It was a confusing time. By the end of the month, the whole country was on edge.

Chapter Twenty-Three

October 1989 was always going to be complicated. October 7 was the GDR's fortieth anniversary, and Gorbachev was to be in attendance of the jubilee. He came to East Berlin a day early for meetings with Erich Honecker and other state functionaries. There were lavish parties, honoring years of Soviet-East German cooperation. But even with all the pomp and circumstance, signs of trouble were unmistakable. Wherever Gorbachev went, crowds lined up outside chanting, *Gorbi, help*!

Gorbachev understood. Part of the reason he had come early was to inform GDR leadership that reform was required immediately, that the status quo could not be sustained. Gorbachev was direct: you must adapt to reality, he said. Then more explicitly, "Life punishes those who come too late."

On the day of the jubilee, there were parades in Berlin, filled with red flags and a procession of tanks. A podium was erected, presided over by men in military costumes. Honecker basked in the glory of the crowds. When they called out Gorbachev's name, rather than his own, it was as if he couldn't hear it.

That afternoon people showed up at the Palace of the Republic to demonstrate. Police beat them back, making mass arrests. The next day demonstrations popped up across the GDR. That was on a Sunday. But Monday, October 9, would be the day for full-scale demonstrations. The previous Monday, the rally in Leipzig had grown to an estimated twenty thousand. Once again the crowds focused on domestic issues, chanting, "We're staying here!" and "Democracy, Now or Never!" Throughout the chant sounded: *"Gor-bi! Gor-bi! Gor-bi!"*

Leipzig, dubbed the City of Heroes, had risen to cult status in the GDR. Across the city were scores of small acts of defiance—police vehicles were denied gasoline at filling stations; children of state officials were sent home from school.

But the state only retrenched. Stasi regional headquarters were equipped with thousands of military-grade weapons. Stasi chief Erich Mielke gave orders to use violence as necessary. Over the past weeks he had been stoking fear, instructing commanders to show their men images of a policeman brutalized by demonstrators in China. Mielke's message was frank: it's them or us.

From early morning, October 9, the city stirred uneasily. By afternoon, as many as seventy thousand protestors had showed up to march in the name of peace and democracy, armed only with signs and candles. They were ready for the shootings, the beatings, the mass arrests. They were ready to give their bodies, even their lives, to the cause. But as the demonstration swelled, police forces shrank back, first withdrawing to the outskirts of the rally, then disappearing completely, taking cover in the Stasi headquarters, the infamous Runde Ecke.

For all their bluster, Mielke's scare tactics had backfired. The Stasi officers were now concerned that the demonstrators might turn into a lynch mob. The crowd marched to the Runde Ecke shouting: "Stasi, out!" and "Occupy the building!"

The following morning, the politburo of the GDR did an about-face, announcing it was willing to start a dialogue with popular opposition groups. A good first step perhaps, but also evidence of the state's utter lack of comprehension of what was happening, of a regime forced to change, but crippled by age and inertia, incapable of figuring out how. Across the country, Stasi officers dutifully continued their work, informing on and monitoring behavior considered threatening to the state—including writing reports about demonstrations right outside their doors.

In one startling instance of bureaucratic inanity, on October 9, the same day as the great demonstration, the Justice Ministry finally approved a draft memo written a month earlier (right after the Hungarian border opening) that the state would adopt a position of tolerance toward those who fled. This statement was comically mild given the circumstances. Moreover, it included a warning that while those who returned would be pardoned, they might still be fined. This was hardly the message of a state even remotely cognizant of the geopolitical fissure on which it sat.

I came across this file in one of my last trips to the Stasi Records Archive; it reads now almost as a curiosity—because of its ideological disconnectedness, but also because of the contrast of colors and sounds. When I envision those days of early October 1989, I see chanting masses and flickering candles. I can smell the sweat of bodies, hear the words as they drift into the night sky. Yet in the archive, there is none of this. The paper is cheap, colorless, the language typed out impassively. There is no reference to the protestors in the street, or to world events. It is not brisk outside, or windy; the morning has not turned into afternoon.

On Monday, October 16, more than a hundred thousand assembled at the Leipzig demonstration. The following day, Honecker was forced out as secretary general of the Party—putatively for health reasons—and replaced by Egon Krenz, who was younger but otherwise little different. This was a last gasp effort by the Party to restore popular faith in their authority. Few thought it would work. On October 23, the protests in Leipzig swelled to three hundred thousand, with other demonstrations countrywide: Magdeburg, Dresden, Schwerin, Zwickau, Halle, Berlin.

In a further attempt to placate the protestors, a few days later, the GDR reopened its border with Czechoslovakia. This was momentous, given that Czechoslovakia had started sending East German refugees on trains to West Germany. In some backhanded sense this meant the border was already open. The move smacked of desperation, but also perhaps a change in strategy. Now that the state was reeling, better to let malcontents leave than keep them home to join the fight.

The winds of change swirled furiously. And through it all, life went on. One evening a man was apprehended at the border. He was so drunk he drove past the barricade. He didn't know where he was and wasn't trying to leave. But he was apprehended anyway. It was a bad time for human accident, teetering as everyone was on the precipice of the unknown.

FOR THE MOST PART WE VIEW COUNTRIES AS DISCRETE UNITS. But at certain times, narratives get upended and national fates converge. As Zoltán Balog had prophesied, Hungary and East Germany appeared destined to advance toward democracy together.

On October 7, 1989, the Hungarian Communist Party held its annual Congress and officially dissolved itself. From that day forth, it was no longer the sole political party in a one-party state; it was just a party like any other. Officially, it became the Hungarian Socialist Party, headed up by reformers in government. Within days, the hardline Communists formed their own party, reclaiming their old name, the Hungarian Socialist Workers' Party, led by Károly Grósz. The era of democratic infighting had already begun.

On October 18, the word "People's" was dropped from the middle of Hungary's name—it was now just the Hungarian Republic. The constitution was revised to declare the state a democracy. These changes were formally announced on October 23 in dramatic fashion by Mátyás Szűrös, the president of the Parliament, from the balcony of that glorious edifice overlooking the Danube. The symbolism was lost on no one: this was the precise date of the 1956 revolution.

Szűrös's announcement was met with raucous applause by the

giant crowd that had assembled. Had he stopped there, the day would have been an unequivocal success. But Szűrös added an ill-advised proviso: Hungary would continue to cooperate with the Soviet Union. Soon the cheers turned to boos. That evening thousands took to the streets to march in favor of independence from Soviet occupation.

Hungary may have already become a democracy in name, but meaningful popular rule remained far away. Old tensions continued to fester, embodied by the presence of the Worker's Guard, the Party's militia. Across the political spectrum, people feared that there could be no transition without bloodshed unless this military entity was disbanded.

When Németh and I talk now about those last treacherous months of 1989, it is to this subject that we return. Try to imagine it, he tells me. Sixty thousand people with heavy artillery and a budget big enough to fund different uniforms in winter and summer. How do you get them to give up their guns?

The prospect of violence cast a long shadow. When Németh called a meeting of his cabinet in early October to discuss decommissioning the Guard, he found little enthusiasm. No one was willing to risk their neck. Finally after an awkward, nearly wordless silence, then some haggling, Németh convinced Ferenc Kárpáti, the minister of defense, to join him.

Kárpáti was an ideal partner. Although aligned with the reformers, he was considered a moderate, and commanded the respect of even the most orthodox of Communists. Still, Németh was nervous. It was the second time that year he felt truly scared. The first was in June, on the date of the reburial of Imre Nagy, when he'd faced the threat of assassination by Romanian dictator Nicolae Ceaușescu.

Németh called a meeting with heads of the Worker's Guard from around the country. That morning, he and his wife, Erzsébet, walked circles around each other, neither broaching the subject. When he turned to leave, she asked: Will I see you alive tonight? They exchanged a weary glance.

A government car pulled up in front of Németh's building. In it, Kárpáti was dressed in full military regalia. Németh gave him an update on what to expect: Feri, he said, major firearms, including machine guns and grenades will be confiscated at the door. But they will be allowed to carry pistols.

Miklós, Kárpáti replied. We have military surrounding the building. If they try to kill us, no one comes out alive.

As the car passed through the city, Németh found himself thinking of his father, what he'd said when Németh first took the job as prime minister. Always look over your shoulder, his father had told to him. That's the only way to avoid the hanging.

Looking over his shoulder now, there was only Kárpáti. Walking into the room, taking his seat upon the dais, Németh mustered his courage. He spoke his piece, and the sea of men before them murmured and grumbled but did not budge. The plan had worked. But now the next challenge: They had to confiscate a quarter of a million weapons.

This intervention was to be staged on the night of October 21 by the Hungarian armed forces. Now it was time for other officials to be afraid. In Sopron, the regional commander of the border guards, István Frankó, was tasked with securing the warehouse where the Worker's Guard stored their arms, making sure they couldn't get in before the national forces took them away.

On the night of the raid, Frankó himself went, along with a unit of local border police and Sopron city police to guard the gate. Guardsmen showed up en masse, stamping and chanting. All those angry people— the mob was strong and Frankó's forces were pushed back against the gate. But then the military trucks arrived and amid the screaming and honking, everybody scattered.

This was a big moment for the forces of change in Hungary— perhaps the biggest. When discussing the raid today, Németh's face takes on a hint of boyish glee. I ask him how many arms they took that night, and his response is succinct: all of them.

OFTEN WHAT WE THINK OF AS A WAVE ISN'T WAVELIKE AT ALL; it's just a million compounding ripples, gathering force.

On November 1, cities across the GDR such as Frankfurt (Oder), Freital, and Ilmenau joined the call for democracy. The next day, it was Erfurt, Gera, and Halle. And while reforms sputtered through official channels, state organs began to atrophy. Officials across Party leadership resigned from their posts, a steady beat of steppings down.

On November 3, Egon Krenz gave a televised address, promising further reform. His tone was upbeat: it will be morning in the GDR, he seemed to suggest. The following day as many as half a million people gathered on East Berlin's Alexanderplatz. Images of the demonstration traveled the world over, as did audio and video recordings. So much noise in a country renowned for silence; so much color in a land of grayscale and sepia. Groupings in as many as forty cities, towns, and villages across the country marched in solidarity.

At the same time, people continued to flee. The sealed trains from Czechoslovakia continued unabated. Across the GDR, civil society was forced to choose: Stay or go? On November 8, the novelist Christa Wolf gave a televised address—a plea—asking that people remain in East Germany. Have confidence in reform, she exhorted. Don't give up on socialism.

The afternoon of Thursday, November 9, was cold. Thursdays were normally quiet, or it seemed so to Harald Jäger, the commanding officer at Bornholmerstraße, a northern crossing point of the Berlin Wall—a port of entry, at least in name; functionally it was a parking lot with a barricade strong enough to keep out military-grade vehicles. At 6 p.m. Jäger took a break for dinner, as usual.

Earlier that afternoon, after weeks of hemming and hawing, the politburo had finally agreed to relax travel restrictions—people would be allowed to leave the country, pending visas. The meeting had been contentious, weeks of pressure having taken a toll on the tempers of everyone present. It was late when Egon Krenz read out the draft travel bill. There was some dissent, calls for more discussion, but these were overridden. It was too late for further delay.

A last-minute press conference was called, presided over by Günter Schabowski, who had been acting as politburo spokesman. He hadn't been at the meeting but was given a note to read out.

The scene is iconic: Schabowski is a large man, visibly nonplussed to be in the briefing room—it was 6 p.m., dinnertime. His eyes are wide and drowsy; his cheeks sag. The statement he reads is short, the question of travel buried among minor details. When he finishes there is silence in the room. Finally a question from the audience: When will it come into effect? Schabowski fumbles with the slip of paper, his fingers thick and clumsy. He flips it over to see if anything is written on the back. *It will come into effect . . . to my knowledge . . .* he stammers, buying time. Then finally: *immediately.*

Ab sofort: words now ingrained in the German consciousness. That man, that room, that uncomfortable shift and shuffle. The words were uttered at 6:52 p.m. The room cleared in a rush, journalists dropping pens and briefcases, dashing out to speak the news. Within minutes, Tom Brokaw was live on NBC. At 7:05 p.m., the Associated Press report was in print. Then, the crush to the border, to the Berlin Wall. To see what it all meant.

The government was not expecting this. They had not worked out the details, hoping to hand the process over to bureaucratic organs that would slow things down. They had only intended to grant GDR citizens the right to apply for visas to visit the West, conditional on the usual rules regarding travel. But Schabowski didn't know that. Nothing accelerates bureaucratic time like accident.

Scores of people began showing up at the border. At 8:15 p.m., the East Berlin police put out statements to guards at all major crossing points. The orders: let no one out.

At Bornholmerstraße, out there in the dark and cold under the chemical yellows and greens of the Wall's protective lighting, the scene was mayhem. In the beginning the masses kept their distance, but with time they pushed closer to the guards, who stood in a line clutching their weapons. And as the crowds got louder, voices could be heard from the other side—West Germans who had come to see what was going on. While the one side screamed "*Open up*," the other responded: "*Come on over*."

And so, the first thing that crossed the Wall was sound, a traffic of words that no barrier could silence. Suddenly the pressure became two-sided and the authorities were squeezed. They could no longer abide the mythology of walling, that they protected their fellow citizens from the darkness on the other side. The voices outside rang loud and clear: these were not enemies; they were loved ones and friends.

As the crowds pushed forth, the question was omnipresent: Would the guards use their arms to reassert order?

The setting is eerily familiar. In August, just a few months earlier, Árpád Bella and his men had stood their ground in Hungary, defensive, uncertain, facing down a throng of bodies while defending a coercive institution breathing its last gasp. Now again, East German masses. Except here it wasn't several hundred, but thousands. This time the responsible guard was Harald Jäger. Like Bella, Jäger walked back and forth unsteadily and called up to his superiors, seeking orders that never came.

At just after 11 p.m., Jäger made his own decision. Open up, he ordered his men. The crowd pushed through the gate yelling and screaming as they passed to the West, just a few short meters away. Like so many institutions of violence, the Berlin Wall was strong enough to stop any man or woman acting alone. But it could do nothing against the force of thousands acting together.

The East German military stood at the ready. As many as twelve thousand soldiers were on high alert in case things got out of hand. But they were not summoned. In a last effort to quell the crowds, at 2 a.m. the Interior Ministry announced via the radio that the border opening was "temporary," that the proper policy would be in place that morning. But no one was listening. History had already been made.

Soon there were people dancing on the Wall, dancing on the Ku'damm, the main shopping street in West Berlin, people not just thinking about freedom but living it and screaming it.

Two of those people were Regina and Lars. Regina had heard the news on the radio. They were not trying to make it West. They had already done this. They were crossing back East, past the Wall, across the Sonnenallee in Neukölln. Just because they could.

They joined the crowds, laughing, screaming, singing songs, and there among the exultant masses, they ran into friends from the East. They kissed and hugged, overcome with wonderment. They stayed up all night and ended up at the only place in the world that made sense at that moment: a McDonald's in West Berlin. The buns are so fluffy, Regina told her friends, helping them cross the same spiritual boundary she had traversed, just a few months before.

And so Regina completed her impossible journey, from Berlin to Berlin and back again. A trip that took thousands of kilometers only to travel an inch. Or by another way of thinking, not to travel at all. The next step, for her and everyone else, would be not geographic, but ideational. They had torn down the Wall. The question now was how to make their once-divided home whole again. To turn it into a place that everyone, East and West, could inhabit together.

PART V

DEMOCRACY NOW

Chapter Twenty-Four

In the beginning it was all joy and celebration. In Sopron, you could nip over to Austria for a coffee and an *apfelstrudel* and be back in time for dinner. Daily life had a fresh feeling to it, as though a new chapter had begun. But transition is a vacuum. Pretty soon everyone gets sucked in. For Miklós Németh, for Imre Pozsgay, for so many other reformers, the fall was swift and hard. It wasn't an easy time to be a Communist politician, even a good one.

For Németh, the transition began on November 10, 1989, the day after the fall of the Berlin Wall—the *Mauerfall*. He came into his office to find a letter, rubber stamped three times by the Soviet authorities, denoting the heights of its issuing office. It stated that all nuclear weapons had been removed from Hungarian soil and transported back to the Soviet Union.

That this massive undertaking could have occurred without Németh knowing was all but unfathomable. The weapons were protected by concentric rings of security. The outer one was staffed by Hungarian military; the inner one, by Soviet officers installed by Moscow. To move nuclear weapons, numerous special train lines had to be requested—it was nearly five hundred kilometers from Tótvázsony, where the missiles had been stored in silos, to the border at Csap, in the Soviet Union (now Ukraine). That meant a lot of people averting their eyes, scared to speak up.

Németh placed a call to his defense minister, Ferenc Kárpáti. The silos are empty, he told him.

For fuck's sake, was the reply.

Even in this waning hour, the Soviet Union remained powerful. But all that time Németh had spent worrying that the Soviets might move against him, under his nose, invisibly, they were moving away.

Meanwhile, the people wanted democracy, *now*.

The opposition groups were so eager to kick-start the transition and hold elections that they prioritized political reforms. Major changes to the economy were tabled, to be resolved once a democratic government had formed. Németh was nonplussed. Doing it this way, he feared, would mean that economic decisions would be made simply with the interests of the ruling party in mind. And that with each subsequent election, new systems would cater to new interests—a recipe for corruption.

Németh preferred what he calls the Spanish Model, named after the transition following the fall of the Franco regime in the mid-1970s. There, they designed political and economic institutions in tandem, to insulate long-term economic planning from the vagaries of politics. Németh tried to speak to Péter Tölgyessy, an opposition leader from the Free Democrats, about this. Let's first establish the fundamentals of the new economy, he told him.

Tölgyessy, a thoughtful man, replied in earnest. You're probably right, he said. But if the public catches word that we are designing the future along with you Communists, we'll get destroyed. The people don't want to share the burden of the past with you. They don't want anything to do with you.

Just as with the fiery sermon of Viktor Orbán on the anniversary of Imre Nagy's death, in which Németh and the other reformers were lumped in with the other Communists, here again he was considered simply part of the problem. He was someone to be moved away from, not forward with.

Németh also called a meeting with József Antall, newly appointed head of the MDF. I know this will be unpopular and hard to accept, he said, but let me stay in office for another year. I will do the dirty work of making this country a functioning democracy with stable economic institutions. After that, I will step down and the opposition will take over once the country is on its feet.

No one would accept this, Antall replied.

Németh's idea was indeed madness: after so many decades of Communism, there was no way the opposition would allow him to retain power—even just for a year. But the exchange is revealing. When we talk about democracy, we usually do so in the language of the social contract—a shorthand for the agreement by which we come together as individuals to live with one another, and the rules that structure this engagement. According to this rubric, we trade off *natural* freedom—to do whatever we want; the freedom of the state of nature—for *social* freedom, a life with security and peace of mind, the conditions necessary to develop our talents and forge common bonds, constrained by law.

The principle that undergirds the social contract is popular sovereignty—the notion that state authority derives its legitimacy from citizen consent. In democracies, citizens are sovereign because they have the final say, up to and including the right to depose the government. In his *Second Treatise of Government* (1690), English philosopher John Locke asks rhetorically about a conflict between the people and their rulers, *"Who shall be Judge?"* He replies, *"The People shall be Judge."*

For most of us, these principles are sacrosanct. This is the problem with Németh's proposal—it certainly *seems* antidemocratic, suggesting he suspend popular rule to retain power. But Németh understood something vital about democracy: that transition might require a technocratic hour (that appears antithetical to popular sovereignty but may be necessary for it). Indeed, while classic texts explicate the principles of democracy, they hardly furnish the path to get there.

Németh was concerned that the opposition groups were rushing forward without first designing sound institutions. He wasn't critical of democracy, per se; he was critical of democracy *now*.

During those last months of 1989, Németh was also concerned about securing development aid. What we need, he told American officials, was a Marshall Plan 2.0—referring to the comprehensive aid package that rebuilt Western Europe after World War II. American interest was lukewarm—they didn't want to meddle in what was still considered the Soviet sphere of influence. Németh also raised the issue to Western European leaders—Kohl, Mitterrand, Thatcher—but without American leadership, the proposal was untenable.

Now that Eastern Europe wasn't the purview of the Soviet Union, it had lost strategic importance. The moment the Wall came down, the United States seemed to lose interest in what lay behind it. Politically, places like Hungary all but disappeared from world attention, like the nuclear weapons, spirited away in the dead of night.

At the Bush and Gorbachev summit at Malta, at the end of 1989, the American position was summed up neatly with the refrain "Malta will not be another Yalta." Meaning: they were not going to decide on the future of Europe. Both powers pledged to maintain the old order, even as it was falling away.

In the lead-up to the Hungarian elections, called for March 1990—the first fully free elections in the region (Poland's 1989 elections had been semi-free)—László was on the campaign trail in Sopron, giving speeches at MDF events. He was not running for office but liked public speaking and answering questions from people in the crowd, many of whom he knew.

After one event, a family friend approached him. He had been a colleague of László's father's—a Communist—whom László had known since he was a child. László embraced him enthusiastically. But when he peeled away, he saw fear in the man's eyes.

László, the man said. What will happen to me?

Pista Bácsi (Uncle István), László replied. Nothing will happen to you. You didn't do anything.

This comforted his friend. But László was shaken by the encounter. In all those years dreaming of transition, he had never thought about this. It had been Manichean in his mind: the bad Communists would be punished, and the good democrats would take over.

But now he understood something different: innocent people would get swept up in the recriminations too. How can you decide who was a *real* Communist, versus every other person who joined the Party just to get by? It's easy to vilify the state. But when it falls, you realize it's just a collection of people. All of whom were someone's Uncle István.

The impact of the elections—the MDF came out on top—was profound. Overnight, a whole society was turned upside down.

DEBRECEN IS THE SECOND MOST POPULOUS CITY IN HUNGARY, with over two hundred thousand residents. It was the capital of Hungary during the revolutions that swept Europe in 1848, and it was there, in the Reformed Great Church—Nagytemplom—that the Habsburg Empire was officially dethroned, putting a period to the lineage by which Otto von Habsburg would have been heir.

The center today bears some marks of its past grandeur, with buildings in the high Secessionist style popular in the 1880s. But generally grand old Debrecen is hard to find. Greatly damaged in World War II, the city had its face reconstructed and, after decades of Communist rule, it fell into disrepair.

Now Debrecen tells the story of Hungary in a different way. The buildings are clean and contemporary, with glass faces and shiny product displays, the streets filled with a hearty mix of bustling off-to-work types, mothers and prams, and elderly denizens making their slow way around the squares. But as with all places that privatized quickly, the commerce consists in characterless chain stores, straight-from-China retail, ready-to-eat food lacking local flavor. The speediness of this transformation belies its history: a capitalist scramble for markets as ravening as the colonial scramble for Africa.

Hungary today has no national supermarket chain. The market leader is Tesco, a British company that took advantage of the opening. Stories of this type are commonplace. Such and such industry is German; or such and such company seems Hungarian, but its profits go elsewhere. The transition to capitalism was abrupt and poorly regulated. People tried to be patient, but in many ways it was a bloodletting. A transition not from Communism to capitalism, but from one form of servitude to another.

In such conditions, of chaos and uncertainty, it was natural for people to long for a sense of order, a contiguity with the past. One border guard I spoke with, Imre Csapó, now curates a private gallery of border memorabilia in his house in Fertőrákos. He talks fondly about his days manning the lake during the Communist times, back when curfews were strictly enforced, and the beaches were patrolled by men in uniform.

There was a beauty to life back then, he says. People today run around *like pigs in the rain*.

I am in Debrecen now to see Mária. She is waiting for me at the station when I arrive. She is with her nephew, Mate, who will act as our translator. When I approach, Mária grips my hands, her eyes wide and welcoming beneath thick glasses.

In her old car we weave through new streets to her home, a modest house set back from the pavement, tucked into a leafy neighborhood on the outskirts. Mária sets the table, a spread of roasted root vegetables, chicken, and salads. Alcohol too. First *pálinka*, the local firewater, and then beer. Please, she says. *Drink*.

She pours herself one. There is no further negotiation.

We start slowly, beginning with the way back, her father's days in the resistance in 1956. One of her uncles knocked the red star from a factory in Debrecen, just as, in 1989, Mária would tear one off the city hall.

She proudly produces a scribbled-over draft of the first program of the picnic, dated July 3, 1989. She was the one who wrote it down; it is the treasure of her personal archive.

When we move on to the present, the tenor of the conversation shifts. The first anniversary celebration of the picnic, in 1990, went by without her. She was not invited; neither was Ferenc. By that time, everything had changed. The Communist era was over. Now the MDF was in power. They made the commemorative event a celebration of the party and an occasion for grandstanding. The new prime minister, József Antall was there, as was a young Angela Merkel, the one-day chancellor of a unified Germany, and Lothar de Maizière, the first and last freely elected leader of East Germany. The event was given a generic title: Europe Day.

Mária was hurt by her exclusion, but she wasn't surprised. So it is with success in politics. Many more claim credit when times are good than participated when they weren't. She offers a quote she attributes to Giuseppe Garibaldi, the famed Italian revolutionary of the nineteenth century: "We were few, however many remained."

Much of the hurt she feels is about Debrecen, her city—the place where it all began, now written out of the story. Debrecen is nicknamed the Guard of Freedom, she says. We don't just accept society; we try and change it.

It was Debrecen, she reminds me, that invited Otto von Habsburg to the same place where his family had been dethroned.

Her paean to Debrecen is familiar; it shares the melody and cadence of her love for her Hungarian brethren in Transylvania. They are both facets of nation.

In the West we frequently dismiss nationalism as regressive. And in many ways it is. But something about it makes sense to me now, especially as regards *place*, its logic of continuity that stays above the vicissitudes of power, that stays true when everything else comes into question.

This version of nation recalls Géza Szőcs's poem the "The Kolozs-vár Horror," from 1983, in which he writes of his beloved Transylvania. One night, concerned there might be a police raid on his apartment, he threw a cassette tape into his hometown's Szamos River. It had been gifted to him by his lover.

> For a long time afterwards, every time I
> crossed that bridge over the Szamos
> I could hear you calling from the water.

I can hear it: the voice of his beloved; the sounds of the police raid too. It is a poem about nation, about place. But as I read it now, I think it also says something about transition. For all our dreams of new beginnings, the past remains with us, for good and bad, recorded in the water.

Chapter Twenty-Five

Contemporary discussions about 1989 often default to inevitability narratives—that the Wall had to fall; that the collapse of the Soviet Union was predestined. But this certainly was not what it felt like at the time. The picnic organizers thought hundreds, maybe thousands, of acts of resistance would be necessary to effect real change. If the refugees had thought the GDR would fall so quickly, they wouldn't have risked their lives trying to escape it.

The time between the picnic and the *Mauerfall* was just two and a half months—an unsteady interregnum between the end of one world and the beginning of another. But it was a time of crippling uncertainty, especially for the East Germans, who wondered whether they would ever see their families again.

Margret Pfitzenreiter's mother was seventy-five at the time of the breach. She thought it would be at least a decade before cross-border travel might be possible. Given her age, that meant she might never see her daughter or grandchildren again.

These were consequential days. In some cases, the damage was long lasting. Simone Sobel came from a Party family. They learned about the breach on the nightly news. A report ran at 8:15 p.m. on August 19, showing video of the breakthrough, and there, front and center, was an image of Walter, clutching their youngest daughter. Simone's family was shocked at what she had done. They felt angry and betrayed. Later, after the Wall came down, they reconnected. But the rupture remained. Simone puts it simply: something broke when I left that couldn't be put back together.

Simone's parents were interrogated by the Stasi. Her father ran into trouble at work. The Stasi threatened to expel her brother from his position studying law. To this day, several members of Simone's family won't forgive her.

It wasn't just a question of those left behind. For many of the refugees, integrating into the West was challenging too. Before they even started their journey to Vienna, Katja and Oskar stopped at a supermarket so Katja could buy sanitary pads. She came back empty-handed, streaming tears. The array of selections, the colors, the prices, it was all too overwhelming. Rather than find one brand, there were ten. She didn't know what to do.

She also fretted about telephoning home. How could she tell her parents she wasn't coming back? She had to be careful with her words. Given the call was international it would certainly be listened in on. Katja steeled herself as she made the call. She didn't wail *Mama* as she wanted to when her mother picked up.

Vienna is beautiful, she said.

Then she hung up.

When Katja arrived at Oskar's family home in West Germany, there were so many people to meet—Oskar's friends and family friends. Everyone wanted to hear her story. But for all she was welcomed in, she felt herself pulling away. She spent much of those first days and weeks thinking about home. She revisited the time before her trip, its normalcy. Eating dinner with her family, as she had every other evening, sleeping under the same roof.

Katja struggled to find her place. One day, she and Oskar took a drive to a large shopping center in a nearby town. They were looking to buy bedsheets. Passing through the aisles they came upon a handsome set—satin, nicer than any either had ever slept on before. They liked them, but Oskar wanted to wait a day to think about it. Katja pushed back. Tomorrow the sheets will be gone, she said.

The idea that the shelves might remain stocked from one day to the next was hard for her to fathom. Oskar's family found these quirks of integration endearing. They all had a good laugh when Katja couldn't figure out the dishwasher. Katja laughed too. But she felt uncomfortable being dependent on Oskar's family, sequestered in their house, without any means of supporting herself.

The challenges of refugee integration are immense, as they always have been. In one of her lesser-known essays, "We Refugees" (1943), Hannah Arendt discusses her own experience after the Second World War. "We lost our home, which means the familiarity of daily life," she writes. "If we are saved we feel humiliated, and if we are helped we feel degraded."

With each passing day, Katja grew more homesick. She also missed her home*land*, Dresden. In West Germany, she was free—she could walk about wherever she liked, talk freely without wondering if anyone was listening in. But if this was freedom, it wasn't what she had expected. It wasn't enough to be free: She wanted to be free *at home*. She wanted her parents to be free too.

The word Katja uses for home here is *heimat*. It's hard to translate. The word *home* doesn't quite do it justice. It is linked strongly to an idea of belonging—the connection we feel to the land of our birth, a stretch of earth we feel we know. It is not home, exactly, but feeling at home in that home.

Katja's homesickness was oppressive, and increasingly it weighed on her relationship with Oskar. By the end of 1989 they had split up; Katja stayed in the West, but moved away to study medicine, as had been her childhood dream.

Katja wasn't the only one to struggle through those first months in the West—so did the Nagler brothers. Stephan was just eighteen, a few years younger than Katja, and Andreas sixteen. They were still, all of them, just kids.

After the refugee center at Gießen, the brothers were resettled to a camp in Schöppingen, in the northwest of West Germany. They slept in a large room with twenty other people, Andreas on the top bunk, Stephan below. At night, they dreamed about return. Within a few days, Andreas collapsed into a fit of crying. He missed their mother.

Stephan took him in his arms. We'll find a way back, he told him.

I'll never forget that, Andreas says to me now.

The power of that embrace is hard to appreciate, for those of us who have never been refugees. They had to choose: to stay with people they loved or go out and find freedom; they couldn't have both. It's an impossible dilemma, because freedom and love aren't separate and discrete. Without love, freedom might be nothing but loss.

After the camp, Stephan and Andreas went to extended family in Bavaria. Like so many *Ossis* who came to meet their *Wessi* relatives, they felt they were greeted coldly, as though their Easternness was a kind of stain. They felt like strangers. Because he was older, Stephan was sent to work at a factory out in the Bavarian woods. He worked long hours with few people to speak to. Back home, Stephan had always been popular in school—friends, girls, a clique he traveled with. At the factory, he felt like a leper.

When the Wall fell, Stephan learned about it at work, where the GDR was ridiculed by his *Wessi* colleagues. You guys are crazy, one of the other factory workers said to him, the *Ossi*, in passing.

———

IT WASN'T JUST THE REFUGEES AND THEIR FAMILIES WHO WERE blindsided by the *Mauerfall*; the same could be said of elites. Despite his lofty rhetoric, West German chancellor Helmut Kohl clearly didn't expect anything imminent. On November 9, 1989, he was on a state visit to Poland. In a televised address he quipped that he felt he was in the wrong place. President George H. W. Bush heard what was happening in Berlin on the news. Startled, he said to his aides. "If the Soviets are going to let the Communists fall in East Germany . . . [they're] more serious than I realized."

President Bush didn't share Reagan's faith in Gorbachev, who he felt was just another Soviet propagandist who would resort to violence if he felt he was losing control. This was the CIA's assessment as well—even after the Wall had come down.

In fact, circumstances were extremely volatile. On the night of November 9, Valentin Falin, the Soviet ambassador in Bonn, threatened to send a million troops to the border to make sure it stayed shut. Gorbachev's foreign minister, Eduard Shevardnadze, later remarked that in those early hours after the breach, they were sitting on the precipice of a third world war.

There were a lot of ways the Wall could have come down. The same can be said about reunification. From the vantage of the present, it seems obvious the two Germanies would get back together. But at the time, the notion of reunification was nothing short of shocking. On September 28, 1989, the magazine *Quick* published a survey on the subject—the first of its kind, with respondents on both sides of the Wall (1,471 in the West; and 1,410 in the East). In the West, most respondents saw it as possible within ten years (56 percent) or thirty years (28 percent). In the East, the most common answer was that reunification would never happen (36 percent).

Six weeks later, the two national histories seemed destined to collide.

On November 13, 1989, just days after the fall of the Wall, during an extraordinary, ten-hour session of the GDR's Parliament, the Volkskammer, speakers publicly denounced the Communist leadership and demanded elections. In early December, a Round Table formed to address the opposition's many demands. Chief among these were the dissolution of the State Security Service—the Stasi.

On December 12, as many as three hundred thousand people gathered in Leipzig, carrying flags and shouting *Wir sind ein Volk* (We are one people).

On Christmas Eve, December 24, 1989, it was decided there would be visa-free travel between the two states. On that day, finally, the Inner-German border went the way of the Wall. For people across Germany, this was the wildest day—especially for the refugees who had just crossed to the West and could now come back East to visit. The borders were set to open at exactly midnight—just as they had on September 11 in Hungary—and huge lines of cars snaked from the still-guarded border.

When Annette slotted into the queue, the scene was mayhem. Everybody was screaming and celebrating. The traffic was so great, the authorities decided to open the border earlier, at just before 7 p.m. She and Frank sped the remaining three hundred kilometers to their hometown. It felt like we were flying, she says.

All these people who just a few months earlier had risked their lives to flee westward were together once again, exultant, heading back home. And beside them, an equally lengthy queue of East Germans headed the other way, to see family in the West. The encounters were magical: equal parts awesome and strange. When Marlies Grunert's parents came to visit them in Bremen, they brought a Trabant-full of gifts: especially food and blankets. They had heard how bad life was out west, and they thought this would be helpful.

The Nagler boys were also visited by their parents. The first thing their mother did when she arrived was slap her sons' faces. Andreas first. She hadn't even stepped off the train.

It was a time of euphoria, but confusion too. For many, this was a future they had not asked for. Jenny Erpenbeck, the writer, was a young woman when the Wall came down, forced quickly to adapt to radically new circumstances, even though she herself never moved from her home in East Berlin. "I am not a refugee," she remarks in a 2018 lecture, "but my past also took place in a different country."

Erpenbeck's feeling of being out of place was compounded by the treatment she received by West Germans. Just before Christmas 1989, a West German man drove over to East Berlin to hand out fancy wrapping paper to passersby. This was intended as an act of kindness, but Erpenbeck found it grating. "The present time that I live in is beautiful," she felt the West German man was telling her. "It is already the future." By contrast, the present time the East Germans were living in, he insinuated, was "just now turning into a 'past present,' that is to say, a past, which might best be left behind in that winter darkness, trampled into the mud."

Another spin on the *Ossi-Wessi* divide—the revelation they weren't just out of place, but out of time—that they would be forced to adapt to a present other than their own.

Hermann and Margret crossed back to the East for the first time in early 1990 to buy back their old Trabant which the GDR authorities had retrieved from the Hungarian borderlands. To return to the West, they had to cross GDR territory and sit for border checks. The experience was unsettling, driving back in their old car, traversing old roads.

Facing the same old border police too.

Stop here! They commanded. *ID!*

That sound of authority, so familiar. Margret felt rage well up inside. They were forced to pay an exit tax, as they were no longer considered East Germans. Margret wanted to say something to the officers, something that carried her contempt at this abuse—of being considered an alien in her own home. She did the best thing she could think of: when they asked for payment, she demanded a receipt.

The *Mauerfall* had been earthshaking, but for all the glimmer of the new dawn, the old order remained ever-present. Nowhere was this clearer than with the Stasi. On January 15, 1990, columns of smoke were seen billowing from the Stasi headquarters in Berlin. Everyone knew what this meant: they were burning files. That day, demonstrators in East Berlin stormed the Stasi headquarters. Agents did as much as they could before the masses swelled outside their gates, pushed through, and occupied the premises.

The past's presentness was a given in the new GDR.

HARALD JÄGER WAS EXPECTING MY CALL. ÁRPÁD BELLA, THE BORder guard who oversaw the breach in Hungary, had helped us get in touch. They are friends now, in that special way of people with shared experiences—like bands of brothers; here, two lieutenant colonels, whose split-second decisions helped reshape the world.

Jäger lives in an apartment on the outskirts of Berlin. He is a large man with a weighty presence, and he speaks in a deep, throaty baritone. When he takes my hand, it's almost swallowed in his own.

On November 9, 1989, at Bornholmerstraße, he did the right thing. But his is not an untroubled brow. Jäger worked for the Stasi for over thirty years—climbing the ranks, interrogating, note taking, stalking. In our conversation, he breezes past these years, but they are there, legible on his face. Our interview is halting. When he looks at me, I sometimes find myself looking away.

Jäger is happy to revel in 1989. But I am pressing him now on something different: not the moment of change, but the kind of world he helped bring about. About this, he has reservations. His speech slows; the tone shifts from the monumental register to a more tragic one.

If I had known then, he says, that by opening the gate I would bring about the end of the GDR, I never would have done it.

His rationale for opening the gate was simple. The regime had gone too far. The Wall was supposed to protect East German citizens from the insidious forces of the West—especially predatory capitalism and unrepentant fascism. But that's not what it was doing: it was locking them in.

He makes the point in structural terms: the Wall was one-sided. If you tried to cross to the West—*out* of the GDR—the Wall's defenses were all but impenetrable. The gate at Bornholmerstraße was strong enough to stop armored vehicles. But heading to the East—*into* the GDR—it could have been pushed open by a bicycle.

After the *Mauerfall*, Jäger was one of many Stasi officials who had dreams of saving the East German state. In this way, their position mirrored those of the opposition. Transition makes strange bedfellows.

In a statement from December 9, 1989, the Round Table claimed its goal was a "new, true socialism," a "third way," something between the capitalist West and the Communist East. They wanted a functioning example of democratic socialism; reunification was not its objective. (Democracy *now*, but reunification *later*.)

So while the people in the streets were increasingly shouting *Wir sind ein Volk*, the position of the Round Table was instead *Wir sind das Volk*. The distinction is important: they were not saying we are *one* people. They were saying we are *the* people.

Nevertheless, reunification steamrolled ahead. The East was bleeding people, and the GDR economy was on the edge of collapse. West Germany took control. Economic institutions of the East were wrapped into and replaced by those of the West. Even basic East German budgetary decisions were becoming subject to West German approval. Any idea that the two states might merge as equals was quickly discarded.

The same was true politically. On March 18, 1990, the GDR held its first free democratic elections. These were putatively East German elections, but West German parties were allowed to compete, and the CDU (center-right) and SPD (center-left) were easily the highest vote getters, with 40.8 percent and 21.9 percent respectively. The leading opposition groups of the GDR—the Neues Forum, Demokratie Jetzt (Democracy Now), among others—won only a handful of seats. The colonial tenor of this process was hard to ignore. Jens Reich, of the Neues Forum, described it as the arrival of "the Bonn Hippopotamus," which came through and destroyed everything in its way.

Reunification was moving so fast that many across the West grew concerned. French premier François Mitterrand's advisor, Jacques Attali, told Németh in Hungary: I will be as a tourist on the moon before we agree upon reunification! British prime minister Margaret Thatcher felt similarly. "I love the Germans so much," she proclaimed, "I would like to see them living in two countries."

But European concerns were assuaged by broader plans for integration that would tie together not only the Germanies, but also everyone else. This would become formalized in 1992, at the signing of the Maastricht Treaty, with the formation of the European Union.

On October 3, 1990, the territory of the GDR officially joined the jurisdiction of West Germany. The word they use for this process is the *Wende*. It signifies something more powerful than simple reunification; it is a turning point, or a reversal. As in: from that point forward, history changed course. There was no going back.

Harald Jäger found himself out of a job and living in a society in which he was reviled. He struggled to find work; when prospective employers learned of his Stasi past, he was swiftly shown the door. Of the many things he thought about in trying to comfort himself during those days, chief among these was a conversation he'd had with his sister, whom he called late in the evening on November 9, 1989.

He told her he'd opened the border. She had been asleep. There was silence on her end of the line as she tried to come to terms with the significance of what he had said.

Did you shoot anyone? she asked.

No.

Good.

Revisiting this three decades later, Jäger breaks into a smile. He is pleased his sister didn't judge him harshly—however significant his actions might have been; whatever new world they might yet usher forth.

Chapter Twenty-Six

In 1992, Mária went to the third anniversary of the picnic, even though, again, she was not invited. They didn't look me in the eye, she says of her reception. She stood about anonymously during the speeches, a face in the crowd. Her worst fears were confirmed. It was just another celebration for the MDF. Debrecen wasn't even mentioned.

Ferenc also attended the commemoration in 1992. He was horrified by the dull political messaging. Our beautiful event had turned into a funereal-like thing, he says.

A few days later, Mária picked up the phone and tried to call the old numbers she had used to get in touch with Pozsgay, hoping maybe they still worked; that maybe he would be there to explain what had happened. But those lines were now dead; new ones weren't easy to obtain.

Pozsgay had run for a seat in Parliament in the 1990 elections but lost. Németh also ran for Parliament in 1990; he won a seat but lasted only ten months. In 1991, he left Hungary and went to work at the European Bank for Reconstruction and Development (EBRD) in London. The bank had been set up to aid the recovery of the former Eastern Bloc, but it was vastly underfunded—hardly the Marshall Plan 2.0 Németh had envisioned.

Németh found it hard to be so far from Hungary; harder still to know the new leadership wanted it this way. Over the subsequent years, Németh frequently received letters from members of the new government. The letters did not suggest, as he had once hoped, that he return home and reenter politics. Rather, they suggested the opposite: they supported him where he was.

There is an adage in politics, that you want your friends close and your enemies closer. But Németh was a liminal figure—neither opposition, nor really Communist—someone no one could quite figure out. They were happy to keep him at a distance.

When I ask him about this now, he demurs. I have no regrets, he says. Politics is the dirtiest business.

One day, when Németh was living in London, he was offered a generous sum of money to return. Two Hungarian entrepreneurs—men who had made it rich during transition—wanted him to start a new party. But Németh sent them away. If I took that money, he says, I would be in their pockets.

Németh's stance is a principled one. But it reveals how ill-suited he was for democratic rule. There is no freedom from money in politics. Thus, the principled road is also no road. Being honest means abandoning politics to those who aren't.

IT WOULD BE HARD TO OVERSTATE THE SPEED OF CHANGE. ON February 25, 1991, the Warsaw Pact formally dissolved. A few months later, on June 30, the last Soviet soldier left Hungary. Finally, the Soviet curse had truly lifted. Across the country it was a day of drunken merriment. The pubs in Sopron offered a deal: *Vodka, 20 percent off.*

That summer, László was vacationing with his family in Italy. One day while getting an ice cream they strolled past an electronics store, which had televisions running in the windows. There, in full color, was Boris Yeltsin, standing atop a tank in Moscow. On another screen, an image of the Duma, breached, fire issuing from its windows.

It was a coup attempt against Gorbachev—the so-called August

Coup, which started on August 19, 1991, precisely two years from
the day of the picnic. This was exactly what everyone had feared. It's
over, László thought. Gorbachev will be gone, the hardliners will take
over. They will march their tanks across the border tomorrow and
take Budapest.

Though the threat passed, fear ran deep in the national psyche—
and remained even later, when on Christmas Day, 1991, the Soviet
Union collapsed. One never knew what horrors might be around the
corner.

József Antall died in 1993 from cancer. It quickly became clear the
MDF would struggle without his leadership. A void was created in the
political scene, soon to be filled, in 1994, by none other than the Socialist Party, led by the resuscitated figure of Gyula Horn—Németh's former foreign minister.

Horn's rise, beside Németh's fall, is a plot twist worthy of high
drama—with the groundwork paved by Németh himself. It was Horn
who was photographed cutting the Iron Curtain on June 27, 1989,
not Németh. Later, on September 10, it was Horn who made the
announcement about the border opening. Both moves made sense—
Horn was foreign minister, after all. But given the transitive power
of television, it was Horn who became linked with these propitious
events, not Németh.

The turnaround verges on farce. Within Németh's cabinet, Horn
had been the one most resistant to opening the border—especially
given the stepwise, ad hoc way things transpired. As noted Hungarian historian and journalist Andreas Oplatka explained it to me, Horn
detested the picnic. But he had no trouble later taking credit. Horn
was a political opportunist who didn't really stand for anything. Or as
Oplatka puts it: He was a politician. He stood for himself.

In the years that followed, 1994–1998, a new cult of personality
rose around Horn, centered on his role, on June 27, in cutting the border
wire. After the socialists came back to power, it took a few years for the
opposition to regroup. But by the next election, the stage was set for the

return of a man, already famous for fire and ambition, who once commanded the Soviets to get out.

Viktor Orbán.

MANY OF THE EAST GERMAN REFUGEES I SPOKE WITH DECIDED TO
stay and make a life in the West. It was comfortable there. But complica-
tions abounded, especially at first. Many were called out for their *Ossi*
ways—stereotyped as lazy, reliant on handouts. The children often
struggled in their new schools, teased for their Eastern clothing, being
told they smelled. One day when working in retail, Annette made a
mistake and a shopper remarked: *stupid Easterner, go back to where you
came from.*

Even the Sobels, by any measure an integration success story, faced
obstacles. When they tried to buy a plot of land to build a house the
owners told them they would not sell to East Germans.

The refugees also faced hardship when they went back East to
visit. People were resentful of how comparatively well-off they were
in the West, earning better money in the stronger economy. This is
another facet of the *Ossi-Wessi* divide: feeling alien in the West, but also
estranged at home.

Margret Pfitzenreiter stopped attending class reunions. They will
just talk about how badly they're doing, she says, as though they have
forgotten what it was like in the GDR.

Hermann thinks the problem comes down to how quickly capitalism spread to the East. Overnight, people became hyper-materialistic,
and bitter at the West even as they enjoyed its freedoms. In the new East
people think freely, Hermann says, but they think mostly about money.

Other refugees returned to the East. In May 1992, Stephan Nagler,
now twenty-two, moved back to the village where he was born. By this
point, he had been working for some time as an apprentice at a window-
making business. Now he was ready to start a company of his own.
Andreas moved back a few years later, in 1996. Either boy could have

gone anywhere in the world, but they decided they didn't want to. In the West, they felt, they would only ever be outsiders.

There is something beautiful about such a homecoming. But for many refugees the return was not easy, as the home that awaited them had little in common with the one they left behind.

Toward the end of 1991, the Grunerts decided to move back to the East. Their reasons included the family house, which they had built with their own hands. Marlies had been twenty-one, Bernd just two years older, in 1978, when Marlies's father had felled the first trees to begin the frame. They borrowed a machine to cut stones, bit by bit culling their home from the material nature of the GDR itself. The house was everything to them. They finished it in 1989, just before they fled.

It was an awkward return. They had been gone only two years but found themselves avoiding a lot of their old stomping grounds. They even shopped in different supermarkets. Marlies refused to visit the village she used to work in, because that way she wouldn't run into people she didn't want to see. It was as though they were living on the outskirts of their former life. By comparison, the *Ossi-Wessi* split seems almost simple. This was something different: a compound fracture that never quite heals.

Wolfgang Hilbig's novel *The Sleep of the Righteous* (2002) tells the story of an Easterner who relocated to the West, only to return, haunted by the ghosts of his not-quite-buried past. He finds himself looking through windows when the curtains aren't drawn, listening for the footsteps of his former Stasi shadow. "In a moment I could expect him to call my name." For the protagonist, the old animosities of the GDR remain fresh.

> No one will believe that you can't help this rage, that it's in your flesh and blood. And that this rage is made of memories that may not even be your own, premonitions or memories that were sunk within you without your really knowing them. Without your knowing it, a time bomb rests within you.

The protagonist feels prisoner to his memories, which meld with the soil of the old GDR, locking him into place. This haunting is the other side of *heimat*—its bounded, always-there-ness.

It's not easy returning to a country once abandoned, especially if in the interim it ceased to exist.

———

USUALLY, WE SEPARATE FACTS FROM THEIR RETELLING. HISTORY from the historian. Politics from the archive. But in post-*Wende* East Germany, these were inseparable. The question of politics *was* the question of the archive.

Though the Stasi itself was officially abolished on the day of the *Wende*, the problem of the files remained. All told, the Stasi had collected records on millions of East German citizens. A debate raged. Should they be destroyed—a true break with the past? But wasn't there a danger in forgetting? And yet, if the files were opened, mightn't this tear the country apart—all those secrets, animosities, and betrayals suddenly out in the open for everyone to see?

The government decided that citizens had the right to view their records. On November 14, 1991, the Stasi Documents Act was passed, after which the archive of Stasi records was opened, allowing citizens to inspect their files.

By this time mountains of files had already been destroyed. So many paper shredders were used to destroy files; when they gave out, agents resorted to ripping up pages by hand. Additional shredders were purchased in West Berlin. Destruction was also in miniature: individual Stasi employees went through their own records and eliminated any they considered damning. Like soldiers in the snow, they dragged branches behind them to cover their tracks.

Even so, millions of records remained—with new ones recovered every day. The Stasi were so organized in their manner of ripping up documents—often depositing whole files into a single garbage bag—that they ultimately facilitated the process of piecing them back together. There is a collective in Nuremberg—popularly called the puzzlers—who reconstruct the files by hand. They use conventional methods—tape, tweezers, gloves—but also increasingly a digital instrument referred to as the unshredder, which pairs shards of paper based on the shapes of their edges.

This is an important part of reconciliation, but also a curse. With each new record comes secrets exposed, betrayals unveiled—among neighbors, coworkers, family members, friends.

The problem wasn't just the files; it was also people. By the time of its fall, the Stasi organization had as many as ninety thousand official employees and nearly two hundred thousand unofficial ones— *inoffizielle Mitarbeiter*, or "informal collaborators" (IMs). What would become of them? They were still around.

Wolfang Hilbig's novel, *The Sleep of the Righteous*, returns us to this moment, and the lingering presence of the IMs. What he portrays is a double game: informers, incapable of letting go of their pursuits; the informed-upon, beset by paranoia. Neither is able to let go of the past, until the other is gone.

One day when he is back home, Hilbig's protagonist finds himself confronted by the Stasi agent who had followed him. It is long after the *Wende*, and the interaction unnerves him. Back home, he tries to recall the face of this informer.

> I tried to remember how he looked, his face, his build . . . and strangely, as I did so, I looked into the mirror, as though I could remember his face only with the help of my own.

Seeing him again later, the protagonist realizes that only by killing the former agent can he rid himself of this stain. "How could I describe the strange feeling that seized me at this moment?" he asks once the deed is done. "It was a *sense of home* that came to me."

In fiction we can rid ourselves of our demons. In the real world, they are not so easily dispatched.

Generally, former Stasi officials stopped hunting their former prey, but they struggled to find work. Some of the old Stasi hands took jobs at Western corporations expanding into Eastern markets. No one knew how to navigate these waters better than they did. Perhaps the skill set—exploitation, expropriation, data collection—is more compatible than we like to admit. These days, in our era of expansive security protocols and omnipresent digital surveillance, we say that *data is the new oil*. But the Stasi always knew this. For them, data was the old oil too.

Economic transition was terrifically hard in post-*Wende* East Germany—with joblessness, the continued flight to the West, factories falling into disuse, and towns abandoned. The numbers are stark: in April 1990 the number of unemployed in the GDR was sixty-five thousand. By the end of 1991, it ballooned to between five hundred thousand and two million. But shortly these conditions began to improve, due in large part to the "German Unity Fund," which distributed billions of Deutsche Marks toward reconstruction—precisely the kind of funding that Németh wanted for Hungary, but which he never obtained. The first transfer payments to East Germany came in June 1991 to the tune of 143 billion Deutsche Marks. In 1992, this rose to 173 billion. And so it went, year after year, up to 200 billion in 2000. The total for the decade amounted to 1.6 trillion Deutsche Marks.

It was not easy for Westerners to foot the bill. And it was not easy for people in the East to feel they were entering the union as beggars. But with each passing year, the economies grew more intertwined.

In 1994, at the end of August, nearly four full years after reunification, the last Soviet troops finally left the territory of the former East Germany. Five years later, in 1999, Hungary, the Czech Republic, and Poland joined NATO. It was a whole new world.

Chapter Twenty-Seven

It was 1999, the precipice of a new millennium. For the organizers of the picnic, this meant the ten-year anniversary. They felt some urgency to reclaim the event. If they didn't tell the story correctly, the truth might be lost forever.

Starting in 1997, László Nagy, László Magas, Pál Csóka and others decided to create the Pan-European Picnic '89 Foundation. They would draft an authoritative account of the events of August 19, 1989, and collect the memoirs of everyone involved, compiling these documents as part of an archive. For the anniversary, they would organize a conference at the Pannonia Hotel in Sopron. Their motto was a quotation from American social theorist and author Thomas Sowell: "There are only two ways of telling the complete truth—anonymously and posthumously."

A lot had gone wrong in the telling of the story. It wasn't just the MDF and Horn who had perverted its meaning—it was politicians across the political spectrum.

The 1999 event was a grand affair. As many as five hundred people squeezed into the opulent conference room of the hotel in Sopron. Leaders from across Europe showed up. As did the poet Géza Szőcs. János Rumpf made a photograph exhibit in the lobby. In the evening, they held a concert in Fertőrákos, in a theater carved into a cave. Prime Minister Viktor Orbán was a special guest.

This time, both Mária and Ferenc were invited. An honorary Bell of Freedom was gifted by the city of Debrecen to Sopron to mark the occasion. It is now at the border, on the site of the breach. In his speech, Ferenc attempted to restore the spirit of the picnic. All this dirty politics, he said, takes away from the power of the story, which is about human morale.

This morale, he said, is what brought down the Berlin Wall.

Ferenc had hoped to elevate the proceedings above the squabble over credit-taking. But the 1999 event did as much to generate disputes as resolve them—especially regarding the role of Árpád Bella. Until this anniversary, Bella was an obscure figure—the organizers didn't even remember his name. But in 1999, he rose to prominence. This ruffled many feathers.

Bella's path was not easy. In the weeks and months after the picnic, Bella worried that the political winds might shift. That he would be forced to stand trial. For the first anniversary events, Bella was nowhere to be seen. It was ten years later, when László started to organize the anniversary events, that he came into conversation with the editor from *Kisalföld*, a small newspaper in western Hungary, which had previously run a story incorrectly crediting a different man—István Róka—as the border guard who stood the line that day. Róka had been happy to take the credit and repeated the claim to advance his own political career. But now the editor gave László the correct name: Árpád Bella.

László called Bella and invited him to speak. Bella was distrusting, but eventually agreed. At the conference, before hundreds of onlookers and the glinty eyes of video cameras, Bella spoke directly: he was angry that his orders hadn't been clearer, that he was left alone out there on the crossroads of history.

Bella ascended to central stage. But his speech would not be the final word here. Indeed, the conflict to come had already been foreshadowed. In 1999, Viktor Orbán arranged that Bella be given an award for his service—the Officer's Cross for his humane behavior at the border. But Gyula Kovács—Bella's superior—had won that same award, for the same reason, in 1994, when the Socialist Party was in power.

The past keeps changing, László had told me when we first met. I'm beginning to understand what he meant.

———

THESE DAYS, FERENC LIVES IN AN ART AND POETRY GARDEN ON the outskirts of Lake Balaton. It is an enclosed fortress with high walls and a wooden gate, with the letter *F* etched into the center and the word *Galeria* strung above the top. If tearing down the Iron Curtain was an attempt to forge European openness, this little sanctuary is a way of finding freedom of another sort—a contemplative space away from the clamor of modern society.

It is here, sipping fizzy drinks beneath the shade of a broad and leafy tree, that I glean something essential about the picnic. On the outside, social movements often appear as a single, homogeneous mass. But on the inside, they are composed of lots of independent voices. They march in the same direction, but that doesn't mean they are all saying the same thing.

For Mária Filep, the picnic was a humanitarian intervention—a care for refugees initially motivated by the Hungarians in Transylvania. For Magas, it was a political cause, toward bringing about a democratic Hungary. For Ferenc, it was something more abstract. It was about gathering a community of people who wanted to write and think and talk like he did.

Walking through Ferenc's garden, this vision is still manifest, his wooden gate like a portal to an almost mythological world. Everywhere along the curated path are inscriptions of poetry and philosophy—etched into trees, painted on stones, woven into artworks. Chief among these are the writings of German philosopher Friedrich Nietzsche.

"Those who know they are profound strive for clarity," reads one placard screwed onto a wooden stake. "Those who would like to seem profound strive for obscurity." (*Wer sich tief weiß, bemüht sich um Klarheit; wer der Menge tief scheinen möchte, bemüht sich um Dunkelheit.*") The quote is from Nietzsche's *The Gay Science*. The appeal of such lines to Ferenc is clear—he, of humble origins, who had a rough introduction to the world of intellectuals. And of politicians.

In our conversation, Ferenc hopscotches between ideas, drawing liberally from history and philosophy, often drifting into allegory. Imagine you are enclosed in a barrack, he says. A barrack, where the ceiling is so low you cannot stand up straight. You must sit on your knees and crane your neck to see the light. In addition, the people who made this barrack are tiny. They see no problem with this confined world. They dislike you and distrust your discontent.

This is what it was like in Communist Hungary, he says. That is, if you tried to think for yourself. You had to crouch on your knees and suffer insult when all you wanted was to stand up straight and tear away the goddamn ceiling and see what it was that was really out there.

The hope was that with the help of the MDF we could tear away this ceiling, he says.

It is a powerful image. It bears the imprint of Plato's cave. In Book VII of the *Republic*, Plato introduces his famous allegory via a dialogue between Socrates and his interlocutor, Glaucon. We are asked to imagine prisoners chained up in a cave, facing inward into its depths. Before them are inverted images projected against the stone. Since the prisoners cannot move their necks, these images are all they know of the world.

These are "strange prisoners you're telling of," Glaucon remarks.

"They're like us," Socrates replies.

This is the nature of society, the dialogue suggests. We are all bound in place and have come to mistake our constricted viewpoints for truth. Plato's critique remains resonant. It also clarifies the problem of freedom. The point isn't just to be free from the cave; but to be free from illusion.

The freedom Ferenc sought from Communism wasn't just about travel, or assembly, or any of the other classical markers of liberalism.

What he wanted was for people to expand the aperture of their gaze. To break free of the bounds of their social world and realize the artifice by which it was constituted. Yet Ferenc escaped Communism only to find himself caught in a similarly constricted worldview: nationalism. This was an illusion too.

Plato's allegory of the cave closes with a note of admonition. Let's say one man breaks free, Socrates posits. He escapes his shackles, comes up to the light and sees the world for how it really is. What will happen to him once he goes back into the cave and tells the others? Will they so easily be convinced their worldviews were misguided? "Wouldn't he be the source of laughter?" Socrates asks. And if the others were able to get their hands free of their shackles, "wouldn't they kill him?"

Ferenc left the MDF in 1990. The party made clear to him that he was not wanted, that his ideas were too unruly and contrarian and no longer fit the image they were trying to cultivate, the party they were trying to become. Ferenc struggled through the transition years of the 1990s and remains angry about the course the country has taken. But he is not giving up. The most important thing, he thinks, is vigilance.

Barracks keep being built, he says. But if we are stubborn enough, we may yet tear them down.

———

UWE BERGANDER NEVER LEFT THE GDR BEHIND. WHEREVER HE went, it followed him.

It wasn't long after crossing the border, on September 11, 1989, that he began to feel the pull to go back. He and Anja had gotten as far as Salzburg, to the nearby lake town of Mondsee, encircled by the majestic Alps. Just a few kilometers ahead was the West German border.

It was all so clean. The grass was cut so nicely; Uwe felt bad walking on it. He turned to Anja. I can't stay here, he said.

They drove back to the exact gate they had just crossed so many hours before. But they didn't have visas to enter Hungary. And so, the Iron Curtain again: the same barrier that had once prevented them from leaving the East now barred them from going back. Uwe was devastated. He felt he had just earned the right to free movement. And he had. He was free to go anywhere except the one place he wanted. Home. He felt resigned to his fate: that wherever he went, there the Wall would be.

Uwe had been eight years old when the Wall went up. He was troubled by it, even then. He was kicked out of school for making critical remarks, but later reinstated after apologizing. He battled with depression throughout his childhood.

At university in Berlin he met an exchange student from France named Silvia. They walked the city and she brought him books from West Berlin, which they would read together in the cocoon of his apartment. There he was, suddenly impossibly happy, their conversation, a nourishment for which he had so long been starved. But one day he came home to find his closet rummaged through, a book taken away—a forbidden volume about the opposition in Poland. Uwe rushed over to Silvia's student house, but she was gone.

When he returned to his flat there was a letter directing him to report to a local Stasi office. There, an officer addressed him curtly. You have contacts with the French secret service, the man told him. For this you should go to prison. Another officer questioned him, then another. Uwe sat in shock. He knew he would be kicked out of university, if not worse. And as he sat, the hole into which he had fallen grew deeper and deeper. Finally, he agreed to help them look for her, Silvia, this girl he also loved.

Uwe informed for the Stasi for thirteen years. He closed himself off from the few friends he had. If he didn't see them, he couldn't learn anything dangerous, that's how he reasoned it. The world around him shrank. He grew deeply paranoid. He felt the Stasi could read his mind. He started work on a novel—maybe if he came clean with his thoughts, he would have nothing to hide. He started attending readings, in the process of which he befriended an established writer named Fritz Rudolf Fries, who encouraged him to publish. Uwe's novel, *Balance*, came out in 1988.

It was an exhilarating time. But hanging out with Fries and the other writers of East Berlin meant Uwe was suddenly immersed in a world of opposition figures. The more he spent time with them, the more uncomfortable he felt. He didn't want to have to report on these new friends, so he broke ties with them too. This group of independent, creative thinkers, the very community he had always sought, he felt he could only protect by turning away.

Later Uwe learned that Fries was working for the Stasi too.

This is how it was back then. The Wall was everywhere, even within. There is an expression for this: the *Mauer im Kopf* (the Wall in the head). Here again, the problem of Plato's cave: to escape what binds you, you must also escape the mindset it imposes.

Those first years after transition, Uwe was beset by nightmares in which he found himself working again for the Stasi. Several times he contemplated suicide. Throughout the 1990s, stories broke about writers and intellectuals in the GDR being outed as Stasi informers. Uwe read the newspapers with dread that his name would appear, that he would be smeared as a liar, a backstabber. A Judas.

One of those writers, outed as a Stasi informant in 1993, was Christa Wolf.

Uwe moved to Munich in part because it was far away from his former life in Berlin. There he could be free of the people he was ashamed to see. To Bavaria, no less: the corner of West Germany least hospitable to Easterners, where, in 1997, during the so-called Leaflet Affair, flyers were passed around to incite violence against *Ossis*, claiming that the Wall should be built back up.

Before the fall of the Wall, Uwe used to dream about West Berlin, and a street—an unnamed, imagined avenue—to which he returned. This, it seems to me, is the story of Uwe's life, a street he looks for but cannot find.

Chapter Twenty-Eight

A whole world ended in 1989; and in 2001, a new one was birthed. It was a journey from one September 11 to another, you might say. Gone were the days of the Cold War, the Soviet Union, the *evil empire*; in came the likes of Osama bin Laden and Saddam Hussein, Afghanistan and Iraq, the *axis of evil*. The euphoria of the *Mauerfall* was replaced by a new desire to build walls—between Israel and Palestine, along the US-Mexico border, around the EU. The age of borderlessness proved short-lived.

We don't talk anymore about freedom like we did in 1989—freedom for collectivities, continents even; freedom for people fleeing oppression, wherever it is they were coming from. Now freedom is a bounded construct. It is for people within the polity. Walls quickly became reimagined as instruments not just to stymie security threats, but to bar passage of those who needed it most. *Refugees* were now *migrants*, and migrants might bring terror, or at the very least, crime.

Within a few years, the old Cold War geopolitical logic had all but vanished. On May 1, 2004, the European Union oversaw its greatest expansion—letting in many of the states of the old East, including Hungary and Poland, alongside others. Hungary was now formally as much a part of Europe as Austria. And the idea that there were once two Germanies was one for the history books.

And yet, even as the world of the Cold War receded into the past, the same questions persisted: of refugees and walls; in and out; us and them.

In both Hungary and the former GDR, politics in these years emerged directly from the residue of earlier eras. Angela Merkel's story is an East German fairytale. She entered politics during the revolutionary days of 1989 and quickly caught the eye of Chancellor Helmut Kohl. In 1991, he brought her into his government, and in 1998 when Kohl stepped down, she took over as general secretary of the Christian Democratic Union (CDU). On November 22, 2005, she was elected the chancellor of Germany—the first female to hold the office; and the only East German.

Merkel took a progressive stance on immigration. But with the rise in refugees, especially after 2015, came a populist backlash—similar to trends that in the UK produced Brexit, and in the US enabled the rise of Donald Trump—especially from the AfD (Alternative für Deutschland), a nationalist party with Nazi-charged rhetoric, that wanted a Germany for Germans. Ironically, the breeding ground of this backlash was the territory of the old GDR, once the bastion of anti-fascism.

In 2015, demonstrations emerged in Dresden, self-consciously mirroring the famous Monday Marches of Leipzig in 1989—once aimed at progressive reform, now directed against immigrants. They were termed Pegida Demonstrations. Pegida stands for Patriotic Europeans Against the Islamicisation of the Occident (Patriotische Europäer gegen die Islamisierung des Abendlandes). That same year, the movement's founder, Lutz Bachmann, briefly resigned after images surfaced of him dressed up as Hitler—in case the nasty undertones of the movement weren't sufficiently clear.

In January 2017, the AfD received 12.6 percent of the votes nationally and entered the Bundestag.

In Hungary, Viktor Orbán's first government, 1998–2002, was

short-lived, with Fidesz voted out in favor of a reinvigorated Socialist Party. The seesawing continued (right, then left, then right again). In 2010, Fidesz and Orbán returned with a vengeance, riding into power partly on a wave of EU-skepticism. For many Hungarians, the process of joining the EU was humiliating; they felt berated by European institutions for their failure to meet codes and requirements. Emotionally, it was as though they had just freed themselves from the shackle of one master—Moscow—only to fall into the arms of a new one—Brussels. The feeling of subservience grated on the Hungarian psyche.

Among the organizers, this feeling was especially strong for María—it reminded her of the humiliation of Trianon, after World War I, when the Western powers first tore Hungary apart. There is a border stone on the Austrian border, she tells me. Every year when I go back to the border I stand on that stone and face West, she says. *Then I spit.*

In Hungary, nationalism and the legacy of Trianon are inextricably linked. As a result of that treaty, the Hungarian empire was reduced overnight to a simple nation-state, with millions of Hungarians living in neighboring lands—Romania, Yugoslavia, Czechoslovakia. László puts it well: Hungary is the only nation in the world that borders itself.

This generates a complicated kind of nationalism—a transnational nationalism. The original redrafting of the constitution, in late 1989, stated that the Republic of Hungary "bears responsibility for the fate of Hungarians living outside its borders." In 1990, József Antall described himself as the prime minister for "fifteen million Hungarians in spirit."

In 2010, when Orbán returned to office, one of the first acts of the Fidesz-led Parliament was to transform this transnational nationhood into law, declaring that Hungarians "subjected to the jurisdiction of other states, belong to the single Hungarian nation." It is this narrative positioning that anchors Orbán's exclusionary stance vis-à-vis migrants. Our priority is uniting our own people, he is essentially saying. We don't have time to deal with someone else's.

On September 30, 2015, Orbán staked this ground to great political effect in front of the General Assembly of the United Nations. That same year, Orbán started building a wall on Hungary's southern border with Serbia—replete with several rows of razor and concertina wire fencing, as much as thirteen feet tall.

Hungary: the place that demolished walls, was now building them up. And by Orbán, no less, the man who once declared *Soviets Out!*

The turnaround is whiplash-inducing. But perhaps we shouldn't be so surprised. In the West, we took the Hungarian opposition in the 1980s to be inherently democratic. It was. But it was also sovereigntist. Getting rid of the Soviet Union would mean Hungary for Hungarians; the same could be said of getting rid of migrants.

Building a wall makes sense for Orbán's anti-immigration politics. But actually the policy wasn't easy to justify, due to Hungary's transnationalism. Building a wall would seem to legitimate Hungary's borders, thereby excluding the millions of conationals cut out of the polity. Here, the one national objective (to reunite Hungarians) and the other (to exclude migrants) seem to conflict. To square the circle, Orbán had to revisit an older Hungarian mythology—not the tragedy of Trianon, but the triumphant battles of the 1500s, by which the forward expanse of the Ottoman Empire—of Islam—was halted. Orbán was not subtle. The wall, he declared, was "Christian Europe's defensive line against the invading Muslim immigrants."

It was a new version of the old notion *Antemurale Christianitatis* (Bulwark of Christendom). It was not Hungary's wall, but a wall for all of Europe. We still believe in the dream of a unified Hungary, Orbán could thus maintain. But first we need to save civilization from the barbarians.

Such language is not new to Hungarian politics. It mirrors Otto von Habsburg's message, read by Walburga at the picnic, which declared that "Without Hungary, Europe would be incomplete, since throughout history our nation has been a bastion defending Christianity."

At a meeting with German politicians in 2015, Orbán remarked that now, given its positioning as the bulwark of Europe, Hungary was practically the border of Germany. Hungary was the border; and

Orbán, performatively the border guard. He was the new Árpád Bella, but rather than letting refugees cross into the West, he was making sure they stayed outside.

It was about this time that Orbán started getting closer to Putin's Moscow. It was as though 1989 had never happened.

IN THE MIDDLE OF THIS TIME OF FORGETTING, IN 2009, CAME A reminder: the twentieth anniversary of the picnic.

It was a bright day in high summer, and a grandstand was erected in the field where the border had been breached. The stage was filled with smiling faces, many bearing the marks of age. Imre Pozsgay, now seventy-five, rested his cane on his belly; he leaned on it heavily when he stood. Németh sat back, taking in the sun; now back in Hungary, he had settled into a life outside of politics and was pleased to revisit old glories.

After the speeches, László approached Pozsgay—deferential, as the old hierarchy reasserted itself. You know, Pozsgay said to him, speaking earnestly. If the Soviets had cracked down, we would have protected you.

Unless you were put in prison too, László replied.

Pozsgay laughed. True, he said. Then it would have gone very badly.

It was a dialogue cut from a different time, a moment in history still fresh among those who lived it, even as it had drifted away for everyone else.

As such gatherings go, this anniversary was generally scandal free—perhaps the last event surrounding the picnic for which this would be true. It was a reunion in a new sense as well: many East Germans showed up. This meant the organizers could actually meet the people who'd fled. It also meant the East Germans could reconnect with one another.

On the night of August 19, 1989, the Pfitzenreiters, the Sobels, and the Naglers had taken the train from Vienna together. Before parting, they exchanged the addresses of the friends and relatives to whose houses they would travel. But this promise of togetherness proved ephemeral. The Pfitzenreiters and Naglers managed to retain contact. But the information they had for the Sobels dead-ended. It was only in 2004 that they found each other again—via a film about GDR refugees that publicized their stories. They got in touch through a chain-link effort of phone calls and letters. They all returned for the anniversary in 2009.

Perhaps the most emotional in their return were the Sobels. For the twenty-year reunion, they decided to camp again, just like they had in 1989—to park where they parked, to sleep where they slept, only now with a camper van rather than tents. They came with their children, also their grandchildren.

The Nagler boys also returned for the twentieth anniversary—in part to see the Pfitzenreiters and Sobels. These relationships still mean a lot to them, especially the Pfitzenreiters. At one point during our conversation, in 2019, in their hometown of Bischofswerda, Stephan takes a picture and sends it to them. I like this small act of inclusion—as though I were part of an extended family, my own life now intertwined with theirs.

The Naglers had also returned for the ten-year anniversary, but skipped the conference. Instead, they took a video recorder out to the border and re-created their escape, laughing and making jokes as they pretended to cross into Austria.

Both the Naglers and the Sobels took well to capitalism—the Sobels out in the West; the Naglers back in the East. The Pfitzenreiters were a bit different. They stayed in the West, but while they integrated, they forged something of a middle way, keeping in their manner and behavior a bit of the character of the East.

The second time we meet, I visit the Pfitzenreiters at their house, just south of Mannheim, in the plush lands of the Rhine. Neither Margret nor Hermann speak English; both seem somewhat removed from the modern world. They do not carry cell phones or use email. They are fervently anti-Communist, but also anti-consumerist. It is a position born of experience: they lived long enough in the East to treasure the freedoms of the West, but not to need all its stuff. Maybe this is what I find so interesting about them, that they consciously retain their in-betweenness.

At one point in our conversation, Hermann walks to a chest of drawers and pulls out an old atlas of the GDR. He shows me their little corner, called the Eichsfeld. It's a unique spot. After the Second World War, when the Allies claimed they wanted part of Berlin, the Soviets demanded a swath of land from the West as compensation. This is what they took. It still upsets Hermann, how arbitrary it all is: born in the East pressed up against the West; or born in the West, pressed up against the East.

As much as Hermann and Margret retained their identity as Easterners in the West, they have also never lost their sensibility as having come from the borderlands. The mountain on the Inner German border they used to live beside was called Sonnenstein. To this day, Hermann, who wrestled himself free of the border, carries a lucky stone from that mountain in his pocket.

The house is filled with treasures of their past. Some time later, Hermann pulls out their son's Alf doll—a tiny thing, not larger than my thumb. Then some GDR currency—which they call *Ostalgie* coins (referring to nostalgia for the *Ost*, or East)—as well their vinyls. The very albums Margret had hidden in the hay just before their escape.

When we are feeling festive, Margret says, we put these on and dance.

The Pfitzenreiters return to Sopron frequently. They still think fondly about the East. Sometimes Margret and Hermann wonder aloud whether they might move back to the hill country where they grew up. This is the freedom the West affords: they could, but they might not. It's up to them.

———

I AM BACK IN LÁSZLÓ'S OFFICE IN SOPRON, IN MY USUAL SEAT, NES-tled into a corner of the room I now know, beside a stack of books and some empty bottles of his homemade alcohol. I am the best *pálinka*-maker in Sopron, László tells me with a twinkle in his eye.

His secret: pears that grow wild in the borderlands, hidden in the overgrown bits where the Iron Curtain used to stand. He promises to give me a bottle before I go.

It is spring 2019, just a few months before the thirtieth anniversary celebration. We are looking through documents, this time focused on the growing scandal surrounding the figure of Árpád Bella. Many felt he was taking too much credit for his decision not to use force to stop the refugees. His many detractors include several of the organizers—especially Mária—as well as Miklós Németh.

These disputes have been simmering since 1999 when Bella first rose to prominence, but found new life in 2014, when the socialist old guard restarted the tradition began under Horn (1994–1998), of celebrating 1989 through the June 27 wire cutting, not the picnic. Always the same dividing line: between the former socialist left (following the line of Horn) and the nationalist right (following Orbán). Soon the former socialists organized conferences and commemorative events of their own, with different heroes—specifically, Bella's superior, Gyula Kovács, who claims to have circulated a memo about the East Germans prior to their arrival, urging border guards not to react violently.

It has developed into a war of words. Papers too. László has reams of documents, many of which he got from Bella; so does Gyula Kovács. Interestingly, many of the documents are the same.

Reading through these files today, I find little to go on. There was a lot of vagueness about the border regime between May 2 (after Németh's first cutting of the electric wiring) and August 22 (the death of Kurt Werner Schulz). It was only then, and really after September 11, that rules became formalized. Prior to this, the Iron Curtain was being *de facto* dismantled, but *de jure* remained intact. As Andreas Oplatka puts it: taken together the evidence suggests "that illegal crossing of the border had to be prevented and did not need to be prevented at the same time."

The contestation is not legal, but political. Everybody wants to be seen as heroic and just, to feel they are on the right side of history. But to look for heroes is to go about history the wrong way. Transition is messy. It took a lot to stay nonviolent—not the action of one person but many, acting together. This was true at the heights of power—as with Németh and Pozsgay—but also on the ground. From one day to the next, the border guards went from being respected standard-bearers of the state, to being told (loosely) to turn a blind eye to border transgressors. This was a period of indeterminacy, beset with risk. But by and large the guards acted nobly. Try a few kilometers to the east, some told the refugees they encountered. Others carried slips of paper in their pockets with arrows drawn on them and the words "the border is that way."

Bella and Kovács are part of a larger human drama of changing systems—as are Németh, and Ferenc and Mária. Bella's choice to eschew violence was virtuous and consequential—all it would have taken was one bullet to have changed history forever. But the decision arose constituent with the reforms Németh had put in place, the courageous acts of the picnic organizers to bring their vision of united Europe out to the borderlands—perhaps Kovács's memo to the border guards too.

The fact that so many people were involved in building up to that moment is what makes the story worth telling. The rest is just politics.

I leave László's office with several bottles of his homemade *pálinka*. Before I depart, conversation returns to the subject of the thirtieth anniversary of the picnic, which is on the horizon. Orbán will speak; so will Merkel. There will be a pavilion by the border with food and drinks—a *picnic!*—followed by a concert in the cave theater in Fertőrákos.

Still, many of the organizers are worried the event will be tarnished by scandal.

László's parting words are cryptic: the disasters are coming.

Chapter Twenty-Nine

It was not a single party in 2019, but a year of parties. The events of 1989 happened a long time ago. As far as Viktor Orbán was concerned, there was a lot to commemorate—the end of Communism, the end of Soviet occupation. Also, him. The government commissioned a video commemorating 1989 that would play on television and at events throughout the year. The focus was Orbán himself, specifically his speech on June 16, 1989, at the reburial ceremony for Imre Nagy.

The video begins with the graphic demolition of a red star, then a montage of 1989. There, at the center, is Orbán, in grainy black and white footage, flanked by caskets, delivering his fiery oration. Two themes are foregrounded. First, the reclaiming of Hungarian sovereignty from Soviet oppression, a narrative that focuses on Orbán's speech. Second, Hungary's central role in German reunification. For this, the picnic was portrayed as a crowning achievement of the Hungarian opposition—in which Orbán's Fidesz played a crucial role. Optically, both events were focused on him.

In this rendering, Orbán comes off as an autocrat like any other, creating a cult in his image. But political lineage is a tangled mess. One must consider both faces of Orbán: the revolutionary of yesteryear and the politician of today. Central to his speech in 1989 are references to "the ideals of 1956," the impetus to get rid of the Soviets; he is speaking the language of liberty, of democracy, the things the West cherishes. But the words are also laden with nationalism. The Hungarian people should rise up against the occupiers, he is saying. The Hungarian nation should become self-determining.

Back in 1989, calls for national freedom had a beautiful ring to them. Now that they assert a xenophobic vision, they no longer do. But the calls themselves haven't changed. It's just that in 1989 we were so deafened by our own ideology, we couldn't hear what they were saying.

It is June 16, 2019, and I am in Budapest to attend the rally on Heroes' Square on the anniversary of the reburial of Imre Nagy. It's been thirty years, about as distant in time from the reburial, as the reburial was from Nagy's death.

Approaching the square, the boom of the festivities is audible from afar. Vendors sell light-up pinwheels and noisemakers from makeshift carts. Others sell cans of beer and baked goods. Thousands show up. The event opens with Orbán's video, projected onto a massive screen. The proceedings are a mixture of speeches and music that build up to an emotional final act.

There is a pause before the finale and the stage goes dark. Shortly, a solitary figure ascends the stage. He is quiet for a beat, two beats, an uncomfortable, expectant pause, then comes a familiar whistle. Within seconds, the crowd erupts. It is a cover of the 1991 Scorpions classic, "Wind of Change," about the end of the Cold War. The whistle is followed by a strum of tinny guitar. Then lyrics that people across the East know by heart. By the chorus, the square erupts into a beery, heavily accented sing-along.

The final set is epic and the crowd departs in a haze of drunken glory—exactly as the architects of the event intended. It is well later, as I make my way from the garbage-strewn square, that I realize something was absent from the festivities: any reference to Imre Nagy.

Yes, the politics of burial and commemoration are complex. But this is extreme. What was celebrated was the occasion of Orbán's speech—no more, no less. Nagy was all but circumstantial. In retrospect, this shouldn't have been surprising. Just a few months earlier, on December 28, 2018, a statue of Imre Nagy was relocated from central Budapest to a less prominent location in the city. Like everything else in Hungary, his legacy has become a subject of bitter debate. Records allegedly reveal Nagy to have been more in bed with Moscow than previously understood. This view is popular among Orbán's supporters; critics see it as historical revisionism.

The turns that history takes: the critique of Nagy originally came from people like Kádár and Grósz, the old Communists; now it is taken up by Orbán, the nationalist. Both ends of the spectrum find Nagy's legacy threatening. It is a heroism discrete from their own.

Nagy's grave in the Rákoskeresztúri Cemetery in Budapest, Plot 301—where his body was reburied in 1989; where Oskar and Katja visited in August before their trip to the border—is a quiet spot, out in a corner of the burial ground. Before attending the rally on Heroes' Square, I made a pilgrimage there. It was empty when I arrived, but with time, a small procession appeared, mostly the now-elderly children of fallen 1956 revolutionaries, dressed in white and bearing flowers. They formed a ring and held hands. They read poetry and gave speeches, then departed. Nothing like the festivities that would come that evening.

Everything in contemporary Hungary is dual—and dueling. Just as there are two commemorations on June 16, so too are there competing events about the border opening.

A week later, I attend the event organized by the Hungarian left to celebrate their own version of 1989, hinging on the June 27 clipping of the Iron Curtain by Gyula Horn and Alois Mock. This is the competitor event to the picnic celebration, which would come in August.

The left is out of power, and it shows. Their event is held out in the border city of Hegyeshalom, in a midsize room filled with dusty flags and the shifting bodies of mostly elderly men. It receives little media attention and proceeds without fanfare save for intermittent and tepid applause. The tone is drab and overserious—or as Ferenc would put it, "funereal." Németh speaks, as does Kovács.

During one intermission I sit with Németh. He is upset. There is almost no press. And he detests the cult of Horn as much as that of Orbán. They are each building their statues, Németh says dismissively about the dueling commemorations.

He is certainly right. But one can't help but feel that something else is at play too. Németh is upset that no one is building a statue for him.

Németh was invited to speak at the thirtieth anniversary of the picnic, but he pulled out when he saw the program. Németh's panel was titled "Breakthrough and Collapse"—meaning the breach of the border by the East Germans and the dissolution of the Communist state. He rejects both claims. It wasn't a "breakthrough," he contends, as the government had been aware of East German crossings, and was even trying to facilitate them. And he doesn't like the term "collapse," as it undercuts all the work he put into trying to cultivate reform.

But if the picnic retelling is so filled with inaccuracies, why not go correct them? I ask.

Németh looks at me with disappointment. If I show up I legitimize the lies, he replies.

Then he adds: *I live here.*

Hungary is his house, his *heimat*. It is the center of his world. This is the unspoken truth buried in the silences of our conversation. I have invested many years in this story, but I am an outsider here. At any point, I could pick up and leave. I am looking forward to the thirtieth anniversary of the picnic, scandals and all.

———

IT IS EARLY EVENING, AUGUST 17, 2019, AND THE MAIN SHOPPING street of Sopron is blocked off to traffic. It's balmy and the city is aglow with lights. The conference starts the following morning; but

the weekend kicks off with a concert. I am here with some research assistants who will help with translation. One of them, Eva, picks a spot on the pavement, while I run off to buy beer.

The show starts slowly with some speeches and folk dancing, before Beatrice, a Hungarian rock band, takes the stage and brings down the house with sentimental classics. A sign at the back of the stage reads "Fuck the 20th Century." Beatrice claim to have been the first band to criticize Communism in Hungary.

A giant crane dangles a Trabant above the stage.

There will be several days of events—panels, talks, concerts. On the 19th, they will re-create the picnic on the field where the breach took place, now named Pan-European Picnic Monument Park. The final day is reserved for speeches by Merkel and Orbán.

The conference takes place in a stately municipal building in the center of Sopron. The discussion is fairly pat. Positions have ossified by this point, so disputes—about Bella's role, for instance—have a warmed-over quality. More interesting is the perspective of the East Germans. Hermann and Margret Pfitzenreiter are part of the formal

program, but displeased about the number of Fidesz politicians present, including on stage. These politicians strike a nationalist tone; they
object to letting too many migrants into Hungary, especially Muslims.

The new Iron Curtain—the *Antemurale Christianitatis*.

Margret and Hermann can't believe their ears. And in Sopron,
no less, at a conference putatively celebrating the passage of refugees.
It's degrading the way they speak about refugees, Hermann says. Like
we're some sort of mob.

I was asked if I would shake Orbán's hand, Margret adds. I said no.

Their concern isn't just the callousness of the Fidesz remarks, but
something broader: that we might celebrate the past but not learn from
it. The Pfitzenreiters are here as time witnesses—offering public tes-
timony about their experience—a role they have begun to embrace
over the last years, availing themselves to German high schools. It is
an effort to correct what they see as a shortcoming in the curriculum
about basic GDR history. One year, when they were speaking in front
of a school in the west, a student asked if former East German premier
Erich Honecker had started the Second World War.

Throughout the weekend, chartered buses take attendees out to the
border. I head out on Sunday, when they re-create the picnic.

The field by the border is now an open-air museum. It's a beautiful place, with paved walkways wending through the grounds, and
wooden posts that detail the history leading up to the picnic. In one
area, a stretch of barbed wire is preserved; looming above is the rickety
old watchtower. At the center of the field is a concrete monument to the
fall of Communism. To one side is the Bell of Freedom, gifted by Debrecen; a bit farther down, a segment of the Berlin Wall. And in the middle,
a road cuts through the field, heading to the open border, marked out
by two metallic signs a few meters apart. The one reads Magyarország
(Hungary), the other Österreich (Austria).

Much of this had been built up over the years, so I had seen it before.
New for the thirtieth anniversary is a visitor's center, with black and

white photographs along the walls, and displays of Communist-era kitsch. Another new fixture is an experience machine—a dark chamber, wrought of rusted iron, in which you find yourself compressed against metal statues. Before you is a small window of light, looking forward onto barbed wire. It is supposed to re-create the pressure you might have felt making the dash to freedom, and summon the horrors that lie in your path.

I find the space moving; appropriate to the story it is meant to tell. And on this day, the grounds are swelling with people. A giant tent plays video footage of the breach; speeches are held out in the open, notably by Magas; a band plays. Another tent provides refreshments, and toward the evening, a great meal—a picnic. True to Ferenc's thirty-year-old dream, there was even a barbeque.

It's a grand reunion. Marlies and Bernd Grunert sit at one table chatting gaily; Magas and Rumpf sit at another. Stephan Nagler walks around wearing a #piknik30 wristband. Both the Sobels and Pfitzenreiters mention taking a trip to see Aunt Ágnes.

And as always, new bits of the story are revealed. At one point, László rushes up to me: you'll never believe what I just learned, he all but yells. *They were keeping count!* He is referring to a story he heard from Annette. She was number thirteen. She remembers hearing the number said aloud as she passed.

On the final day, Angela Merkel and Viktor Orbán speak—each highlighting their interests. For Merkel it's the humanitarianism of the guards, who "put their humanity above their orders." Orbán focuses on the question of sovereignty.

Politics: always.

I am left with an unresolved feeling, as though I've watched a drama missing its last act. I am reminded of the division in Shakespeare's canon between tragedies and comedies—tragedies end in death; comedies in marriage. But the story of contemporary Hungary is neither comedic nor tragic. The dueling thirty-year anniversary celebrations are like weddings in a way. But the tragedy is that there are two of them.

It is not a death, but a division. Not a marriage, nor a divorce, but something in between. Maybe politics is always this way.

Before I leave Sopron, I return to László's office for a coffee. He is tired from the planning, but proud of how it went.

Next up is the fortieth, he says with a grin. Who knows what new things will have happened by then.

———

I AM ON A TRAIN FROM BERLIN TO DRESDEN, WHICH IS LOCATED in the southeastern corner of what had once been the GDR. Once beyond the housing blocks of Berlin, we pass outskirt-villages-cum-commuter-suburbs with plaster buildings and red roofs, then more remote settlements intermixed with woods. It is surprisingly destitute in places, even though it's been thirty years since the *Wende*, almost as long as the GDR was in existence.

It is strange to think there were two Germanies once. Unified Germany is a body I recognize; the map is its face. Maps that say otherwise seem out of place. They look like maps of somewhere else.

Sometimes the train passes an urban area with new high rises or older buildings with fresh coats of paint. But this does little to change the face and smell of the ex-GDR. It is a slapdashing, a half-remedying; less a re*new*al than an un*old*ing. Our present moment but a tiny respite, before these buildings become old again. Maybe the GDR will be reclaimed after all.

For parts of the trip the internet connection is slow; the map on my phone shows my location the last time I checked, not where I am now. In the ex-GDR, this is somehow fitting. We are in one place and another at the same time.

It is February 2, 2020, and I am in Dresden to meet Katja and Oskar, whose story I first heard in Sopron at the thirtieth anniversary and have waited half a year to hear again. I recognize them instantly from the window of a bar in the city center. He is sturdy, she is slight; her raincoat seems to slide into his as they walk.

It is my last interview before the COVID-19 pandemic takes over and the world changes anew.

After Katja and Oskar split up, in late 1989, they went years without contact. Both tried to move on from each other, from that life-altering experience at the border. Katja never went back to Mörbisch, the town near the hole in the fence where she had first crossed into Austria, even when she was living close by in Vienna. It raised questions she wasn't ready to answer.

Oskar frequently dreamed about making a pilgrimage back to the border, but never did. It was a place and a time of his life wrapped up with Katja. He didn't want to do it without her.

Katja lived in the West for fifteen years, finally moving back to Dresden in 2004. She married and had children. Oskar stayed in the West. He married and had children too.

It was many years before they got back in touch, in 2000; longer still before they arranged to meet. By that point, things had changed in their lives. In 2009, they separately wrote to the authorities to look into their Stasi files.

The following year they decided to go look at them together. Twenty years had passed since they had been a couple. If they were going to see each other again, this was how it made sense to do so: by looking into the files that might have torn their lives apart.

In summer 2015, they took a trip together to Fertőrákos; for each it was their first time back. The date was August 21—the precise anniversary of their crossing, twenty-six years before. In the evening they went to Mörbisch for dinner and Oskar asked Katja to marry him. She said yes.

A dream nearly three decades deferred, was suddenly real.

They retraced their steps across the border, tried to locate the exact spot where they had come upon that border stone, with the M and the Ö. They were once again living their fairytale, looking for the bread crumbs they had scattered so many years before.

The grassy patch they believed they had crossed was overgrown with bushes. And although they spotted some border markers, it was hard to tell which was theirs. While Oskar looked about, Katja knelt down and put her fingers into the dirt. Back in 1989, during those long hours hiding in the cornfields, Katja had passed the time by digging in the ground, where she came across some slender mollusk shells—like fossils from an ancient ocean. Katja put a few in her pocket and carried them with her, through her time in the cell where she was detained, back to the camp outside Fertőrákos, then across the border to Mörbisch, and all the way to West Germany, where she began her new life.

Returning to the border with Oskar, she dug until she found some more shells—her bridge to that long-lost sea, which once covered this land they twice trod. That covered everything that is now Hungary and Austria and their interlocking borderlands, and the Iron Curtain that once divided East from West. An ancient sea, as inscrutable as memory itself.

They have been back to the border by Fertőrákos three times since 2015. When I casually suggest they should buy a house there, they say it is something they are already considering. They have several projects on their hands. Recently, Oskar found the photographs taken by the journalist he had met in 1989. One is a picture of their border stone, which has a number on it. They resolve to go back soon, to retread their path and see if they can find it, with its painted *M* and *Ö*.

Even if they don't, they have already found in each other what they were looking for. Not the past, exactly, but the traces we carry with us into the present. A past we sometimes can't let go of; which also won't let go of us. Even as it changes.

This is the past's presentness.

It is the voices of those we love, calling from the water.

Epilogue

FREEDOM'S PRICE

S opron today is a well-kept, untroubled place, with a walkable medieval center defined by a crumbling stone wall. The streets that radiate outward from this core bear the hallmarks of Habsburg architecture—pastel coloring, often yellows and pinks, plastered facades and neo-classical ornamentation. A pedestrian street is lined with ice cream shops for afternoon strolls and pizza spots for evening merrymaking. At a glance, it's hard to imagine this place as a forward garrison of the Cold War.

In the years since I started coming to Sopron, I have formed something of a routine. There is a small guesthouse off the center where I stay. It is inexpensive yet overpriced for what it offers. The room is without a desk or chair, and there is no possibility of arranging coffee outside circumscribed hours. Like many places in Hungary, the smell of Communism seems to linger on the furniture—wooden relics, including an oversized dresser that vastly exceeds the use any traveler might put to it. Even the receptionist seems cast from another era.

For all those still living in Sopron—László, Magas, Rumpf—their daily lives are contiguous with this history. One day while sitting in his office, László shows me a photograph of the luncheon attended by the picnic organizers at the Lövér Hotel on August 20, 1989, the day after the picnic. László is positioned beside a state implant, Lajos Farkas. I ask what happened to him, whether he is still alive. László waves his hand dismissively.

Of course, he says, I saw him two days ago.

From the outside it's easy to overlook the stickiness of *place*, its persistence in time. But if it's your home, this is the main thing. They are all still living it: the picnic, the glorious days of 1989; the aftermath too. It's all here, written into the streets.

Aunt Ágnes is ninety-three when we meet. We are standing on her screened porch. She reaches out to me with cold and swollen hands, striated with wine-dark veins. I don't see well anymore, she says, then touches my cheek.

When we sit, she produces a box of postcards from all over the former East and West Germany—Dresden, Rostock, Hamburg, Hanover. Ágnes had a request for the East Germans she helped: wherever you end up, send a postcard telling me you got there safely. Soon enough, cards started coming in. She can't read them anymore, but she knows what they say. Many of the East German families still keep in touch, and occasionally visit. She remembers them all by name.

Fertőrákos is her home. She is part of the internal logic of the village, which preceded the picnic; which succeeds it too. The strength of this local bond, its moral economy, comes out in her relationship with Imre Csapó, a local border guard, putatively responsible for catching refugees.

Did Csapó know you were leading East Germans to the border? I ask.

Of course, she replies. I told him.

He didn't command you to stop?

No. I was friends with his father.

It's easy to dismiss relationships like these. But to do so would miss something fundamental. Empires fall, geopolitical lines shift, but the village remains.

History for Ágnes is everywhere; it anchors her understanding of the world. She was living in the east of Hungary, in the village of Tisza-lök, in 1956, when the Soviet tanks rolled in. She was thirty, already the mother of three. Out in the village they did not face Soviet violence. But a strange thing happened. One night an unfamiliar train pulled into their railway station, headed for the Soviet Union. This was suspicious. After dark, some villagers snuck onto the tracks and opened one of the wagons only to find it filled with coffins—exactly what they had feared. But when they opened them up they found they were filled with corn. For the villagers this was shocking still. They'd come dreading one kind of imperial violence and found another.

That's why I dislike Orbán, Ágnes says to me now. Anyone who cozies up to Moscow cannot be trusted.

The past is stuck to us. We may be free to do many things, but it's not so simple to change how we think, how we see the world—the essential bits of our being. The past is like the village. Even as it changes, it stays constant too.

Oral history emerges from the belief that it is through peoples' stories that we come to understand the world around us. The air Hungarians breathe today is continuous somehow with the winds awhirl in 1989; the same winds that swirl about the rest of us too. Yet, the process is humbling. Not just because I am a stranger in the village, but also because there are so many stories I cannot retrace. I never got to meet Pozsgay; he died in 2016. Gyula Horn passed away in 2013. When I met Andreas Oplatka at the beginning of this project, in 2018, he offered me a piece of advice: You better hurry up with your research, he said. These people aren't young anymore.

Oplatka passed away in 2020. Ágnes died at the end of 2019. She missed the COVID-19 pandemic by a few months. Géza Szőcs died in 2020 because of it.

Some of these stories may never be told again. But the questions they raise are eternal—they speak as much to their world as to ours. Especially the questions about freedom.

IN 1958, POLITICAL PHILOSOPHER AND THEORIST ISAIAH BERLIN
delivered a lecture entitled "Two Concepts of Liberty," outlining different ways of understanding this foundational ideal. Negative liberty,
he explained, is concerned with freedom from interference—the area,
like a fortress around the self, that the state cannot enter, where we are
left to do as we please. This is the concept of liberty most recognizable
to those of us who grew up in the West. When we think of the private
spaces of our lives, a bedroom we share with intimates, a well-lighted
office in which to read, it is this kind of liberty we invoke. It is the core
of what we think of as liberalism, and the values it embraces—free
speech, free association, free movement. It is also what the Communist
states, especially draconian ones like the GDR, failed to provide. These
societies sought total obeisance.

But Berlin also highlighted a second form, what he calls positive
liberty. This is concerned with self-mastery, the ability to determine
who or what we are. It is positive in that it defines the content of freedom. "I wish to be a subject, not an object," Berlin writes of the imaginative space this freedom captures, "a doer—deciding, not being decided
for." Thinking about freedom in this way, as self-fulfillment, helps
explain why the ideal is so powerful. It is the pathway not just to self-
hood, but into our *better* selves. The selves we wish we were, whom we
will ourselves to become.

On positive liberty, Berlin expresses a concern. Once you allow
that in each of us there is a higher self—the path you would have taken
had you only known better—it puts others (the state, the clergy, the
nation) in a position to say they know what is best for you. Let us help
you, the state says, to be the better citizen, the better comrade. It's
thinking of liberty in this way, Berlin contends, that opens the door for
totalitarianism.

In Berlin's writing, the shadow of the Soviet Union looms large.
Its brand of Communism was one in which there was only one path to

redemption—state ideology. And the state was going to take you there, even if it meant stripping you of your land, of your political voice, your critical capacity. This was the notion of positive liberty taken to its logical extreme: by forcibly making people who they might be, it destroyed who they actually were.

Berlin's essay remains pertinent. But, in returning to it now, something rings hollow. It's hard to imagine thinking of negative liberty as glowingly as Berlin did. These days, when we speak about freedom in the West it sounds more like *license*—as though being free means simply doing what you want and not having anything stand in your way. This notion of freedom-as-individualism is extreme too.

In the United States, as for much of the West, the problem was readily apparent during the COVID-19 pandemic, when for many freedom became synonymous with the right *not* to wear masks, even if doing so might be beneficial for others.

Something has gone wrong in our thinking. We live in complex, interwoven societies. They function in part because of the accommodations we make to one another. This is the essence of the social contract. And yet, we have lost the ability to speak about freedom in such terms: where we are not free on our own, but among others.

This theme recurs in my conversations with the East German refugees. When they speak about the freedom they sought in the 1980s, they use the language of negative freedom—the freedom of the West. And yet for so many of them, the accession to these values brought disappointment. Many found people in the West to be more selfish and self-serving—*individualistic*—than the world they knew in the East. What they wanted was not exactly freedom, but freedom and community together. Without the former, you had simple totalitarianism. But without the latter, life feels cold, almost inhuman.

Some have been saying this all along. Hannah Arendt's essay "What Is Freedom?" (1961) offers a different governing idiom for freedom: it is not the private sanctum—Berlin's sphere of noninterference—but the ancient Greek polis, "which provided men with . . . a kind of the-

ater where freedom could appear." Arendt's freedom feels and sounds
very different from Berlin's: it is loud, messy, sweaty, with lots of people
gathering to speak their minds on the public square. Her point is that
for freedom to be meaningful, we must commit to a shared political
domain, rather than try to escape from it. The problem with liberal
views of freedom—like Berlin's—is that they privilege the sovereign
power of the individual over all else.

For Arendt, this vision of sovereignty is futile due to the irreducible
fact of human plurality. As she puts it in *The Human Condition* (1958),
"No man can be sovereign because not one man, but men, inhabit the
earth." Given the condition of plurality, to be sovereign one must ultimately be alone, or above all others. It is a dangerous fantasy—"an
illusion"—that carries within it projections of power and domination.

If we value individual freedom above all else, Arendt tells us, we
will always place other values, like solidarity, community, equality, on a
lower rung. In the Communist states, by contrast, these values were considered central. "From each according to his ability, to each according to
his needs," as per Marx's famous phrase. Certainly there wasn't solidarity in the darkest days of the GDR, when people were driven into their
pods of loneliness. Communism as a *practice* was often anti-solidaristic.
But the point here is neither to defend Communism, nor to revisit its
excesses. Rather it is to ask whether anything of value has been lost.

My own perspective on this has changed since I began work on
this project. I no longer view the fall of the Berlin Wall as marking the
straightforward triumph of democracy over authoritarianism. Nor do
I associate the West cleanly with freedom. If anything, I now see 1989
as the year we failed to reign in liberalism's more dangerous impulses.
In the West, we don't usually think of ourselves as experiencing transition at the end of the Cold War, but perhaps we should.

Coming back to Isaiah Berlin, I now see his argument as very much
a product of the Cold War—a defense of liberalism that makes sense
in circumstances where the ties of community are strong (nothing
makes friends like a common enemy, they say). It's as though there was a

hidden value, a baseline of solidarity, that made negative liberty—the liberty of the West—less callous than it appears today.

I have been teaching Berlin and Arendt side by side for years. When I teach Berlin, students are instantly receptive. By contrast, Arendt's insights are harder to communicate, as though they come from circumstances wholly different from our own. They do and they don't. Across the West, society has become more atomized and divided. We need to relearn how to live together. Maybe this means bringing back welfare institutions from the 1950s and '60s (when Berlin was writing), which did more to stem inequality than those we have today. Maybe it means inculcating civic responsibility—more central to educational systems in the old Eastern Bloc but jettisoned along with the Wall. Maybe it means experimenting with democratic socialism—as many had once hoped for the GDR.

But the main thing is finding a way to view freedom as but one value among many. In the West we used to value such pluralism. Much of this was lost after 1989. It behooves us to see whether it might be regained.

———

THERE MIGHT NEVER HAVE BEEN A BERLIN WALL. ON MARCH 10, 1952, only a few years after the partition of East and West Germany, Stalin put forth a plan to reunify the two states as a neutral power. This became known as the Stalin Note. Western powers rejected the idea, perceiving it as capitulation. The offer never came again.

In the aftermath of World War II, as the Axis powers surrendered and the Red Army pushed west, another plan had been on the table: Austria would be divided, just like Germany. Under this model, Vienna would have been cut up between Western and Soviet spheres. There might have been a Vienna Wall instead.

Monumental historical narratives paper over so much luck and randomness. They render inevitable what was, and obscure what might have been.

When I hear the Naglers' story, I wonder: what if they had decided not to cross, would their lives have been so different? Heiko, Stephan's friend, did not cross the border to the West in 1989. He went back to the GDR. He and Stephan are still close. They live near to one another. There is something poetic in this: the two boys, separated on that fateful day, ending up in the same place.

These stories are not unique; history is *always*, implicitly, a question of counterfactuals—events that never occurred; decisions unmade, actions untaken. All the more reason to be humble about what we know and what we don't.

When Katja and Oskar looked in their Stasi files, they expected to find a massive cache of their correspondences. But they found nothing—not a single letter. Speaking about it today, Oskar almost seems disappointed. Think how they could have blackmailed us, he says.

This is the nonstory of the archive. The absence between pages. Perhaps it is simply evidence of state decline—by 1989 the Stasi edifice was collapsing beneath the weight of its own investigations. But maybe there is a more elegant story here too: of a nameless bureaucrat tasked with reading the letters of these two young lovers, yet choosing not to flag them. The everyday morality of looking the other way.

Several of my interlocutors gave me permission to examine their personal files. This takes a lot of paperwork, as the Stasi Records Archive is protective of its subjects' privacy. But after the documents are submitted and an appointment is made to view the files, I find almost nothing.

The search for the names Bernd and Marlies Grunert produces only a slender folder, containing files from *after* their flight. We know the Grunerts were interrogated by Hungarian guards; if the Stasi have no records, it means the Hungarians didn't write anything down. If they did, they chose not to send their notes to Berlin.

One day at the Stasi Records Archive I approach my stack and find a note placed at the top. It is from an archivist, Herr Andreas Bogoslawski. He had heard of my project and asked whether I wanted to speak about it. He had been a refugee too.

Bogoslawski joined the Stasi Records Archive in January 1991, during the first wave of hires. He jumped at the opportunity to look behind the wizard's curtain, but like so many others he was shocked to learn how little the Stasi actually knew. They had no record of his flight. Most of his file was from his younger days, when he took a Polish class in high school—this was at the time of the protest movement in Poland. But by the end of the 1980s the Stasi were missing basic things. Once, in 1988, Helmut Kohl paid a visit to his hometown; Bogoslawski was part of a group that took him around—he was practically the tour guide for the chancellor of West Germany. There is no note of this in his file.

I ask what he thinks he's learned, now thirty years immersed in Stasi documentation. He pauses a moment to reflect before replying. The archives tell the story of power, he says. What the powerful knew; what they thought to look for. This can only be partial.

November 9, 2019, marked the thirtieth anniversary of the fall of the Berlin Wall, #Mauerfall30. Thousands thronged the city; there were days of celebratory events. The concert at the Brandenburg Gate was a feast of color and light. But just as it felt tone deaf in Hungary to discuss refugees in the age of Orbán, so here it was uncomfortable commemorating walllessness at a moment in which new ones were everywhere being built.

Monumental stories are usually the easiest to tell. But there is so much they leave out, details they cover over or hurry past. This is why oral history is so important, why we listen to what people like Ferenc and Mária and all the others who lived through that miraculous year, 1989, have to say. To consider events of the past with all their idiosyncrasies. Their lingering resonances too—the ideas we can't let go of, the retrenching of valor and pain. Memories are tricky things; they shapeshift to accommodate the uses to which they are put, the thoughtscapes they also engender.

Ferenc's comments about Nietzsche in his art and poetry garden got me reading *The Gay Science* again. This time, I am noticing different things—specifically Nietzsche's reflections on history, his fixation on the past's presentness. Take his famous proclamation, "God is dead," for example. The passage is concerned less with God's end, than his lingering presence.

> After Buddha was dead, his shadow was still shown for centuries in a cave—a tremendous, gruesome shadow. God is dead; but given the way of men, there may still be caves for thousands of years in which his shadow will be shown. And we—we still have to vanquish his shadow too.

We could say the same for all ideas, all time periods, all eras. The Soviet Empire has died out, but it still lives on in ideas—as we can see in Putin's invasion of Ukraine. As does Hitler's eugenicist fascism—consistently reworked by the fringes of the American and European right. Thinking evolves slowly; the past is always revisited and revised.

Importantly, in Nietzsche's account it is a madman who proclaims that God is dead. The reason he is thought mad is because he has come before his time. Like the one who breaks free from Plato's cave only to return and be ridiculed, this prophet too finds that people are unready for his message. They want to stick to their old ways—their old Gods. It is dangerous to come too soon.

In some ways Nietzsche's parable isn't about God at all, but simply the terror of new beginnings. It is a story of transition.

The picnic was beautiful, as was the *Mauerfall*. But freedom as an ideal doesn't take form easily in the world. This is the greatest challenge: giving the values we cherish their earthly embodiment. It is why we seek history as our guide, why we study the past and read the classics. Crises come constantly. As Ferenc puts it: barracks keep being built. So do walls. Tearing them down is the first step; the next is finding a way to build something lasting and noble and true after they fall.

Acknowledgments

Books are massive undertakings; they are rarely written alone. This is certainly true of this project, which depended greatly on the kindness of strangers and a fair amount of serendipity. From our first meeting in Sopronpuszta, László Nagy has been exceedingly generous with his time and experience, far beyond what any researcher could reasonably ask. Without him I would never have even known about the picnic, let alone been able to write about it. My thanks go out to him first and foremost. I am also exceptionally grateful to Machteld Venken, who convened the Association for Borderlands Studies World Conference in 2018, which included a trip to the Austrian-Hungarian border, where I first got the chance to hear László speak. Simply put: without this felicitous encounter, there is no book.

This project also would not have been possible without a great number of research assistants to help with translation and interpretation. I am especially grateful to Mika Bauer, Eva Berger, and Szonja Hajdú, who came out to Sopron for the thirtieth anniversary celebration in 2019 and spent several tireless days in the unforgiving sun helping me conduct interviews. They saw the project through from beginning to end. Without the hours they put in, a research project of such epic and gangly proportions could never have come together. Others I would like to thank include (in the rough order in which they joined the project): Réka Eltar, Hannah Vögele, Áron Gebe, Maria-Sophie Hehle, Milán Szabó, Manuel Neubauer, Calam Gallacher Roig, Elizabeth Friedrich, Ayman Mekkaoui Alaoui, Alena Kanitz, Zsófia Maris, Markku Hepokoski, Mira Kurtović, Paulina Medek, Mathis Böhm, and Jada Henkel.

In addition to these dedicated assistants, I am grateful to several institutions that helped facilitate this research. I wish to thank the Leiden University Institute of Political Science for its support throughout these years, and David Atkinson at handmademaps.com for the beautiful maps at the front of the book. I have also profited greatly from the access provided to me by the Pan-European Picnic '89 Foundation in Sopron, as well as the Stasi Records Archive (Stasi Unterlagen Archiv) and the Berlin Wall Foundation (Berliner Mauer Stiftung) in Berlin.

I owe special thanks to my agent, Pamela Malpas, and my editor, Alane Mason, for believing in this project from its earliest stages and for committing so much time and labor to helping me bring these stories and characters to life. I am grateful for their readership, as well as that of my parents, Genny Kapuler and Gianni Longo, Mike van Mantgem, Ellen Akins, and especially my wife, Nina, without whom this book would have been longer and considerably less refined.

I like to think my daughters, Freya and Oona, also helped. The bulk of the writing of this book took place during the COVID-19 pandemic, where we were often huddled at home and I found myself sharing with them many of the stories featured here. This project started before either of them could really read and has ended with them each unable to tear their eyes from the page. One day, I hope they will read this book too.

Notes on Sources

The primary source material for this book came from interviews, conducted mostly in Hungary and Germany, between September 2018 and February 2022. All Hungarian names are printed in full in the text, using the Western convention (first name last name) rather than the Hungarian one (in which the order is reversed); some of the East Germans I interviewed requested to be kept anonymous. In these cases, I have used pseudonyms or hidden their names.

To establish the general historical record, I drew heavily from journalistic, academic, and narrative accounts of 1989. Chief among these were Michael Meyer's *1989: The Year That Changed the World* (Simon & Schuster, 2009), Timothy Garton Ash's *The Magic Lantern: The Revolution of '89 Witnessed in Warsaw, Budapest, Berlin and Prague* (Vintage, 1990), Anna Funder's *Stasiland: Stories from Behind the Berlin Wall* (Granta, 2003), and Rudolf Tőkés's *Hungary's Negotiated Revolution* (Cambridge University Press, 1996). On contemporary Hungarian politics, I also drew from James W. Scott, "Hungarian Border Politics as an Anti-Politics of the European Union," *Geopolitics* 25, no. 3 (2020): 658–77; James W. Scott and Zoltán Hajdú, "The Carpathian Basin as a 'Hungarian Neighbourhood': Imaginative Geographies of Regional Cooperation and National Exceptionalism," *Eurasian Geography and Economics* 63, no. 6 (2022): 753–78; and Gela Merabishvili, "Defending Europe at the Trianon Border: Geopolitical

Visions of Nationhood and the Remaking of Hungary's Southern Border," *Geopolitics* (Online First, 2022).

For texts specific to the Pan-European Picnic, I used Andreas Oplatka's *Der Erste Riss in der Mauer: September 1989—Ungarn öffnet die Grenze* (Zsolnay, 2009); László Nagy's "The Pan-European Picnic, and the Opening of the Border on the 11th of September 1989," in *Gazdaság & Társadalom: Journal of Economy & Society* (2014); Terry Cox's "The Picnic on the Border: An Interview with Laszlo Vass," *Europe-Asia Studies* 63, no. 9 (November 2011): 1627–38; and György Gyarmati (ed.), *Prelude to Demolishing the Iron Curtain: Pan-European Picnic, Sopron 19 August 1989* (2012), especially the chapters by Ignác Romsics, László Borhi, Krisztina Slachta, and Andreas Oplatka.

This book quotes several sources from political philosophy and especially the writing of Hannah Arendt, who accompanied me during this project like a muse. I cite several of her books, *The Origins of Totalitarianism* (Penguin Classics, 2017), *Eichmann in Jerusalem* (Penguin Classics, 2016), and *The Human Condition* (University of Chicago Press, 1998), as well as her essays, "What Is Freedom?" in *Between Past and Future* (Penguin Classics, 1961), "We Refugees," in *The Jewish Writings,* Jerome Kohn and Ron H. Feldman (eds.) (Schocken Books, 2008), and her "Introduction" to Walter Benjamin's *Illuminations* (Harcourt, Brace & Jovanovich, 1968). Many more of her texts were consulted for reference but didn't make it into the book.

Additional cited works of political philosophy include: Allan Bloom (ed.), *The Republic of Plato* (Basic Books, 2016), Jean-Jacques Rousseau, *The Basic Political Writings* (Hacket Publishing Company, 1987); John Locke, *Two Treatises of Government* (Cambridge University Press, 2014); Friedrich Nietzsche, *The Gay Science,* translated by Walter Kaufmann (Vintage, 1974); Karl Marx, *Selected Writings* (Hackett, 1994); and Isaiah Berlin, *The Proper Study of Mankind* (Farrar, Straus and Giroux, 1997). The discussion of these sources was also aided by several secondary sources. These include Seyla Benhabib's *Exile, Statelessness, and Migration: Playing Chess with History from Hannah Arendt to Isaiah Berlin* (Princeton University Press, 2018); Michael Taussig's *Walter Benjamin's Grave* (University of Chicago Press, 2006); and Samantha Rose Hill's "Walter Benjamin's Last Work," *Los Angeles Review of Books,* December 9, 2019.

In this book, I also drew heavily from Hungarian and East German literature. Among these were István Bibó's *The Art of Peacemaking* (Yale University Press, 2015), translated by Péter Pásztor; quotations from Imre Nagy were taken from http://www.nagyimreemlekhaz.hu/en/imre-nagy.html; Géza Szőcs, *Liberty, Rats and Sandpaper*, translated from the Hungarian by Paul Sohar (Iniquity Press/Irodalmi Jelen Konyvek, 2017); György Konrád, *The Case Worker*, translated by Paul Aston (Harcourt Brace Jovanovich, 1969; English translation, 1974); György Konrád, *A Guest in My Own Country: A Hungarian Life*, translated by Jim Tucker, edited by Michael Henry Heim (Other Press, originally published, 2002; English translation, 2007); Christa Wolf, *They Divided the Sky*, translated into English by Luise von Flotow (University of Ottawa Press, 2013); Jenny Erpenbeck, *Not a Novel: Collected Writings and Reflections*, translated from the German by Kurt Beals (Granta Books, 2020); Wolfgang Hilbig, *The Sleep of the Righteous*, translated by Isabel Fargo Cole, introduction by László Krasznahorkai (Two Lines Press, 2015).

Additional evidence was provided by archives. Two in particular warrant note: the Pan-European Picnic '89 Foundation archive in Sopron (unindexed), as well as the Stasi Records Archive in Berlin. From the Picnic archive, I drew from a number of primary sources, these include the speeches given at the picnic (notably those from Ferenc Mészáros, György Konrád, László Vass, and Walburga von Habsburg), as well as numerous diaries (especially those from Mária Filep, Ferenc Mészáros, Márta Magos, and Ákos Gali), as well as several official documents and letters, among which include 1989.08.16 Ker. Pk. 034-1989 Intézk. 1; 1989.08.22. Ker. Pk. 035-1989 Int. (1) - 1989.08.22. Ker. Pk. 035-1989 Int. (4). The archive was also home to countless flyers, maps, official documents, and various and sundry other files which I perused during the course of this research but which are not cited directly in it. Notably, the Pan-European Picnic '89 Foundation is the source of most photographs reprinted in this book.

In the Stasi Records Archive, I culled from numerous files—too many to list. The most important of these files were the following: MfS, Bdl 5198; MfS, HA IX, 8817; MfS, HA IX, Fo 527; MfS, HA IX, Fo 526; Mfs, HA XX, Fo 143; MfS, HA IX, 5602; MfS, HA IX, 5897; MfS, HA IX, 8740; MfS, HA IX, 8817; MfS-ZAIG 21887; MfS, HA IX, 25364l; MfS, HA IX, 3628; MfS, HA IX, 4996; MfS, HA IX, 8342; MfS, HA IX, 5530; MfS, HA IX, 4411; MfS, HA IX, 17128. From the Stasi Records Archive I have also reprinted several images; these are specified in the Illustration Credits.

Illustration Credits

Index